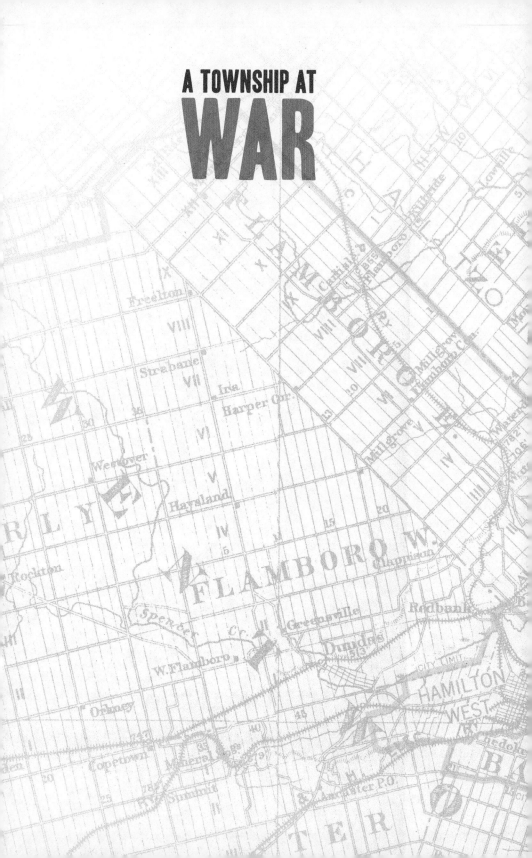

A TOWNSHIP AT
WAR

A TOWNSHIP AT WAR

JONATHAN F. VANCE

WILFRID LAURIER
UNIVERSITY PRESS

LAURIER
Inspiring Lives.

Wilfrid Laurier University Press acknowledges the support of the Canada Council for the Arts for our publishing program. We acknowledge the financial support of the Government of Canada through the Canada Book Fund for its publishing activities. This work was supported by the Research Support Fund.

Library and Archives Canada Cataloguing in Publication

Vance, Jonathan F. (Jonathan Franklin William), 1963–, author
    A township at war / Jonathan F. Vance.

Includes bibliographical references and index.
Issued in print and electronic formats.
ISBN 978-1-77112-386-0 (hardcover).—ISBN 978-1-77112-388-4 (EPUB).—
ISBN 978-1-77112-389-1 (PDF)

    1. East Flamborough (Ont.) —History—20th century. 2. World War, 1914–1918—
Ontario—East Flamborough. I. Title.

FC3099.F575V36 2018   971.3'52   C2018-902962-5
                                                        C2018-902963-3

Cover design by Michel Vrana. Front-cover photo by Will Reid (author's collection); front-cover map shows a detail from a map of the County of Wentworth (author's collection). Back-cover photo by Will Reid: Waterdown, 1916 (author's collection). Text design by Lime Design Inc.

This book is printed on FSC® certified paper and is certified Ecologo. It contains post-consumer fibre, is processed chlorine free, and is manufactured using biogas energy.

Printed in Canada

RECYCLED
Paper made from
recycled material
FSC® C103567

TO MY GRANDPARENTS,

Harold M. and Isabell (Fleming) Vance,

whose childhood was lived

in the shadow of war

———◆———

CONTENTS

—◆—

LIST OF ILLUSTRATIONS

A NOTE TO READERS

IN CHRONICLING THE EXPERIENCE of the township of East Flamborough during the First World War, I have been guided first and foremost by the archival documents, rather than by the history of the period as I know it and teach it. The 1910s was a tumultuous decade in Canadian history, and the war years particularly saw bitter conflict over a wide range of issues, including woman's suffrage, French-language education in Ontario, prohibition, the nationalization of the railways, and industrial relations. Were I writing a general history of Canada during the Great War, these episodes would loom large.

But in East Flamborough, they caused scarcely a ripple at the time. The fortunes of industrial unionism were of no concern in a township without unions. French-language education was irrelevant for no one spoke French, much less wanted to be educated in French. I imagine that some people in East Flamborough were passionately concerned about votes for women, but in the archival record I could find no one who mentioned it, either privately or publicly. Not even the Waterdown Women's Institute was sufficiently interested in the subject to discuss the matter at its meetings.

The same might be said for a dozen other flashpoints that one might expect to find in a book set in Ontario during the First World War. They are important in the march of history, but there is absolutely no evidence that they were important to the people of the township at the time. Even conscription, which brought violence and bitterness to parts of Canada, looked very different in the villages and on the concession roads of East Flamborough.

This is a roundabout way of saying that anyone who writes about the past must always be sensitive to the voices they are reading. We must put aside what we think historical actors *should* have thought or *must* have been interested in, and instead let them tell us what their concerns *actually* were. I would certainly like to think that my ancestors in East Flamborough were wise enough and worldly enough to ponder things like the franchise, minority language rights, or social democracy, but I can find no evidence that they did. The state of privies in Waterdown, the likelihood that the Progreston dam would survive another winter, the price of a train ticket to Hamilton – these were matters of real concern to locals. Regulation 17, the Ontario Temperance Act of 1916, or the missteps of the Hearst government, apparently, were not.

A historian must bring many qualities to the task. One of the most critical is humility. The voices of the past will tell us what was important to them; our job is to avoid assuming that we know better than they do.

Introduction – Clare

THE DOOR TO THE RETIREMENT HOME closes behind me with a sort of vacuum whoosh, and I am struck by how quiet it has become—as if the noise of a busy day in suburban Toronto has been sucked into a void. Classical music plays softly on the sound system and I hear the gentle click of billiard balls. Any other noise is swallowed up by the plush carpets and brocade upholstery. There are a few residents around the lobby, chatting or playing cards, but they seem to be outnumbered by the staff, who are all smiling, calm, and utterly unflustered. My work has taken me to a good many seniors' homes, and my first thought is that the place must cost a fortune. My second is that, since one must grow old, this wouldn't be a bad place to do it.[1]

I follow the hallway around to the left and eventually come to a door adorned with a little straw and flower arrangement. Even my knock sounds muffled and there is no noise coming from inside the apartment to suggest that anyone is home. I'm a little startled when the door opens. The man before me is small and very neatly dressed in a striped golf shirt and a chunky bolo. His glasses are stylish and obviously new, and his steel grey hair is perfectly combed. He offers his hand—the skin is thin, almost papery, and covered with blemishes. But what strikes me most powerfully are his eyes. Although he dabs them with a handkerchief, they are clear and bright, with the kind of piercing gaze of a person who has seen much. And the man before me has seen more than most people. At age 102, Clare Laking is the last of the residents of the southern Ontario township of East Flamborough who went away to the First World War.

He has been waiting for me, he says, and shows me around his small apartment. On the back of an armchair is a Toronto Maple Leafs jersey, a gift from the team when he went to a game on his ninety-ninth birthday. A sliding door opens to a small patio, and Clare tells me about his tomatoes. He's very proud of them, but can still chuckle happily as he describes watching a determined squirrel wrestle his best one from the stalk and manhandle it off the patio. I see his *Légion d'honneur*, given to him by the French government in recognition of his service in that war so long ago. And then he shows me to an overstuffed floral couch and takes a seat himself, a small pile of papers on his knees.

The first thing he tells me is that he doesn't *really* consider himself to be from East Flamborough. The Lakings were farmers who had settled in Nassagaweya Township, at the north end of Halton County and along the road that marked the boundary between Nassagaweya and East Flamborough. Clare was brought into the world on a raw night in February 1899 by a doctor who came in his cutter from a village six miles distant. As soon as the young lad was old enough to handle a team, he guided a stone boat around the fields, picking up rocks to be used for building fences. He went to School Section #2, some three miles away—before Highway 401 went through, cutting off the bottom end of Nassagaweya from the rest of the township. One day when their teacher failed to arrive at school, Clare and some of his pals broke into the school, stoked up the fire, and spent the day catching mice to hide in the girls' pencil boxes. When he was ten he missed almost a whole school year to take care of his infant sister while their mother was desperately ill. He smiles fondly as he talks of waking up to find the tot's arms wrapped lovingly around his neck.

But if Clare was thirty-odd yards away from being an actual resident of East Flamborough, he still knew the township well. When he was a teenager, his parents enrolled him in a six-month course at a business college in Hamilton, and every day he walked to the CPR station at Guelph Junction to catch the southbound train. The long trip to Hamilton took Clare through the centre of East Flamborough, past the stations in Carlisle, Waterdown, and Aldershot, along Grindstone Creek, whose rushing waters drew settlers to the area long before the Lakings arrived, and down the escarpment that separated the northern part of the township from the lakefront lots. He played baseball in East Flamborough, went to picnics and parties there, walked out with girls from there.

When he finished business school, Clare got a job as a clerk with the Bank of Nova Scotia in Campbellville at $300 a year. But it wouldn't last. War had broken out in August 1914, when Clare was just fifteen, and he had watched many of his friends enlist and go off to fight. In April 1917, he decided to do the same and joined the Canadian Field Artillery in Guelph. His father, a severe Methodist who allowed neither dancing nor card-playing in his sight or his home, was outraged. Convinced that soldiering was a sure road to moral ruin, he forbade his son from leaving. Clare, perhaps because his father was so determined, was equally determined to be rebellious. He left anyways, and his father told him that, even if he survived the war, he needn't bother returning to the family home.

But Clare describes even that angry confrontation with a smile, for he doesn't like to dwell on dark things. He is full of amusing stories of his youth, and enjoys a good joke. He laughs heartily after each of his yarns, but the laughter always ends in a wheeze as Clare pauses to catch his breath for a few moments. Only then is it evident that this is a man who has lived for more than a century. I watch his eyes as he talks, hoping that he can help me to see the township as he saw it nearly a hundred years ago, before the war came to tear apart minds, bodies, families, and communities. To travel back in time is a rare opportunity, and I had been thrilled to hear that Clare was willing to take me on the journey. I was born in 1963, so my memories of East Flamborough go back only a few decades. Like many people (and perhaps most historians), I live with the knowledge that I've already missed most of my chances to learn. My grandparents, my great-aunts and -uncles, my great-grandmother, the older men and women who had been fixtures of my childhood—they had all lived in the township during those terrible years. There were any number of occasions in the past when I could have asked them to tell me some stories. But I didn't. Although my ancestors were among the township's founding families, my knowledge of the area's history was spotty. Clare was pretty much my last chance to fill in the gaps by talking with some-one who had been there in the golden years before the First World War, when East Flamborough's possibilities seemed limitless.

The research I had already done had shown me how little I understood life in a rural community a century ago. I had assumed that any such village, especially one that was close to a big city, was something of a backwater. Progress flowed past it like a river, with East Flamborough an eddy off to the side, its people as leaves that were constantly moving but only in circles, so that they never actually got anywhere. I had grown up among people who, I was sure, had never been more than ten miles beyond the township boundary in their lives—and that was all right with them. But I had learned that East Flamborough was nothing like an eddy holding generations of families in its clutches. Modern war is a highly bureaucratized affair that leaves masses of paperwork in its wake; before meeting Clare, I had spent many hours searching for the people of East Flamborough in the war's written record. That quest revealed that they had been far more adventurous than I realized. At a time when national borders didn't matter very much (unless, of course, you wanted to invade France), people apparently thought little of selling up and moving—across the province, across the continent, even to another part of the world. Before 1914, the township's sons and daughters had scattered and the war continued that diaspora—less a deluge, as British historian Arthur Marwick famously called it, than a whirlwind that picked people up and deposited them around the world.[2] I had already found descendants of East Flamborough spending parts of the war in every corner of North America, the British Isles, France and Belgium, Germany, Italy, Australia, Siberia, the Balkans, Palestine, Egypt, the Dardanelles. Where else would I find them? Despite this scattering, their ties to the township were carefully cultivated. They remained connected with relatives and friends who stayed there, and craved news of their old stomping grounds, gleaned through letters, local newspapers, and even during chance meetings near the battlefield. No matter where they were, the pull of home was strong.

I appreciated that myself. I had started this research long after moving away from Waterdown, pecking away at it, moving on to complete other projects, but always being drawn back to it. It became an inner compulsion to make up for years of opportunities I had never taken—penance for my failure to talk to the Generation of 1914 in my own family when I had the chance. I've asked myself, too, if the very decision to write this book was partly out of arrogance. My township means a great deal to me, so obviously it should mean a great deal to other people. After all, we historians are always deciding what parts of the past are read about, and what parts are left to moulder in closets and attics. Was this process really any different? Had I simply decided that East Flamborough was more important than other townships, and should be the subject of a book that I expected others to read? It did produce a Victoria Cross winner—but Leo Clarke will always be more connected to Winnipeg, where he worked and lived (on Pine Street, later renamed Valour Road, near two other eventual VC winners), than Waterdown, where he was born and baptized. The Clarke family returned to England while Leo was just a boy and I can't imagine that many people in East Flamborough recalled the family—at least until the *Hamilton Spectator* proclaimed "Flamboro Boy Winner of the Victoria Cross" when Clarke's award was announced not long before he was killed on the Somme in October 1916.

I know myself well enough to know that there was likely an element of arrogance in my thinking. But it's much more than that. In her wonderful book on the London district of Kentish Town, historian Gillian Tindall admits her personal attachment to the place, but writes that she chose Kentish Town not because it is special, but because it is archetypal:

> I dwell on particular local events, personalities or structures ... because I am using them to demonstrate a pattern, geographical, historical and social. I am using Kentish Town to give a local habitation and a name to the expression of something far more general, and in the hope that some readers may perhaps be sufficiently interested and inspired to look at other, comparable, areas with fresh eyes afterward.[3]

———————◆———————

I CHOSE TO WRITE ABOUT EAST FLAMBOROUGH in the First World War partly because it means so much to me, but mostly because its experience was replicated countless times across rural Canada. Throughout English Canada were similar townships; the names were different and the geography certainly varied, but there were fundamental commonalities in how the people interacted with each other, the country, and the world. East Flamborough, and indeed almost any rural township, was, like Kentish Town, at once unique and archetypal.

But why rural Canada? The nation had been urbanizing through the late nineteenth century and the centres of gravity seemed to be shifting to the burgeoning cities. The people who spoke and wrote for rural Canada had long been concerned that the movement of young people to the cities was becoming a stampede. At risk was not simply the crops they grew to feed the nation, but their very way of life. And then, the 1921 census revealed that almost half of Canada's people lived in urban centres. Rural Canada was being eclipsed; the Canada of farms and villages, townships and hamlets, was rapidly becoming a thing of the past. In light of this hard demographic reality, surely it makes more sense to study Canada's cities in the First World War, as have Ian Miller (Toronto), Jim Pitsula (Regina), Jim Blanchard (Winnipeg), Terry Copp (Montreal), and others.

But for too long we have focused on a rural/urban tipping point without looking into what the census actually revealed. "Urban," according to the census definition used until 1951, didn't mean somewhere with skyscrapers, streetcars, factories, and slums. It meant any incorporated city, town, or village, regardless of population. As far as the 1911 census was concerned, urban Canada was more than Vancouver, Toronto, Montreal, and other growing cities and towns. It included Garden Island, Ontario, with a population of 150; New Glasgow, Quebec (131); and Birmingham, Saskatchewan (31). And did the Dominion Bureau of Statistics tell the sixteen residents of the incorporated village of Spruce Grove, Alberta, that they were living in an urban area in 1911? Waterdown, with a population of 756, was a veritable metropolis among incorporated villages. All of this suggests that rumours of rural Canada's demise were greatly exaggerated, or at least premature. It may have been in decline, but it wasn't as far along the road to irrelevance as we might have imagined. Throughout the war years, rural life remained the dominant Canadian experience. And an intimate look at one township can tell us much about a war that has largely been interpreted through an urban lens.

Tindall's reference to "fresh eyes" is also important, for her book is as much about seeing the past as it is about writing and reading of the past. The historian should always try to conjure up for readers mental pictures of their subject. But first, they must see their subject in their own mind's eye. And that's why my visit with Clare is so special—I will be listening to a man whose visions of East Flamborough extend back farther than anyone else's. I am not disappointed. As he talks, the years fall away—his recollections are so vivid that the village I have known since childhood starts to change in

A rural childhood—fishing near Grindstone Creek, ca. 1910. Photo by Will Reid. (Author's collection)

my mind. Gone are the strip malls and subdivisions, the fast food joints and traffic lights, the big box stores and skateboard parks. In their place, the Waterdown of Clare's youth takes shape. Coming slowly into focus are horse-drawn buggies and high, starched collars, barefoot boys in wide-brimmed hats scampering down a dirt street to the creek, Daughters of the King meetings, box socials and livery stables, Lydia E. Pinkham's Vegetable Compound, pargetting, bargeboard, and a thousand other things that have all but vanished from our world. The East Flamborough that Clare sees is very different from the one I know so well ...

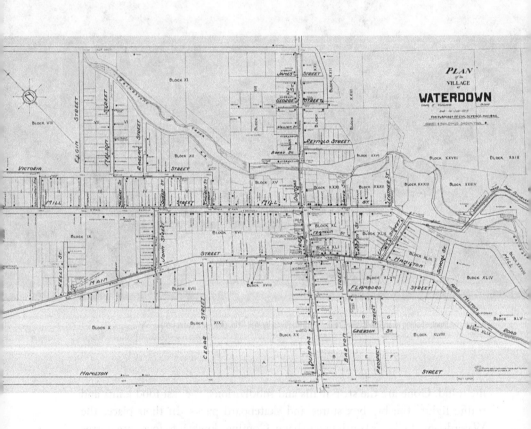

PLAN
of the
VILLAGE
of
WATERDOWN

1

BEFORE

———◆———

At the heart of Waterdown stood the Bell House, an ugly clapboard
building that had squatted on the north side of Dundas Street since 1874.
Any passer-by could tell it had been designed on the back of an envelope,
and even then there had obviously been some disagreements between those
responsible. It had the kind of false front that was intended to look imposing,
but any grandeur was spoiled by a crooked balcony tilting crazily over the
sidewalk and a side addition that might have been left there accidentally by
a passing builder. For all its faults, it had long been the administrative centre
of Waterdown, the scene of the first municipal elections in 1878 and the first
village council meetings. It also acted as the 3rd Divisional Court for the
County of Wentworth, the garage for the fire department's hand pumper,
and, on the rare occasion that someone broke the law, the village lock-up.

The building had a single distinctive (and distinguished) feature: an ele-
gant cupola that rose four stories above the street and held the village bell.
Every morning and evening, Jim Simmons, the blacksmith, crossed from his
forge on the south side of Dundas Street to toll the beginning and end of the
work day; any local emergency also demanded that he ring the bell. For this
duty, the village council paid him the extravagant sum of five dollars a month,
an amount that some of Waterdown's more practical folk considered was far

more than the effort warranted. But they weren't disposed to quibble about it—the bell had always been rung; it must be rung still, even if Jim Simmons was a rascal for taking so much money for the job.

Once in a while, Jim had to climb to the top of the cupola, the highest point in the village, to strike the flag (half-staff was out of the question because the pole was so short). If the day was fine, he yanked a filthy rag out of his back pocket, ran it thoughtfully across the back of his neck, and surveyed the surroundings. From that vantage point, he had a clear view of all the roads that shaped the fortunes of East Flamborough.

The view from atop the Bell House, looking east along Dundas Street towards Vinegar Hill. (Author's collection)

In front of the Bell House, through the heart of Waterdown, ran Dundas Street, one of the oldest roads in the province, whose origins as a military route date back to the late eighteenth century. It ambled eastwards over a rickety wooden bridge across Grindstone Creek, where some of the first settlers erected their cabins on the east bank where the soil was rich and the views sublime. The road then climbed Vinegar Hill, named for the smell of fermenting cider rendered from the windfall apples in the many orchards lining the road. On the north side lay the Union Cemetery, established in the early nineteenth century as a rare cooperative venture by the often fractious Wesleyan

Photographer unknown. (Author's collection)

and Episcopal Methodist churches. Beyond the township boundary, the road dropped away steeply before passing through the tiny town of Nelson and continuing to Toronto. West of the village, Dundas Street ran straight until it crossed the King's Highway at Clappison's Corners and entered West Flamborough township, moving through a rolling landscape covered with clumps of oak, maple, beech, ash, and chestnut, great stands of pine that capped the ridges, and cedar swamps in the low areas. Continuing on that road eventually took the traveller to London; a road to the south, down the escarpment, led to the industrial town of Dundas.

The 4th Concession road was the northern boundary of the village of Waterdown; above it lay nine concessions of farmland, the agricultural heartland of East Flamborough. Centre Road ran like an arrow through the middle of the township, through small settlements that sprang up along the stagecoach route. Nestled in a hollow north of the 5th Concession road was Bakersville, which boasted the stylishly named Rising Sun Hotel and, for three glorious years in the 1860s, its own post office. Flamboro Centre, at the 6th Concession road, was next, a hamlet of fifty-odd souls who were occasionally paralyzed by the debate over whether or not their settlement's name should use the final "ugh." Three concessions farther north was East Flamborough's second centre, the village of Carlisle, originally named Eatonville after its founding family. John Eaton, a veteran of the Battle of Stoney Creek in 1813, had an ancestor who had landed at Plymouth, Massachusetts, on the *Mayflower* in 1660. His wife Catherine was a cousin of Laura Secord, the heroine of the War of 1812. In 1824 the couple was granted 400 acres east of Centre Road and south of the 9th Concession; by the end of the century, their descendants were scattered throughout the township and beyond, and Carlisle was a thriving town of 200 people that owed its prosperity (not to mention its four hotels and daily stagecoach service) in part to being halfway between Hamilton and Guelph. This geographic advantage had given it the leg up on its sometime rival Progreston, still known to a few locals by its original name, Progresstown, christened by an early settler who confidently predicted its future as a showcase of the latest industrial technology. But the years had not been kind to Progreston, and by the end of the nineteenth century only the die-hards saw it as anything but a suburb of its neighbour. It was a bitter irony that its last surviving factory made coffins.

Above Carlisle and the nearly forgotten settlement of Stoney Battery, the flat farmland gave way to lumpy, ragged fields strewn with glacial debris,

left behind as the ice sheet retreated northwards over the millennia. These
northern concessions had been granted in 1817 to the four brothers of Isaac
Brock, the hero of the Battle of Queenston Heights, and remained wild long
after the rest of the township had been put under the plow. Here, farming
was more challenging, and as late as 1924, the reeve of the township admitted
that the upper concessions, "owing to the nature of the rough country, can
hardly be called a producing Section."[1] Some people thought the settlers of
the northern concessions were as rough and poorly cultivated as their fields.
Roger Maynard, who left the civilized streets of Listowel, Ontario, in 1862
to take up the teaching appointment in Mountsberg's log schoolhouse, wondered at the backwardness of the people in the upper concessions. "The worst
undisciplined school that ever was my lot to enter," he complained sourly in
his diary and then, as if to underline his displeasure, he fell ill two days after
arriving and was out of the classroom for three months.[2] But the families
that first cleared the land, the Lakings, the Maddaughs, the Doughertys, the
Emmonses, the Mounts (who gave the settlement of Mountsberg its name)
tended to stay there—they were loath to give up the land they had struggled
to clear, especially since it was worth up to a third less than cleared land in the
lower concessions. They had faith in Mountsberg, even though it had fewer
than fifty people at the turn of the twentieth century. Its time would come.

To the west of Centre Road, the main road between Hamilton and
Guelph marked the dividing line between East and West Flamborough. It
was anchored in the south by Millgrove, opposite the 5th Concession road,
and in the north, opposite the 10th Concession road, by Freelton, a village of
some 200 people. The cold logic of the surveyed boundary put Millgrove and
Freelton in West Flamborough, but a combination of tradition, family and
business connections, and a kind of virtual imperialism effectively annexed
them to East Flamborough. To the east of the township was Halton County,
although it was sparsely populated north of the lakeshore villages of Burlington and Freeman. Only Kilbride, east of Carlisle, and Campbellville, east of
Mountsberg, attracted the attention of East Flamborough—and then only
because their baseball teams were frequent visitors to the township.

But from the beginning, East Flamborough's lifeline was to the south,
where the Waterdown Road dove down past the Great Falls of Grindstone
Creek before carrying on through the lower concessions until it reached Burlington Bay at the western end of Lake Ontario. It was from the south that
the first Europeans came; arriving by water, their first glimpse would have

been of the stands of oak lining the shore. Behind them, pine, hickory, and sugar maple trees, some upwards of two hundred feet tall, jostled for space on the fertile sandy plain that had once been glacial Lake Iroquois. Despite the cedar swamps and the rattlesnakes that infested the area (one early surveyor reported killing 700 in a single summer), it looked deceptively inviting. "From the distance the trees stand from each other," recalled one early visitor, "the great tract under them has more the appearance of an English Gentleman's Park than the wild land in America."[3]

The forest hid something that was very forbidding: the limestone and shale Niagara Escarpment that rises to 750 feet above sea level. This apparently insurmountable barrier to settlement was slashed by salmon-filled streams— Grindstone Creek and its tributaries—that rushed towards the bay through steep ravines whose banks were dotted with native yellow orchids and lavender bird-on-the-wing flowers.[4] The first inhabitants of the region found that the valley of Grindstone Creek was the easiest route up the escarpment, so their trail from the bay followed the stream (the aptly named Snake Road now traces their original path), then went along the heights of the escarpment to the Great Falls, and finally up the creek valleys to their settlements to the north. These people were the Attawandarons. Though of Iroquois extraction, they stayed out of the fights between Iroquois and Hurons, earning themselves the designation Neutrals—although they were not above sweeping down occasionally on the inhabitants of the Illinois country to the west. Their territory covered much of what is now southern Ontario, with East Flamborough probably marking the eastern limit of their lands. Their villages dotted the township, particularly above the 8th Concession, and their major settlement in the area was Tinawatawa, in what is now Beverly Township, on the other side of West Flamborough.[5]

It was to the Neutrals that the Europeans turned in their quest for all that North America had to offer—including an easy route to the fabulous wealth of Asia. Étienne Brûlé, the original *coureur de bois*, probably met them in 1615 when he reached the thin strip of land that divided Burlington Bay from the western end of Lake Ontario, but it was René-Robert Cavelier de La Salle who has gone down in posterity as the "discoverer" of the region. In 1669, after the Jesuits dismissed him as a novitiate on grounds of mental instability, La Salle added his name to the long list of explorers, adventurers, and crackpots who believed that the best route to the riches of the East lay through North America. On the strength of an entirely false claim to speak the Iroquois language, he left Montreal on 6 July 1669 with nine canoes, a ton of supplies, native guides, and two Sulpician priests who had been despatched by a Montreal seminary to take Christianity to the heathen natives. After many weeks of travelling, they stopped at a Seneca village near present-day Rochester, New York, where they found a guide who promised to take them to Tinawatawa. The party set out on 12 September and eventually reached the shore of Burlington Bay. La Salle celebrated his landfall by falling into a fit of fever which, in the Sulpicians' increasingly jaundiced opinion, was caused by "the sight of 3 large rattlesnakes he found in his path whilst climbing a rock ... there are a great many of them at this place, as thick as one's arm, six or seven feet long, entirely black."[6] Once La Salle had regained his faculties, the party began the trek up the escarpment, using either the route up Grindstone Creek or another path a mile or two to the east, along what is now Waterdown Road. When they reached the mountain brow, they followed the creek system west to Tinawatawa.[7]

La Salle's triumphant entry into the Neutral town was spoiled by the realization that, after all that effort, he was not even the first European to arrive. He had been bested by a man named Jolliet, who had been despatched by the Governor of New France to find a legendary copper vein of great purity. But both men were to be disappointed. Jolliet never found his copper, and La Salle never found his northwest passage to the Far East. After a number of disastrous expeditions that severely tested the organizationally challenged La Salle, he was murdered by his own men while exploring the lower Mississippi in 1687. As one historian put it, "the wonder is that his men had not killed him long before."[8]

Not for a century did the first white settler appear in the area, in the person of David Fonger, who fled his home in New Jersey during the American Revolution. In 1783, he established himself—"squatted" is perhaps more accurate—along the ancient native trail running between the lakefront and the escarpment. But Fonger's blissful enjoyment of free land was not to last. Refugees from the Thirteen Colonies followed him in such numbers that in 1788 four new administrative districts were created to cope with the influx of land-hungry settlers. Fonger, once a law unto himself, now found himself in the middle of the District of Nassau, running from the Trent River in eastern Ontario to Long Point, on Lake Erie. The Land Boards came next, and in 1792, the first surveyors arrived to lay the groundwork for settlement. They began by surveying the broken front (the term that contemporary surveyors used for a range bordering a body of water) and the first four concessions, and completed the township on subsequent journeys in 1794 and 1796. The fourteen concessions (an extra chain length between lots 7 and 8 eventually became Centre Road) and surrounding land for the garrison town of Dundas were amalgamated into the Township of Flamborough. In 1798, as part of the boundary realignment of Upper Canada, the township was divided into East and West. David Fonger's idyll was about to end.[9]

Most of the new land parcels went to absentee landlords who promptly sold or traded their grants so they could acquire more desirable plots in York or Niagara. The crusty homesteader David Fonger was forced to buy back from its new owner the land that he himself had cleared and developed. Another large parcel eventually found its way into the hands of Alexander Brown, late of the North West Company, who became the first white settler above the escarpment. In 1805, Brown built the area's first sawmill above the Great Falls. Two years later, another settler built the district's first grist mill in the lower valley of Grindstone Creek. In an all-too-common story that has Monty Pythonesque overtones, it burned down in 1812, was rebuilt, burned down again, and was finally rebuilt to stand for some fifty years in the area that became known as Hidden Valley.

It is no slight to those early settlers of East Flamborough to say that their experience was unremarkable; even the first historian of Wentworth County admitted as much: "To give a detailed account of the adventures and vicissitudes of these men would be at once useless and superfluous. The early history of one township in the county is much the same as another. In each township there was the same monotony of forests and swamp; the same climate, and the same number of wild beasts. The early settlers in the different townships belonged to the same class of people, and went about their work in much the same way. One was as far from the civilized world as the other, and there was with all of them the never changing monotony of hard work and poverty."[10]

It was only as settlement expanded that townships started to develop their own particular character. Within a few years of Alexander Brown's arrival in the area, Waterdown Road overtook Snake Road as the major route between Burlington Bay and East Flamborough. In the 1820s, Brown built a wharf at the foot of Waterdown Road that eventually became the township's door to the outside world. For decades, it anchored the busiest trade route in the area. Gangs of teamsters hauled up supplies for the influx of settlers and hauled down produce to be shipped to urban markets—and, in the 1850s, locally quarried stone to build the new university at Toronto. Brown contracted with a shipping company to supply fuelwood for its lake steamers; by the 1860s, his workers were sending 5,000 cords of wood from the wharf every season, and the operation was so busy that it spawned a new settlement, Aldershot, just north of the wharf and the massive tree known as the Old Sentinel Oak. Ship's captains watched for the tree as they approached the wharf and teamsters used it as a beacon in wintertime, when stinging winds whipping along the shoreline buried the road under drifts of snow.

With Brown's business interests taking more of his time, he decided to sell 360 acres of his empire, the land that would eventually become the village of Waterdown, to a man whom local lore regards as the founder of Waterdown: Ebenezer Griffin.[11] Griffin was born in the Niagara Peninsula, but in 1823 he threw his lot into East Flamborough, purchasing the parcel from Brown, as well as another 200 acres to the south. Some of this land he transferred to his brother Absalom, and soon the two of them were busy entrepreneurs. Together they had a mercantile business; Absalom operated a cloth and carpet mill, while Ebenezer ran a sawmill and a flour mill on Grindstone Creek, just above the Great Falls. By the late 1820s, he was shipping flour as far east as Montreal and Quebec. He also became a real estate tycoon, breaking his parcels into smaller lots and selling them to other settlers. One of Ebenezer's eleven children was responsible for improving Snake Road and erected a tollbooth to pay for the work: sheep, pigs, ducks, and goats passed for one cent, a saddle horse and rider cost four cents, and a loaded wagon with two horses or oxen cost ten cents. Anyone going to a funeral or to church enjoyed free passage.

By the time of Confederation in 1867, land grants and toll roads were things of dim memory. The Township of East Flamborough had been incorporated seventeen years earlier, giving it the power to impose property taxes. In the early days, statute labour was often given in lieu; a settler with a small section of land owed three days' work spreading gravel on the township's roads. That was important, because it was as a crossroads that East Flamborough seemed ideally placed to prosper. Straddling the main highway between London and Toronto, with an outlet on Burlington Bay, and on the route between the burgeoning industrial cities of Hamilton and Guelph, the township was bullish about the future and greeted Confederation with a sense of profound optimism. To represent the area in the Dominion's new parliament, the electors chose James McMonies, who had come from Scotland in the 1830s as an ambitious young man. By 1867 he and his adopted home had prospered in tandem. He was one of the township's cattlemen, and had been one of the five members of the first township council in 1850. James McMonies was a gaunt man with grey mutton chops. In his official portrait as a Member of Parliament, I see a distinct resemblance to my grandfather, his great-grandson, and I have the eerie impression that to look at him in 1867 is to see what I will look like in old age. Like my grandfather, James was a man of few words—not the best quality in a politician. He uttered not a single sentence in the House of Commons in the four years he represented Wentworth North. The experience confirmed for him that he was happier at home in East Flamborough—he declined to stand in the 1872 election, and went back to his cattle.

Every township in Canada had its own James McMonies—to tell the story of East Flamborough in the decades around Confederation is to tell the story of a hundred other townships. Each had its churches, at least one for every denomination, and its schools, known not by name but by number. They all had baseball teams, mostly with mismatched uniforms and hand-me-down equipment, that played in local leagues or special holiday tournaments. Waterdown, like many other rural communities, also boasted roller skating, an English invention that had taken off in the 1870s. Beginning in the 1880s, it spread through rural North America as many small towns put up roller rinks where women in petticoats and men in straw hats teetered and clattered around in what passed for circles. It was cheap (both for the entrepreneur who wanted to build a rink and for the people who wanted to use it), appealed to all classes, and could be done in any weather. Waterdown's roller rink, south of Dundas Street, was no more than a barn with a raised wooden floor that amplified the sound of a few dozen skaters into a thunderstorm that could be heard throughout the village. And the main street in one rural village looked pretty much the same as another's—butcher, baker, general store, blacksmith, barbershop, pool room, hotels. The proprietors' names were different, but not much else was.

Many a rural community also had a militia unit, which often look a lot like the baseball team—mismatched uniforms and equipment brought from the barn. In 1837, when William Lyon Mackenzie's rebels rose up against the ruling elites and sowed panic throughout Upper Canada, the Waterdown Guard mustered twenty-three men who were ready to defend their homes against the dastardly republicans.[12] The Fenian threat of the 1860s, when Irish nationalist sympathizers in the United States launched raids into British North America to help along the cause of Irish independence, brought a vigorous response from the Waterdown company of the 77th Regiment, and from James McMonies Jr., the son of the MP:

> Shoulder to shoulder we'll be seen, boys,
> In that call which our country has made;
> To fight in defence of our Queen, boys,
> We'll each leave our calling and trade.
> Our country, our sweethearts and wives, boys,
> Will confide in us all when afar;
> These treasures we'll guard with our lives, boys,
> If should sound the dread tocsin of war ...
>
> Our Captain no danger will shun, boys,
> He'll instruct and command us all right;
> To handle our bayonet and gun, boys,
> And lead in the front of the fight.
> Where duty demands we'll be found, boys,
> Every one, both the rank and the file;
> And true British cheers shall resound, boys,
> As they did on the banks of the Nile.
>
> Our cause and our laws we'll uphold, boys,
> And our colors we'll nobly defend;
> Despite all greenbacks or gold, boys,
> Fenian, Traitor or Yankee can send.
> Then hurrah for our brave Volunteers, boys,
> With defence of our country in view;
> We will join in three hearty cheers, boys,
> And, 'Tiger,' for the red, white and blue.[13]

No, young James wasn't much of a poet, nor was he much of a businessman. A few years before writing this poem in 1866, he signed a promissory note that he couldn't cover and found himself declared insolvent, everything in his small store, from Brazil nuts to bodkins, seized by the court; twenty years later, he did a runner to Nebraska, leaving another batch of worthless IOUs in the hands of angry creditors. James was a rogue, but his poem did capture the spirit of the community, and its determination to fight for the values it treasured. To capitalize on that spirit, a year after Confederation, the federal government built a drill shed on a small lot on Main Street, south of Dundas. The Department of Militia and Defence went to no great expense—paint was deemed an unnecessary luxury on a building that had neither floor nor interior fittings—but it provided a modicum of shelter for East Flamborough's citizen-soldiers to go through their paces.[14]

We can catch only brief glimpses of life in the township in the decades before the First World War. Newspapers then were as obsessed with the sensational as they are in the twenty-first century, so the stories that have come down to us highlight the tragic, the violent, and the odd. Among the horrific industrial accidents, the family tragedies, the occasional suicide, and the two murders that occurred in the township between Confederation and the First World War, a few curiosities stand out. There was a one-woman crime wave in the person of Mary Jane Lintz, who was collared after a long and lucrative shoplifting career. She freely admitted her guilt to the court but insisted that she had turned to theft in the hope that she might be arrested and so separated from her husband. The magistrate found her confession refreshingly original; he assured Lintz that "her prospects were fair of being separated from society in general for some years" and observed that "the effort to procure a separation from her family, by the peculiar method adopted, had evidently been pursued with commendable patience and assiduity."[15] An inquest was held into the death of a Carlisle woman, who succumbed while being treated not by a real doctor but by what the newspaper called "a Yankee skedaddler" with neither the training nor the knowledge to practise medicine.[16] Augusta James (she went by Gustie, which offered an unintended clue as to her temperament) was given a settlement of twelve dollars when she complained to Waterdown village council after slipping on a sidewalk—which in those days simply consisted of wooden planks laid end to end.[17] A gang of burglars broke into the American Hotel and the homes of four of Waterdown's leading citizens, Messrs. Eager, Griffin, Sawell, and Whalley, taking a sizable haul in money and goods.[18] A complaint about the sale of cigarettes to minors and the number of children roaming the streets at night brought a promise from the town constable that the law would be enforced more stringently.[19] And one frosty night in February 1910, a police raid broke up one of the more popular (and illicit) forms of entertainment in the village: a cockfight in Gilmer's wagon shop. Shortly after midnight the Dundas police chief and five constables surrounded the building, which was immediately plunged into darkness. Some

A pre-war church choir. Judging by the young woman on the left, not everyone took hymns seriously.
Photographer unknown. (Author's collection)

of the luckless bettors rushed for the windows, while others tried to hide in various corners of the building, but police rounded them all up—thirty-two men from the area and seventeen birds, fifteen alive and two dead.[20]

But these are only flashes. East Flamborough was rarely newsworthy, and such stories tell us little about the everyday in the township. Life went on placidly, the occasional petty theft or accident doing little to disturb the settled calm of the rural world. As they were in most rural townships, the people of East Flamborough were relentlessly social and obsessive about organizations. The great irony of our modern age of social media is that, a century ago, people were far more social than we are today, with a penchant for organizing groups and holding get-togethers that would leave most of us breathless. No occasion was too insignificant that it didn't call for a party, and no issue was too small that it didn't demand a committee—even better if the two could be combined. As Agnes Macphail, Canada's first female MP, observed, rural women were so clubbish that they "often kept organizations about nothing running for years."[21] There were all the municipal bodies that we would expect—the village and township councils and the boards of trade, education, and health, and each church spawned a handful of committees, associations, craft circles, and leagues. Beyond such things, there was a whole host of other clubs, societies, and interest groups to ensure that people were never idle—agricultural societies, Masonic and Orange Lodges, Women's Institutes, Daughters of the King, temperance leagues, missionary societies, literary and debating clubs, youth groups, and organizations whose names give no clue as to their purpose. At the turn of the century, little Millgrove had barely 200 people, but those 200 people were members of more than a dozen clubs, societies, and committees for everything from farming to choral singing. Almost every night of the week in any rural township, a group met in someone's home to address some pressing and essential matter. Typically, the evening's business consumed about ten minutes, leaving the rest of the night for chatting, socializing, entertainment (you never went to a meeting without having a song or a recitation ready to perform), and an immense buffet, often well after midnight. Only illness was a sufficient excuse to stay home of an evening.

Outside of the endless meetings, the sun and the seasons governed the tempo of life in the township, for East Flamborough's prosperity still lay in its farms. The lower concessions, with their sandy soils and flat plains, were dominated by market gardens and orchards, and every fall gangs of First Nations men came in from the Bay of Quinte or Moraviantown to pick fruit. North of Waterdown, from the 4th Concession road to the Puslinch Township line, market gardening and orchards gave way to grains, root vegetables, and livestock. Farm families grew oats, barley, potatoes, turnips, and wheat, most of it to be trundled down to Brown's Wharf and loaded on steamers for the first leg of the journey to markets in Ontario, Quebec, the Maritimes, and England.

In that agricultural environment, the important seasonal rituals were plant-
ing, harvest, and the fall fair every October—East Flamborough boasted two,
one in Waterdown and one in Freelton. The fall fair was the rural world's
chance to celebrate itself, to show off the year's best grains, fruits, and vegetables (and also the worst, for every fall fair worthy of the name had an ugliest
vegetable category), the baked goods and preserves, the embroidery and fancy
work—and maybe even take home a ribbon or two. There were horse races
(just for fun, not for wagering) and novelty events—the egg-and-spoon race,
the three-legged race, the wheelbarrow race. Children could play coconut shy
or bob for apples, and if they were lucky they might be able to watch the great
Hamilton-born runner Billy Sherring take on all comers—and usually win.[22]
It was an occasion for one-upmanship, for gossip, for reunions, for courting.
The closest thing that East Flamborough had to a poet laureate, Robert Kernighan (who actually lived in Beverly Township, but that was near enough),
sang the praises of the Freelton fair:

> When I go up to Freelton Fair,
> I hope the girl I love is there,
> She is a lively sight to see;
> She comes from Stoney Battery,
> She is a peach, she is a pear,
> A sweet muskmelon, rich and rare.
> I hope the girl I love is there
> When I go up to Freelton Fair.
>
> Lots of girls at Freelton Fair
> From Bullock's Corners will be there.
> From Waterdown and Platterville,
> From lovely Greensville on the hill.
> From Crook's Hollow by the rill,
> From Hathaway's historic mill.
> From Little Ireland on the Brock,
> From Hayesland built upon the rock,
> And girls from ancient Aberfoyle,
> And from Shaw Station's fertile soil;
> But I'll have only eyes to see
> The girl from Stoney Battery.

When I go up to Freelton Fair
I hope the girl I love is there.
They'll race their horses all in vain,
I will not see the roots and grain,
I will not see the squash—a beaut—
Nor glimpse the honey or the fruit.
Fruit, punkins, crazy quilts, avaunt!
My girl is all the show I want.
She's an inducement and a lure;
Blindfold me and I'll find her, sure;
And if ten thousand filled the park,
I'd find my sweetheart in the dark.
I hope the girl I love is there,
When I go up to Freelton Fair.[23]

But like most other farming communities in Victorian Canada, East Flamborough wanted more. It had bigger dreams—dreams of industry, of factories churning out finished goods for distant markets, of a vast army of skilled workers living in trim cottages, patronizing local services, spending their wages in local shops. And Waterdown had more than just dreams—it had the fast-flowing waters of Grindstone Creek, which acted as a magnet for factories and mills. They dotted its banks in the north end of the village and fought for space in the south end, where dams had been built to harness the waterpower. The dams fed millraces that shot past the Great Falls and rushed down the escarpment to Burlington Bay, powering factories in such numbers that waterpower occasionally had to be rationed, with a tannery using the millrace on Monday, Wednesday, and Friday, and a turning mill using it on Tuesday, Thursday, and Saturday. Woollens, pot and pearl ash, leather, turned goods, rakes, snaiths, cradles, fence pickets, wagons, baskets, barrels and heads, finished lumber, sashes and doors, brass—at one time or another, the mills along Grindstone Creek produced them all. The pride and joy of local business interests was the state-of-the-art flour mill built in the 1850s. Four storeys high and with a 300-foot-long bran shed, the Torrid Zone Mill could produce over 170 barrels of flour a day, making it the largest at the western end of Lake Ontario.[24] Jim Simmons still rang the village bell at the end of each work day, but now he was competing with a new kind of man—the

Mills around the Great Falls in Waterdown, ca. 1910. Photo by Will Reid. (Author's collection)

timekeeper, perched on a stool in the mill office, a servant to the hands of the clock that told him when to sound the factory whistle.

Within a little more than a decade around the turn of the century, most of those whistles fell silent. The waters of Grindstone Creek, once the key to the township's prosperity, started to drop because of land clearance and swamp drainage in the northern parts of East Flamborough and intensive water use in Waterdown. More and more mills started to turn to steam, which offered stable year-round power, but with a costly trade-off. Steam engines relied on boilers, and boilers were prone to exploding, in those days, with alarming regularity. And when they didn't explode, the vast quantities of wood or coal needed to heat them were vulnerable to stray sparks. One by one, the mills of Waterdown were consumed by flames. The death blow came on a frigid night in February 1910 when the Torrid Zone Mill, still the crown jewel of industrial Waterdown, burned to the ground.

The aftermath of the Torrid Zone Mill fire. Photo by Will Reid. (Author's collection)

One visitor to the ruin the next day was Will Reid, who lived with his parents and sisters on the banks of Grindstone Creek, by the Union Cemetery. Will was something of a misfit. His father did a bit of everything—mill owner, farmer, home builder, cabinetmaker—but Will did as little of anything as possible. He picked up odd jobs here and there, worked occasionally for his father, raised a few chickens and cows to trade the eggs and milk, ran errands for neighbours on his rig. Many people thought he was too lazy by half, but in fact most of his time and energy went into his one true love: photography. He got what he needed to live by barter; any money he earned went to photographic supplies. With a simple bellows camera, Will created a remarkable visual record of a rural township in all its many moods. He had no formal training, but he had a natural eye for composition and contrast, and took hundreds of portraits of East Flamborough and its people that practically quiver with vitality and life. He had the soul of an artist trapped in the body of a subsistence farmer. On that cold morning in February, Will Reid drove down the Waterdown Road with his camera and photographed the aftermath: the mill's burnt-out shell, still smoking, with Will's horse-drawn cutter standing incongruously in front. In a single image, he captured the death of East Flamborough's dream of becoming a little Manchester on Grindstone Creek.

The great irony was that the end of its industrial aspirations coincided with the township's introduction to the modern world. For decades, East Flamborough had matured slowly, at a measured pace, growing but barely changing. For all the pride (and smoke) they generated, the factories were small, a few dozen hands at most, so there had never been any sudden influx of industrial labourers. The biggest industry to survive the mill era was the Wentworth Orchard Company, and it was doing exactly what East Flamborough farmers had done for decades—packing apples into barrels and shipping them to urban markets. The only new industries to come to the township after the mills fell silent were just as dependent on the earth as the farmers. The area just north of Aldershot had the good fortune to rest upon the only deposit of Medina shale clay in Ontario, ideal for manufacturing sewer pipes and fireproof bricks.[25] The Dominion Sewer Pipe Company and the National Fireproofing Company were hardly known for romantic products—not like the fine woollens or delicate spindles the township had hoped would be its stock in trade—but at least the growth of Ontario's cities guaranteed an endless market for sewer pipes and chimney tiles.

What the area really needed was farmers, not factory workers, and in the years before the First World War, many communities suffered from a severe shortage of agricultural labourers. The files of the Immigration Branch in Ottawa are filled with pleas for help. Frank Whitley worked a fifty-acre farm near Millgrove with his wife and small daughter and in 1908 was desperate for any man who "would hoe or work in a garden or build a load of hay ... will there be any boys of sixteen that will be honest and truthful for there are so many that can't be trusted."[26] Another Millgrove farmer offered $80 a year for a man under thirty, only to be told that "an experienced man would scarcely stay with you for that much money."[27] In Carlisle, one man was offering $100 a year plus board and promised good accommodation and no other work.[28] In 1911 James Evans in Waterdown asked for "a man that is decent, has good habits and kind to horses and cattle." But by that time, the labour crunch was even worse, and Evans was told that he might have to pay $300 a year to secure help.[29] Much of the farm work fell to sojourners, young men who had been squeezed by the economic downturn in Britain and who looked to Canada to improve their fortunes. There were also thousands of children, teenagers and younger, who came to Canada under a number of philanthropic schemes, often spearheaded by churchmen. The idea was to remove British children, either orphans or from families who could no longer care for them, to the wide-open spaces of Canada, where they could grow, prosper, and become productive members of society—and in doing so, help to address Canada's growing shortage of agricultural labourers. At best, these Home Children, as they came to be known, ended up in loving homes where they were welcomed as members of the family. But many were treated abominably, left to sleep in a barn and take their meals with the animals. As soon as they were old enough to move on, they did. Dozens of these itinerant labourers passed through East Flamborough in the early years of the twentieth century; only a few opted to stay there.

Still, there were enough newcomers in the first decade of the twentieth century to push Waterdown's population to 756 and East Flamborough's to 2,646, making it one of only two rural townships in Wentworth County to grow during that decade. And the people who came to East Flamborough in the years before the First World War were the same kind of people who had always come—English, Irish, and Scots, in that order. The 1911 census revealed that the township was nearly 90 per cent British by ethnicity, a figure that had changed little in decades. About 85 per cent of the township's residents were Ontario-born, probably most of them within ten miles of East Flamborough's boundaries. Considering that new immigrants tended to be attracted to Aldershot and the lower concessions, Waterdown and the concessions to the north were even more local in origin, with nearly 90 per cent of the people being born in Ontario. Over half of the residents were Methodists, with Presbyterians and Anglicans making up another third (36 per cent). Among the smattering of other faiths were Lutherans, Brethren, Disciples, and a single Mennonite.[30] Like most rural communities, East Flamborough didn't see much change in the character of its population; when change came, it was slow, orderly, and gradual—much like the people themselves.

Income levels are difficult to gauge because that column in the census return is usually blank—either East Flamborough's census-takers didn't ask, or residents didn't tell. But what numbers there are reveal a community with a relatively small gap between the rich and the poor. Leaving aside the fabulously wealthy horse dealer Daniel Bowman, who reported an annual income of $25,000 (which is so far above the average that one suspects an error), the biggest earners were the prosperous market gardeners of the southern concessions, whose incomes were in the vicinity of $3,000–$4,000 annually. Below them, at roughly $2,000 per annum and under, were the professional classes—the high school principal, the bank manager, a storekeeper or two, factory owners, nurse Gertrude Walker ($1,150), and barber and pool room owner "Dad" Alton ($1,265). At that point, any connection between class and income seems to disappear. Some labourers report higher incomes than some clergymen, a brick worker made more than a schoolteacher, and a lineman earned the same as a carriage maker. Farm labourers reported annual incomes up to $625, more than double what a store clerk typically earned, and people who listed their trade as "odd jobs" or "jobber around" sometimes out-earned both the farm labourers and the clerks.

What emerges is a community whose social hierarchy was fairly flat—not only because of the relatively small income gap between rich and poor, but also because only a small minority of the township's population consisted of wage workers. Not many people worked for someone else—most were farmers, smallholders, self-employed, or worked in a family enterprise. Not beholden to others for their living, they could interact with them on more equal terms. When the worker/management wage relationship is so uncommon, the power dynamics accompanying that relationship are also absent.

The township's people were also largely self-sufficient. At the height of the mill era, the township had many small factories producing a wide range of goods, rather than a single industry. This had always been the approach; factories sprang up to serve local needs first. Ferdinand Slater opened a planing mill because the people of the township needed doors and window sashes; export was an afterthought. The upshot was a township that was largely self-sufficient. It had little need of imports—almost everything the people of East Flamborough needed, from baby carriages to coffins, was produced within five miles of the Township Hall in Waterdown. The village was only a few miles from Hamilton, but it maintained a kind of splendid isolation—the still centre of a moving universe. The township wasn't cut off from the outside world; it was the outside world that was cut off from the township, and the locals were quite happy to have it that way.

Within a few years, that splendid isolation abruptly ended. The communications revolution had reached Waterdown in 1882, when the first telephone came to J. T. Stock's store on the northwest corner of Mill and Dundas Streets. For over twenty years, there were no other telephones in the village and locals thought it was just a bad investment by a poor businessman—a suspicion confirmed a few years later when Stock, who also served as Wentworth County's treasurer, was found to have dipped into the public till to the tune of $9,000 to cover losses from his store.[31] It was 1908 before the village had a telephone exchange, but from then the technology took off. Within four years, the new North Wentworth Telephone Company had over 240 subscribers and telephone poles were going up all over the village, putting the outside world just a call away. The automobile era overtook East Flamborough at around the same time, and soon there were enough vehicles passing through Waterdown that, in November 1913, council instructed the village clerk to purchase six speed limit signs for the village.[32] Hamilton, Dundas, Burlington, Guelph, and even Toronto were now within easy reach.

The biggest revolution came with the railway. Until the beginning of the twentieth century, the railway age had largely bypassed East Flamborough. Despite its strategic location, the township had watched new lines go around it rather than through it. There were railway stations in the far north and south, and since the 1890s various groups had floated schemes to connect the two, but none of them were able to overcome the escarpment, which gave the route the steepest grade in all of southern Ontario (climbing 586 feet in only five and a half miles). Not until 1910 did the South Ontario Pacific Railway, part of the CPR system, announce that it would build a sixteen-mile-long line to connect the Canadian Pacific at Guelph Junction in the north to the Grand Trunk near Hamilton. Construction began in May 1911 at the north end, with the line slowly pushing through the township. Carlisle's station (called Flamborough) was completed later that year, and then Waterdown North, just above the 4th Concession road. When

A day out in the punt on Waterdown's millpond. Photo by Will Reid. (Author's collection)

construction reached Waterdown, villagers saw how their world would be changed by the modernity that had long been kept at bay.

The biggest dam on Grindstone Creek had been built to power the mill then owned by John Reid, Will's father, and it had unintentionally created one of the loveliest spots in the village: the millpond. It was the sort of place we imagine as typical of Victorian Canada. A favourite with fishers and swimmers, its banks were dotted with scattered groves of trees whose boughs nodded and bobbed into the water. A few barns, greying and weathered even then, stood on the east bank, leaning slightly to one side or the other, as if they were relaxing; beyond them, the headstones of the Union Cemetery were strewn across the hillside like dominoes. A courting couple might drift across the water in the communal punt—no one seemed to own it, but it was always there, pulled up on the shore and waiting to be used. Children splashed and chattered at its margins, while elders gazed into its mirrored surface as they debated and solved the world's problems. It was tranquil, unspoiled, and idyllic. But it couldn't coexist with the railway. The creek bed was the best route through the village and down the escarpment, and everything in the railway's path must be sacrificed to progress. Reid's dam was dismantled and the pond drained; the creek was moved a few feet to the west and diverted into a narrow stream, barely ankle deep in spots. Gangs of railway labourers, living in tents along the track (the surveyors and engineers lived in the village), and smoke-belching steam shovels sliced through the land to create a rail bed. John Reid's fields were chopped away, and the stately willows and oaks hacked out. The acrid tang of creosoted railway ties hung over the construction waste and the few shattered tree trunks that littered the ground. The clang of hammers and the raucous shouts of the navvies split the air. Where there had once been green, lush fields of grass, the scent of buttercups and lilies of the valley, the gentle bleat of John Reid's goats and the buzz of his honeybees, now there was only a wasteland. All that had been green was now brown.

At the south end of the millpond sat a large white house, hard by the rushing waters of the millrace. Since 1901, it had been the home of Ada and John Vance. Ada, the granddaughter of James McMonies, MP, was descended from one of the township's founding families. John, whose grandfather had been one of the earliest settlers in Carlisle, ran a flourishing tinsmithing and undertaking business in Waterdown. As a local politician, he would complete the rare trifecta, serving as reeve of the village of Waterdown, the township of East Flamborough, and the County of Wentworth. His sister was a nurse, his brother a dentist, but behind the family's success was an embarrassing secret that didn't come to light until the 1990s, when an email from a cousin I never knew existed revealed the amusing, if sordid, story. Sometime in the 1880s, the patriarch, Robert Vance, vanished, leaving his wife Annie to raise their children on her own. What most people didn't know, and the family never discussed, was that Robert had taken himself out to Athabasca country, declared himself a widower, and, at the age of forty-one, married a sixteen-

The railway moves past the old Vance house. The millpond has been drained and the creek rerouted.
On the hillside behind is the Union Cemetery. Photo by Will Reid. (Author's collection)

year-old girl. He raised another family in the west, but appears to have been singularly lacking in imagination because he couldn't be bothered to come up with different names for them. And so he had two daughters named Ann Vance and two sons named Robert James Vance, one each in Waterdown and in Alberta. In spite of an absent father, eldest son John had prospered, and after marrying, he and Ada settled in one of the most desirable locations in the village. But desired by the railway too—and so the Vances sold their house to the CPR and moved to the north end of Mill Street. From their house, newly renamed Waterdown South Station, the railway line drove inexorably south, across an iron bridge that vaulted over Mill Street, past the mills that had been condemned by the construction, through the lower concessions, and to its rendezvous with the main line near Aldershot.

Were the people of East Flamborough bothered by this despoliation of the village? Did they lament the loss of their beloved millpond, and the construction that turned the creek valley into a no man's land? It seems not, if the 1st of July 1912 is any indication. Vast crowds converged on Waterdown, which itself was unusual. Typically, the big attraction was Carlisle's Methodist Church for the Dominion Day garden party—an extravaganza of baseball, pies and sandwiches, flags and bunting, and an evening concert of comedians, tap dancers, and musicians. But in 1912, there was an even bigger draw in Waterdown: the arrival of the first train to pass along the new line linking Hamilton and Guelph. Soon there would be four trains a day, taking women to Hamilton to sell eggs and butter, or teenagers from the upper concessions to attend high school in Waterdown. Until then, observed the *Hamilton Spectator*, Waterdown had been a quiet country hamlet: "One of the chief reasons for the popular demonstration on this occasion, therefore, was their realization that the line of demarcation between industrial failure and success had been crossed ... The citizens realized that, with the coming of this railway, their little town with its great natural advantages, the gates of which had almost rusted on their hinges for almost a century, would be opened to industrial, residential and social progress; that Hamilton citizens and business men would turn their attention in that direction; that prosperity which for years had remained dormant, would quickly advance; and for the first time in its history, Waterdown would take on an air of modern prosperity and assured growth."[33]

And so it seemed. All around were signs that East Flamborough Township had arrived, pulled into a new era of prosperity by the steam locomotive. In one month in 1914 alone, 6,000 tickets between Waterdown and Hamilton had been sold at seven and a half cents each, but the boom in passenger tickets wasn't the only sign of progress. The struggling Traders Bank, which had taken over J. T. Stock's building on the corner of Mill and Dundas streets, became the Royal Bank of Canada, the first national bank to set up shop in the township. The public library, which was built on the collection from the old Mechanics' Institute, could boast 2,279 volumes—almost one for every man, woman, and child in the township.[34] At a grand ceremony in the roller rink, with Sir Adam Beck himself throwing the switch, hydroelectricity came to the village in 1911, and a local utility began selling power the following year. Down came the old whale-oil street lamps (which hadn't been used in years, not since village council balked at the steadily rising price of whale oil) and up went brand-new electric fixtures. An advertisement from the time promised only sunshine and light: "Come up to Waterdown and be Happy. Come up and look at us anyway. We leave the latch string out."[35] It seemed that the modern world, slowly and inexorably, was overtaking the township and bringing good times with it. And then, in the summer of 1914, the world intruded on East Flamborough in the most unexpected way.

2

1914

———◆———

It could have been any weekend in any summer in Edwardian Canada, that first weekend of August 1914. June had been hot and dry, July hotter and dryer, and the grain was thinner and shorter than it would be in a perfect summer. The threshing crews had just started to bring in the oats, which had done better than most of the grains, and old hands figured that a few weeks of work would clear the township's fields. The lack of rain made it dirtier work than usual, with clouds of chaff and dust sticking to man, horse, and machine alike. The root crops were also a bit disappointing. The early potatoes had already been shipped, but they were small—so were the turnips—because the hard, dry earth had squeezed them tight as they tried to grow. Even the pastures were parched, the hay barely half as tall as it should be. The fruit growers and market gardeners were happier, for the warm, dry days brought a bumper crop. One woman had picked forty baskets of cherries in a single day in the orchard by the Union Cemetery, a record for the township. The tomatoes would be going out by rail soon—there was a good crop this year and prices were healthy—and the apple harvest was shaping up to be one of the better ones.

When the farms of East Flamborough prospered, so too did the villages—and prosperity meant construction. A new grain chopping mill on Main Street was freshly painted and had a brand new stable; it would open for business within the month. Jim Simmons was putting a new hemlock plank floor in the blacksmith's shop across from the Bell House. Labour gangs were working their way along Dundas Street, getting ready to pour new cement sidewalks in place of the rotting planks that had been there for as long as anyone could remember. A block to the south, a new Roman Catholic church was going up, to replace the crumbling building to the west of the village. In Millgrove, workers were finishing a new schoolhouse, a stately, two-room building with a tiny attic that would house the public library. Another school was under construction in Aldershot, although it wouldn't be ready for the beginning of classes in September. Township council had finally agreed to gravel Progreston Road—as long as the residents were willing to cover a third of the cost out of their own pockets. As usual, the work would be done by local men hired by the township, the stone supplied by local farmers. That's the way it had been done for as long as anyone could remember—there was no reason to do things differently now.

There was no construction going on around Waterdown's drill shed. Earlier in the summer, the local MP had informed the Department of Militia and Defence that the shed was slowly disintegrating through neglect. B Company of the 77th Regiment had left Waterdown for Dundas, and in 1911 the building was loaned to the public school to use as a playroom for younger students. But it was no longer safe for even that, and had been given over to storing barrels. Militia and Defence would have to decide whether to foot the bill for major repairs, estimated at $700, or turn the drill shed over to the village to clear the books. In July 1914 the department concluded that it wasn't worth the money. As soon as the necessary paperwork was done, what remained of the building would be given to the village.[1]

But there was little urgency to any of this. The harvest wasn't yet in full swing, so chores could still be put off for another day. There was plenty of time before the weather turned and put a stop to the building projects. In the meantime, a summer haze hung over the township; it was hot and sunny, and everything seemed to move at a slower pace. Will Reid was out in his rig most of the weekend, delivering eggs or shingles, perhaps with one or two children riding shotgun. Will never married but was a benevolent and much-loved uncle to a generation in the village. Whenever he had a delivery to make, he

A hot summer day in one of the township's swimming holes. Photo by Will Reid. (Author's collection)

hung a red rag out his second-floor window, and any kid who fancied a ride was welcome to join him. His other constant companion had always been his bellows camera and photographic plates, but Will had less time for photography now. Ever since his father died in 1912, Will had been running the family businesses, which involved providing for his widowed mother and his one surviving unmarried sister. He had responsibilities now, although he still tended to do things slowly and deliberately. That day, as on every other day, his horse took after its owner, sauntering at its usual unhurried pace. The clouds of dust that followed them along the concession road seemed to hang in the air forever. The June bugs kept up their insistent buzzing, but the crows could summon up the energy for only the occasional squawk. It felt hot, it looked hot, and it even sounded hot.

It was always busy at Alton's barbershop, where the pool tables were rarely idle. It was nothing like a big-city billiard hall, where aimless young men hid from work, their families, or the law. It was more like a men's club that drew all ages—teenagers trying to look older, family men trying to look younger, and old-timers dispensing wisdom and gossip in equal measure. The village charged Alton ten dollars to license the first table and five dollars for each additional one; the click of billiard balls was supposed to stop at 10 p.m. on weekdays, 11:30 p.m. on weekends, but it might be later, depending on whether or not the bylaw officer had been spotted in the area. The licences were expensive, especially when compared to other costs at the time. The village constable was paid $100 a year to be on call when the law had to be laid down (usually only at Halloween), the village clerk and treasurer $150. When Waterdown council covered the cost of hospital accommodation for an indigent resident, the bill came to $31 for four weeks. A load of gravel was worth 50 cents, and the village ordered twenty-five dog tags from a Hamilton supplier for $1.50. Will Reid would sharpen skates for 10 cents a pair or file a saw for 15 cents. He paid 75 cents for a pair of pullets and earned $2 to maintain a single cemetery plot for a year. So, $25 to license four pool tables seemed steep, but with the traffic that weekend, Dad Alton was comfortably making back his investment, a nickel at a time.

For those interested in more genteel pursuits than roller skating or pool, there was always a berry-picking excursion with the McGregors. The township had a few doctors over the years, but none were as popular as Dr. John Owen McGregor. Born in neighbouring Nelson Township, he trained at the University of Michigan and practised in Dundas before settling in Waterdown with his bride Eliza. His first office was on the corner of Dundas and Main, with his consulting room and a pharmacy on the ground floor and a meeting room, known rather grandly as McGregor's Hall, above. The doctor, notoriously cantankerous in a lovable sort of way, was a tireless practitioner. Local lore had it that he got his best rest while travelling between house calls. He would go to sleep with the reins in his hand, and his horse was well trained enough to stop at every crossroads; the doctor would wake up, guide the horse in the right direction, and then go back to sleep until the next crossroads. As he prospered, the doctor expanded his practice and bought the old Scotch Church lot in the centre of the village, complete with the church buildings, one of which became his barn. He hired John Reid to build a big rambling house (and consulting office) that was christened Clunes, in honour of Eliza's birthplace in Scotland. The couple and their seven children were at the centre of village life, both geographically and socially, for they took an active role in all sorts of organizations and activities. The doctor, with his frosty white hair and tidy beard, and Eliza, always the most gracious of hosts, were omnipresent in the township—find a group photograph taken in the village in the early twentieth century and chances are they will be in it. Perhaps on that weekend there was a hike along Grindstone Creek, where the wild berries clustered above the rock faces—perfect height for picking. Then it was back to Clunes to enjoy tea and lemonade with the fruits of their labours.

There had been the usual weekend exodus from the township, as there was all summer long. Stan Sawell tried to convince a couple of pals to sign up for the annual training camp of the 77th Regiment at Niagara, but he was outvoted—and so the trio drove north, a Waterdown pennant pinned to the soft top of their car, for a camping holiday in Muskoka.[2] It was also garden party and picnic season. Knox Presbyterian Church would hold its annual garden party on its lawn on Monday, 3 August, but the big draws were elsewhere. At the foot of Waterdown Road, just west of Brown's Wharf, was Oaklands Park and Pleasure Grounds, which had been operating as a resort since before Confederation. The city of Hamilton had bought it in 1913 and renamed it Wabasso Park, but locals didn't take kindly to outsiders coming in and changing things, so they stubbornly kept calling it Oaklands. St. Matthew's Church in Aldershot would hold its garden party there the following Wednesday, 5 August, in the large park and picnic area that boasted a pavilion nestled in a grove of trees. It would begin with baseball, two Aldershot teams squaring off for the right to play the East Hamilton Progressives later in the afternoon, all to the music of the East Hamilton Conservative Club Brass Band. Launches would shuttle between the Hamilton waterfront and Brown's Wharf every hour, all day and evening.

But there were always just as many people going the other way, to Dundurn Park on the heights on the opposite side of Burlington Bay. Opened in 1878, Dundurn Park had boasted one of Canada's first rollercoasters (or "scenic railway," as it was called then) and was home to the Hamilton Clippers in its 650-seat baseball stadium. The city of Hamilton took over the park in 1899, closing the baseball field, but expanding the zoo and the concert bowl. On the first Tuesday in August, the 4th, the Waterdown Women's Institute would make an excursion to Dundurn for its annual picnic to enjoy one of the many concerts that brightened the muggy summer evenings in Hamilton.

Yes, it was just like any other weekend. Everyone had heard the worrying news from Europe—the Austrian archduke, Franz Ferdinand, had been assassinated in Sarajevo at the end of June—but that had been weeks ago, and it had led to nothing more than Austria-Hungary and Serbia mobilizing their armies, and others threatening to do so. Granted, there had been years of industrial competition and imperial expansion, an escalating naval arms race, hyper-nationalism fuelled by an aggressive popular press, the memory of the Franco-Prussian War of 1870–71 like a burr under France's saddle, the decay of the Austro-Hungarian Empire, and Germany's territorial ambitions, which seemed to be setting the great powers on a collision course. But who could say if a collision was imminent? The summer war scare was almost a tradition—the brink seemed to be where European governments preferred to be. The Balkan War of 1913 had caused barely a ripple in Canada, just like the Balkan War of 1912. The Moroccan Crisis of 1911 had fizzled quite quickly—and hadn't there been another Moroccan Crisis a few years before that? Who knew? Such places always seemed to be in crisis—none of them ever led to anything, so there was no point in getting too worked up over them. The prospect of war did offer advertisers a new angle to exploit—"War—This is likely to mean a big advance in coal. Get it now and save money"—but it was hardly a reason to alter any plans.[3]

A Hamilton sports columnist would later write that at the beginning of August 1914, four things had seemed to be "utter impossibilities": Washington Senators pitcher Walter Johnson losing thirteen games by mid-August (he would go on to win twenty-eight games that season, but lost his thirteenth on 17 August); the Boston Braves finishing at the top of the standings (after a nightmarish 12–28 start, the "Miracle Braves" battled back to top the league, and then achieved the first-ever sweep of the World Series); and the upstart Federal League lasting out the summer (it finished the 1914 and

Facing page:

(*Top*): A Waterdown baseball team in 1914, with Dr. McGregor looking on from the seat of his buggy. Sitting in front are the McClenahan brothers (left, and second from right), both of whom served in France during the war, and Harry Horning (second from left). Behind is Rob Buchan (second from left). Photographer unknown. (Author's collection)

(*Bottom*): The people of Waterdown gather for a community picnic just before the war. Photographer unknown. (Author's collection)

1915 seasons before collapsing in 1916). The fourth utter impossibility was "a general European war."[4]

But over the weekend, the situation deteriorated with frightening speed. On Thursday, two days after Austria-Hungary had declared war on Serbia, Russia's Czar Nicholas II ordered a full mobilization; France followed, and then Germany. The Kaiser's troops massed along the frontier with neutral Belgium, to emphasize Berlin's demand for unimpeded passage through the country to France, its first target in the event of war. The invasion of a neutral state was provocation enough, but it so happened that nearly a century earlier, when Waterdown was nothing more than a scattering of houses and a couple of mills, Britain had pledged to safeguard Belgian neutrality in the Treaty of London of 1839. But would she? Would Britain stand on principle, on an eighty-year-old treaty that Germany had derided as "a scrap of paper"? Saturday's headlines were bleak—"Grim-Visaged War Now Threatens Peace of Countless Thousands"—and worrying enough to draw large crowds at the Hamilton offices of the *Spectator*, where every news bulletin was posted as it was transcribed from the telegraph machine.[5] Even when it was announced that nothing new could be expected from London that night, hundreds of people stayed behind, fearful that they might miss something.

Sunday morning brought a special edition of the *Spectator*. Workers had stayed up all night getting it ready, even though Ontario Sabbath laws made it illegal to sell newspapers on a Sunday. Undeterred, the publisher decided to give them away, and an army of newsboys fanned out across the city and surrounding communities, passing out papers on street corners and door to door, on the morning boat to Toronto, on the train to Niagara Falls. That afternoon, the crowds were back at the *Spectator* office, eagerly devouring any and all bulletins, and on Monday there was finally some news of substance. Belgium had defiantly rejected Berlin's request for free passage, and it seemed certain that German units would soon cross the frontier. Monday's headline made it clear where the *Spectator* stood on the matter: "Honor of Britain Must Be Upheld and Obligations to her Allies Fulfilled." The paper also announced that the concert already scheduled for Tuesday evening in Dundurn Park would become a patriotic evening, for such a program "in these stirring times is sure to rouse the enthusiastic patriotism of the citizens of this city." During the second half of the concert, the band of the 13th Regiment would perform the national anthems of Britain, Russia, Canada, France, and the United States.[6]

By Tuesday, it was clear that the reckoning was at hand. The British government had decided to stand firm, despatching an ultimatum to the government in Berlin: withdraw all German troops from Belgian soil by 11 p.m. London time, or a state of war would exist between Britain and Germany. "Germany Must Reply to England's Note before 12 To-Night," screamed the headlines. "Germany is Prepared to Fight the World."[7] Once again, crowds gathered in downtown Hamilton, where the *Spectator* had mounted a huge screen on which to project lantern-slide images. The hours passed, the clock creeping closer to 7 p.m. When the ultimatum deadline passed, a stifled hush fell over the crowds. What to say? Nerves jangled in expectation, a hundred possible futures flashed through everyone's minds. Quiet—calm but tense. A burble of whispering, the clatter of the streetcars as a comforting reminder of normalcy. And then the news flashed on the screen—it was war.

In an instant, a roar went up from the crowd as a thousand hats were flung into the air. "No more welcome tidings have ever been received by Hamilton people than those which were flashed onto the *Spectator* bulletin sheet last night, telling the crowd that Germany had declared war on England," observed the editor. "Long, loud, reverberant cheers burst from thousands of throats, and were re-echoed again and again." The projector operator was ready. He showed a slide with the words of the national anthem, as if anyone needed a refresher, and then a patriotic device with the bracing words of Admiral Nelson: "England expects every man to do his duty." A huge image of a British lion, "calm, fearless and majestic," was followed by portraits of various British, French, and Belgian leaders. Images of the Kaiser and his consort, and German and Austrian warships drew hisses and boos—loud and lusty, to be sure, but with little real venom in them. The mood was too jolly for such negativity; there was too much to feel good about, not the least of which was the prospect of Canada responding robustly to the call of war. Few Canadians had been looking forward to a fight, but fewer still would shy away from one that was brought to them. And that's how most people saw things in 1914. Germany had been planning for years to conquer Europe and usher in a new dark age. Britain and her allies *had* to respond—to stand aside meant surrendering liberty, democracy, Christianity, and the very foundations of human civilization. The issue couldn't be simpler: it was good versus evil, and Canada would stand with Britain on the side of right. "There is no mistaking," noted the *Spectator*, "how splendidly the blood of centuries flows in the veins of the sons of the empire, nor how splendidly the ties of kinship assert themselves in times like these."

At Dundurn Park, where the Waterdown Women's Institute was taking in the concert by the 13th Regiment's band, there was little of the nervous energy that had been generated downtown by the constant bulletins from London. It was a glorious summer evening, with the sun sparkling on Burlington Bay and dappling the park lawns. The members of the WI were probably feeling satisfied that their outing hadn't descended into inappropriate forms of merriment, like a local lodge picnic held at Dundurn earlier that weekend. Races for stout men and stout women had no place in polite society—even less did a wheelbarrow race where a man pushed a woman. No, Waterdown's gathering had been so much more civilized, and the women basked in that success. A delicious breeze toyed with the trees, and there were lemon ices for anyone who felt the heat. The band of the 13th had rarely sounded better. On such a pleasant evening, who wanted to watch the clock or wonder about deadlines in Europe? But then Hamilton mayor John Allan strode onto the stage between selections. A hush fell over the crowd—he didn't even need to raise his hand to ask for quiet—and as soon as he announced that the Empire was at war, the crowd "cut loose with its enthusiasm" and the band immediately struck up the national anthem and then "Rule Britannia."[8]

Across Wentworth County, and the rest of the country, wherever people were gathered, similar scenes played out. But in rural Canada, where five people might constitute a crowd, the mood was calmer. The office of a weekly newspaper (and East Flamborough didn't even have one of those) wouldn't attract people looking for the latest war bulletins, and there was no armoury to send out a brass band of stalwart soldiers. Jim Simmons saw no need to make a special trip to the cupola of the Bell House to do anything with the flag. Interest in the outside world was neither broad nor deep, and was usually satisfied by the talks delivered at various club meetings. Whether they listened out of a sense of interest, social obligation, or a desire for improvement, is impossible to say. People accepted news of the war and went about their business. The ladies of the Women's Institute caught a late train back to Waterdown, congratulating themselves on one of the pleasantest picnics in recent years. In the back of Dad Alton's barbershop, the billiard balls continued to click as a warm summer night descended on the village. Near Barrie, Stan Sawell and his pals had camped along a concession road and were greeted on the morning of 5 August by a farmer who told them that Canada

The first weekend of the war, and Stan Sawell and his friends go camping. Photographer unknown. (Author's collection)

was at war and that a neighbour of his had already been called to his militia unit for duty. But the boys were on holiday—it was no time to think of war. They packed up their tents, stowed everything in the car, and continued their drive north. After all, they still had over a week of holidays in front of them. War or no war, life would go on.

In the meantime, Canada moved with more swiftness than order to a war footing. Days earlier, with little fanfare, the nation had gone to the Precautionary Stage, meaning that a surprise attack was possible, and militia units were called out to guard potential targets—electrical stations, bridges, government buildings, docks. The exodus of volunteer soldiers had begun weeks earlier, as European armies summoned reservists home to rejoin their units. Reserve obligations had to be fulfilled no matter where one lived, so ex-soldiers began making their way back to Britain, France, Belgium, Italy, Russia, Serbia. The honour of being the first volunteer to leave East Flamborough went to Albert Loosley, who had come to Aldershot in 1912 to work as a groom at Valley Farm, where Ontario's lieutenant-governor, Sir John Hendrie, and his family trained racehorses (one of them, named Waterdown, was a frequent winner at local tracks during the war). Just a week after the declaration of war,

Albert was on his way back to England to rejoin his unit, the Oxfordshire and Buckinghamshire Light Infantry. German and Austrian reservists, who left Canada by the hundreds before the declaration of war, faced arrest at the border if they tried to cross into the US to sail for Europe. It all seemed a bit frantic, but this mass movement went according to war plans that the great powers had been fine-tuning for years.

Canada, too, had a war plan, which called for the raising of an expeditionary force for overseas service—one infantry division from eastern Canada and a mounted brigade from the west. Everything was carefully laid out—the number of men to be supplied by each militia unit, assembly points, travel timetables, concentration camps. On the 6th of August, the Canadian government announced that the state of war created "a menace to the well-being and integrity of the Empire"; Canada had no choice but to participate, "to provide for its own defence and to assist in maintaining the integrity and honour of the Empire."[9] It was time for the well-oiled war machine to swing into action.

But not on Sam's watch. Canada's Minister of Militia and Defence was Sam Hughes, a mercurial Orangeman from Lindsay, Ontario. He was a man of remarkable energy, capable of bursts of activity that exhausted his younger subordinates. He was passionate and patriotic, but also pig-headed and fiercely partisan. He was wedded to the militia myth, the idea that Canada's best defence lay in its citizen-soldiers, who mobilized only when the nation needed them. He distrusted career military men, and despised their war plans. Canada's mobilization scheme, in Hughes' eyes, was cold and bloodless. At such a great moment in the life of the nation, it simply wouldn't do. Canada was at a crossroads—it was no time for movement tables and train schedules, for bureaucrats filling out endless forms. It was time for a summons to arms, a clarion call to the far corners of the nation, to bring Canadians together to defend all they held dear.

The quotas of the pre-war plan were tossed out. Instead, militia units were directed to take the particulars of volunteers, submit the men to the most searching medical examination, and then forward to Ottawa the names of the fittest and keenest who came forward. Militia headquarters would make the final selections and communicate to each unit the names of the chosen. The men should be between eighteen to forty-five years old—preferably unmarried, though married men, with or without children, would be considered as well. Artillerymen had to be five feet seven inches in height, while five feet three inches was the height standard for most other categories. "In regard to musketry and general proficiency," read the directive, "a high standard will be required." This assumed that volunteers would have at least a modicum of military training. The members of the new Canadian Expeditionary Force (CEF) would be collected at Valcartier, a militia camp in Quebec, where the best of the best would be selected to join Canada's overseas contingent. Anyone who wasn't chosen for the 1st Contingent would have to wait for another opportunity.[10]

There were no armouries in East Flamborough, and it wasn't easy to enlist if you lived outside of a big city; the men of the township had to make the trek to Dundas, where the 77th Regiment was headquartered, or Hamilton, home of the 13th and 91st Regiments. Only a few did so. Will Humphreys had been in Canada for only a little over a year, but he left the family fruit farm in Aldershot to enlist. His older brother Thomas, the first of the family to emigrate, stayed behind to finish the harvest. From Waterdown went Marcus MacKay, a genial Scottish painter with a craggy face and a thick Highland accent that many villagers found unintelligible. William Gillies, who had come to Canada as a nine-year-old Home Child in 1903, walked to the Waterdown train station from a farm in Flamboro Centre, paid his fare to Hamilton, and signed up. But Humphreys, MacKay, and Gillies notwithstanding, most of East Flamborough's early volunteers, about 70 per cent, were Canadian-born, unlike the 1st Contingent as a whole, which was about 70 per cent British-born.

The common denominator was that these first volunteers all had military experience—or so they claimed. The call to arms had made much of the high standards that would be expected; there was a preference for men with some military experience, because no one knew how much training time would be available before they had to be sent into battle. Early volunteers, desperate to be among the chosen few, were prone to exaggerate their military background or even invent it outright, knowing that no one was likely to check. In the rolls of the first volunteers are a surprising number of men who served with various South American navies or with imperial mounted units bearing strange and whimsical names. A good number claimed service in one of Canada's militia units, of which there were more than 200—although given that some of them can't be found on militia rolls, there was some dishonesty behind their claims. And in many of those militia units, training was cursory at best and men like Stan Sawell and Will Humphreys were drawn to them mostly by the chance to hike around the countryside and enjoy the large summer sham battles—or "shambles," as one wag called them.

As far as the public was concerned, however, it was seasoned military veterans who were filling the ranks. On Thursday evening, the 6th, there was a great rally in Hamilton's Market Square for British military and naval veterans—time-expired reservists who were no longer obliged to return to the colours or men who had been part-time soldiers in Britain's Territorial Army. The secretary of the local Army and Navy Veterans Association stood in the middle of the crowd, recording names, addresses, and regimental affiliations to be forwarded to Ottawa—and to be published in the next day's newspaper. Worn out after hours on his feet, he retreated to his house, pursued by straggling ranks of old soldiers eager not to be left behind.[11] It was the beginning of a blur of patriotic rallies that would preoccupy the country for the next three weeks. Military bands marching around downtown streets, lines of volunteers waiting patiently to be enrolled, squads of soldiers drilling in front of adoring crowds—such things became part of life in August 1914.

And then they started to go—by the dozen at first, and then, on 22 August, by the hundred. Not until the night before did the first large group of men from the 13th and 91st Regiments know for sure that they were leaving Hamilton—they expected to have the weekend at home, but returned to the armoury after another parade through the streets to learn that their departure had been fixed for the following morning. The great drill hall of the James Street Armouries was thrown open to family members who wanted to make the most of the last hours before departure. In one corner, there was an impromptu baseball game. In another, a bunch of volunteers clustered around a fellow playing "There's a Hole in the Bottom of the Ocean" on a harmonica. It looked, observed the *Spectator*, like "they were about to start off on a little holiday jaunt." Then a bugle sounded and the men fell in for roll call. The count was taken and the colonel called them to attention for a few words from the mayor. The last thing the men wanted was platitudes from a politician, but although they itched to get moving, they stood politely—muscles tight, mouths set, eyes unmoving—until they gratefully took the command to move out, led by the band of the 13th Regiment. The crowds lining James Street were quiet—strangely so, as if no one wanted to break the spell that seemed to keep time from passing. Not until the head of the parade reached the great throng at city hall did the crowd erupt, and then the cheers threatened to drown out even the bands. At the Hunter Street railway station, there was a scene unlike any the city had ever witnessed, the crowds so tightly packed that gunners from the local 33rd Howitzer Battery had to be called in to clear a path so the troops could reach the platform. At last the train from Brantford arrived, soldiers of that city already aboard, and the band of the 13th struck up a march as the men climbed into the carriages. Then came the men of the 91st, with its band playing "Rule Britannia," and soon everyone was aboard. The reporter for the *Spectator* was moved by the pathos of the scene: "Aged women reached worn hands through the open carriage windows to bless the youthful faces which looked back so bravely ... There was a marked silence and much wiping of eyes ... One of the most touching parts of the farewell was the large number of small children who had gathered to catch a last glimpse of their older brothers." Then, with the insistent whistle of the conductor and a belch of steam from the engine, the train drew out of the station, "carrying the Maple Leaf and the Beaver into places where death may be."[12]

Their destination, ultimately, was Valcartier, a small Quebec village on the eastern bank of the Jacques Cartier River, a twenty-six-hour train ride from Wentworth County. The Department of Militia and Defence had acquired the site a few years earlier as a training camp for local militia units; at peak capacity, it was designed to accommodate 5,000 soldiers for summer exercises. But with Sam Hughes' call to arms, it suddenly became the convergence point for as many as 30,000 eager volunteers and all the engines of war. The camp sat on farmland that was granted to British soldiers who had triumphed at the Battle of the Plains of Abraham in 1759. To the north and east were rocky, wooded slopes; dotting the cleared land to the south were swamps, copses, and clumps of scrub brush. There was plenty of room to expand, and the work of clearing more land had already begun when the first party of volunteers arrived on the 18th. Three days later, Valcartier housed almost as many men as it did during the busiest summer camp of the year.

The challenge was to create an army out of almost nothing. The appearance of new drafts of volunteers arriving from across Canada gave a hint of what lay ahead. Some were fine bodies of trained men, marching in tight step and fully kitted out with field gear, a sight that would do any old soldier proud. But they might be followed by a dozen men sent by another militia unit, in civilian clothes, complete with spats and straw boaters, who ambled along in the most unmilitary fashion—or worse, by a handful of men who simply turned up on their own, confident that the army would find a place for them. Everyone would have to be outfitted with standardized equipment,

with boots, puttees, webbing, rucksacks, and khaki serge uniforms that actually fit. One of the 77th Regiment lads was probably only half joking when he
wrote home that they had been "snugly outfitted with 8 dozen shirts, neck size
18 1/2in. and underwear size 44."[13] Each man needed a peak cap, instead of the
strange mix of pith helmets, slouch hats, Stetsons, and glengarries that pre-
vailed. They all needed paperwork—pay accounts, medical and dental evalu-
ations, dependents' allowance forms. "I suppose I will have to make my will,"
observed one Toronto soldier worn out by the endless paperwork.[14] Every
man needed a CEF service number to replace the overlapping and duplicated
militia numbers they arrived with. They all had to be inoculated, something
that took on a new sense of urgency when the men watched a number of
horse carcasses being hauled from the Jacques Cartier River, the source of the
camp's drinking water.[15] There were visiting dignitaries to show off to, curious
relatives to entertain, and gifts to acknowledge and sort—in the case of the
77th Regiment men, everything from knives and handkerchiefs to sweaters
and foot powder.

The men also had to be organized. Canada had offered one division,
which was typically comprised of three infantry brigades, as well as artillery,
engineers, service corps, and various other support units, for a total of roughly
30,000 men. But how many infantry battalions would there be, and how many
men per battalion? A battalion might be eight companies, or six, or four—
which would it be? And how would each battalion be assembled? Militia units
were regional—would CEF battalions be regional too, or organized according
to some other criteria? Canada's various Highland militia regiments could
easily constitute a battalion or two ("they want us to join 48th Highlanders
& wear kilts," wrote one alarmed volunteer to his brother),[16] but they were
spread out across the country, from Victoria to Cape Breton Island. Were
British Columbians and Nova Scotians to be combined into a single unit? And
what to do with the smaller groups like the twenty-one men from Humboldt,
Saskatchewan, or the seventeen from Grand Forks, British Columbia?

Ultimately, most of the newly created battalions were given a regional
affiliation, to foster pride and assist recruiting in the future. Some of the East
Flamborough men, including William Gillies and Will Humphreys, ended
up in the 4th (Central Ontario) Battalion under Hamilton's Lieutenant-
Colonel R. H. Labatt, a member of the brewing dynasty who had first seen
action as a private during the 1885 North-West Rebellion, and another couple in
the 1st (Western Ontario) Battalion. The consolidation of kilted units saw

others, including Marcus MacKay, become part of the 16th (Canadian Scottish) Battalion, which would eventually call Vancouver home. But an awful lot of shuffling went on at all levels before the divisional organization was finally approved. One battalion went through five commanding officers in a single day as men and units were shifted around.

Letters home glossed over the administrative nightmares and focused on things that brightened the days and nights. A few battalions of men were turned out to corral 300 horses that stampeded.[17] Four runaway horses pulling a wagon charged through a wooden latrine, reducing it to matchsticks and leaving its occupant dazed but otherwise unhurt. There were moving-picture shows and, eventually, wet canteens, although the prices were diabolical. Musketry competitions were held, with a gold cup going to the company with the best marksmen. And late on 27 August, sentries stopped a soldier who was out well after curfew. Subsequent investigation revealed that the soldier was actually a thirty-year-old woman from Boston who claimed to have rented the uniform from a costume company and stole into the camp on a bet. Later, she maintained that she had borrowed it from a private so she could write a series of articles for an American magazine; she claimed to have succeeded with the stunt on other occasions. The officer on hand was unimpressed, and ordered her turned over to the provincial police. So much was going on that there seemed to be little time for training. Valcartier had the largest rifle range in the world—it was a shame not to use it.

If only it would stop raining. For the first couple of days, the drizzle kept the men cool as they worked, but soon the ground became waterlogged and everything turned soupy. Water seeped into the tents and it was impossible to keep anything dry. The tops of the hills surrounding the camp disappeared into the low clouds and even when it wasn't pouring, a fine scotch mist hung in the air. At least the rain held off for their final inspection on 20 September. For the men who had been chosen to make up the 1st Division, Canadian Overseas Expeditionary Force, it was a chance to strut their stuff. Not all of their uniforms matched and some lines were straighter than others, but it was an impressive sight. As the 1st Battalion from western Ontario passed the reviewing stand, Sir Sam Hughes was heard to remark, "Not bad for a bunch of farmers, eh?"

The review went off without a hitch, but the departure was a shambles. Hamilton's artillerymen (reconstituted as the 7th Battery, Canadian Field Artillery) had been warned to leave on Tuesday, the 24th of September, but that day passed, as did Wednesday and Thursday. On Friday came the order to move—so everything was packed up and men and equipment set off in the mid-afternoon. They got no more than a mile out of camp when the cancellation order came, so they turned around and marched right back. The next day, another move order—and a few hours later, another cancellation. At 4 p.m., it was back on and five hours later the column moved out again, through a cold and inky black night. At 4 a.m., they reached Quebec's Provincial Exhibition Grounds, and soon after dawn the first elements of the artillery brigade moved to the docks to board waiting steamers that would take them to England. That was Sunday morning—it wasn't until Thursday, the 1st of October, that the *Arcadian*, the last of the thirty big transports, slowly drew away from the dock in Quebec to join the line of vessels in the St. Lawrence.

One Canadian unit was more anxious than most to get going, for it had been cooling its heels in Montreal for nearly a month. Princess Patricia's Canadian Light Infantry had been established by Montreal millionaire Hamilton Gault and offered directly to the British government; so concerned was Gault that he would miss out on the fighting that he pledged to pay the entire cost of raising the battalion, something like two million dollars in current values, himself. With the governor-general's military secretary Francis Farquhar as its commanding officer, the unit had directed its recruiting call at British émigrés, preferably those with previous military experience. The response was stunning. Friends of Gault quickly set up local recruiting stations in Montreal, Toronto, Winnipeg, Calgary, and Edmonton, and within days the first of over 3,000 volunteers had reached Ottawa. Farquhar interviewed every single one of them, and eventually settled on a roster of 1,098 men. Over 90 per cent were British-born, and all but forty-nine claimed to have prior military experience.

Tom Flintoft of Waterdown didn't meet either criterion. He was born in the Niagara peninsula, in southern Ontario, and the few camps he spent with Hamilton's 91st Regiment could hardly be considered to have given him military experience. Nor was he among the "prize-fighters, cow-punchers, and pipers," as Farquhar called the other forty-nine men picked for the unit. Tom was working as a gas fitter in Edmonton when the war broke out, and something about Gault's appeal for men caught his eye. He was among one of the first groups of volunteers leaving the Alberta capital for Ottawa.

The Patricias had been ready to sail for England in August, but the British government had decided that troopships must sail in convoy—Hamilton Gault's battalion had to wait until the 1st Contingent was ready to sail.

Tom Flintoft (right), with a fellow member of Princess Patricia's Canadian Light Infantry. Photographer unknown. (Author's collection)

Some of his officers occupied their time by learning French, for Farquhar had decreed that no officer could accompany the unit to France unless he could read and write a simple message in French. The men of the contingent, however, didn't have to worry about language instruction. On the *Caribbean*, which carried some of the Wentworth County volunteers, the men were in high spirits. The food was good and plentiful and there were only two parades a day, for calisthenics, no easy feat on the pitching deck of an ocean steamer. In the limited deck space, games were improvised—football, cockfighting (but not the kind that went on in Gilmer's wagon shop in Waterdown), tug-of-war, boxing, jumping—and there were nightly concerts by three Hamilton artillerymen; the proceeds were donated to the Liverpool Seaman's Orphanage. Daily news bulletins were posted on decks, and the *Caribbean* even had a newspaper. The paper was current, probably more up-to-date than some of the men got at home; news reports were transmitted to the escort vessels by wireless, and then relayed to the liners by signal flags.[18]

On 14 October, land was sighted—they had spent thirteen days in transit, but some units had been on board for nearly three weeks. The ships had been badly loaded in Quebec, so there was chaos as they were unloaded. The horses were taken off first, because they had suffered most during the voyage, and then units were disembarked as quickly as possible—which wasn't quickly enough for men who were stuck on board in Plymouth harbour for nearly a week. Individual experiences depended entirely on the luck of the draw. Hamilton's gunners disembarked in brilliant sunshine and marched through cheering crowds to the railway station. At every stop, adoring villagers gathered to welcome them; every station platform and every bridge was packed with waving people. At Exeter, they could barely see the station buildings for the crowds. One woman bought up the entire stock of the station café and distributed it among the men as her gift to Canada. It was a heroes' welcome, and the gunners were well fed and happy when they reached their destination at 11:30 p.m. The fifteen-mile march to West Down North Camp, which they reached four hours later, left them in good spirits, although tired, cold, and weary.

Other units began the journey tired, cold, and weary. When the 4th Battalion disembarked from the *Tyrolia*, massive grey clouds had brought an early dusk and the rain was pelting down as the first ranks reached the railway station. By the time they detrained just before midnight it was a proper deluge and the men set off in what they hoped was the direction of their camp. Colonel Labatt tried to go by car with the padre, but the vehicle got hopelessly stuck while manoeuvring around a stalled steam tractor, and they had to do the rest of the journey on foot. More by luck than good management, they reached the camp to find that there was nothing laid on for their 1,100 men— no food, no drink, no accommodation. The officers blundered around in the dark, trying to find someone to assist them, and Labatt finally bumbled into the tent occupied by the colonel of Toronto's 3rd Battalion, who was at least able to direct him to their assigned section. Labatt then found a dining tent and roused the orderlies from bed. None too happy to be awoken, they grudgingly asked how many men needed drinks and blinked in stunned silence when Labatt said 500 now, 600 more in two hours' time. But we have only fifty mugs on hand, one of them stammered. After a few choice words from Labatt, they agreed to brew coffee in batches and serve it to the men in their canteens, so the ranks were told to take shelter in the tents until refreshments were ready. Many of them immediately fell into a deep sleep.[19]

Their new home, when they were able to see it, was the Salisbury Plain in the south of England. It was exactly what the Canadian-born among them might have imagined England to be. Little villages full of thatched cottages, tiny churches with stone floors worn by centuries of worshippers, lush fields and thick hedgerows, ancient monuments emerging from the mists of time, snug pubs with roaring fireplaces and strong ale. But the men could be forgiven for assuming that it was Valcartier all over again, chiefly because of the unrelenting rain. It was the wettest winter that locals could remember, bringing more than twice the usual amount of rain. Roads and fields disappeared under lakes, tents were washed away, and mud seeped into every corner of kit. On many days, it was too wet to attempt any kind of training whatsoever. Blankets and tents were permanently damp and morale sank as the construction of huts was delayed by a shortage of skilled workers. "Give me a snowbank and a sheet of ice in preference to rain and mud for days at a time," wrote one soldier of the 3rd Battalion plaintively. "It is nothing but mud and water around this place."[20]

At first, the army was liberal with leave passes, assuming that a little recreation would help the men endure the miseries of camp life. But overindulgence soon became a problem. The number of VD cases grew alarmingly and, as the *Spectator* reported, "too much British hospitality and too much firewater taken by some of the Canadian troops while on leave from camp" resulted in fifteen privates being dismissed from the ranks and a few lieutenants losing their commissions.[21] General Edwin Alderson, the newly appointed commander of the 1st Division, publicly pleaded with locals to stop indulging Canadians in their quest for alcohol, at the risk of all passes being cancelled, but it made little impact. One Hamilton soldier complained about the bad reputation of Canadians, some of whom "would be a disgrace to a heathen country." Dozens of soldiers were discharged "in the interests of discipline" and shipped back to Canada in November, some of them in irons.[22] In letters home, the good-natured griping about the rain started to take on a harder edge as frustration took hold. "Miserable, shivering, half-drowned, living in a state of unabating mud-soaked misery," wrote one soldier in his diary.[23] The parades, the bands, the cheering crowds of August and September—all of it seemed like another world to the men huddling in sodden tents as an English winter blew around them.

———◆———

WHILE EAST FLAMBOROUGH'S FIRST VOLUNTEERS were paddling in the mud of Valcartier and Salisbury Plain, life in the township returned to a settled calm. There wasn't much else people could do. All signs still pointed to a short, sharp war that would put Germany in its place. That belief goes some way to explaining the enthusiasm that greeted the coming of war. It would last only a few months at most, and it certainly wouldn't continue past Christmas. Anything else was unthinkable. The worry was not that Canada's young men were signing up for a war that would last for years, but that it might end before they even reached the battlefield. Still, until war became anything more than an abstraction, life in the township continued.

And so the seasonal rituals went on—not even war could derail the annual Mission Band picnic at Dundurn Park or the yearly excursion from Waterdown to Burlington Beach. Millgrove's usual late August baseball tournament went ahead, although the big attraction wasn't the visiting teams from Strabane, Carlisle, and Kilbride, but the evening's moving-picture show, supported by songs, recitations, and instrumental music. And soon it was time for the Waterdown Fair. The fairgrounds (as the locals called it—it was really just a big field) were at the north end of the village, beyond the James' house, although the whole village was decorated with bright bunting and flags. At this year's fair, the chatter wasn't about the war, but about the fancy embroidery by Ada Flintoft, Eliza McGregor's asters, and a three-foot-long beet (another farmer had decided against showing his snake-shaped cauliflower, preferring to display it for a wider audience at the *Hamilton Spectator* office).[24] There was a strolling bagpiper for the Scots, and if you kept your eyes open, you might see two well-dressed men and two strapping boys, modelling the latest fall fashions on behalf of Begg & Shannon's menswear in Hamilton.[25] (Most locals didn't see the need to go to the city for clothes, for Waterdown had two tailors to serve the area. "Maybe you did not always get the latest style or the most perfect fit," recalled Stan Sawell, "but you did get a well-made, long-wearing garment of good material.") There were horse races, although not the kind that drew Sir John Hendrie's thoroughbreds from Valley Farm. This was strictly amateur hour, with the star being Nimble Jim, "who was so nimble that when completing the second lap he was overtaken by the other horses doing the third, [and] received rounds of applause as he finished after delaying the following event just five minutes."

In any newspaper, in any region of Canada, you could find similar articles describing very similar fairs—the same games, the same prize-winning flowers and vegetables, the same attractions. But the *Spectator* correspondent brought a note of whimsical fondness to his subject, an understanding of the rural mind that owed something to Stephen Leacock. I tried to find out who was writing about East Flamborough for the *Spectator*, but without success. It was certainly someone who recognized that ambitious small towns tended to take themselves too seriously, but whose affection for those communities didn't suffer because of that recognition. Reading through the *Spectator* for the war years, I came across a handful of articles about events in the township, all in the same insightful but tongue-in-cheek tone. For obvious reasons, I was especially taken by an account of a court case that followed an episode in Carlisle on a Sunday evening after church. Carlisle had voted years earlier to go dry—the village's hotel had long since become the Temperance House—but that didn't stop a few young men from a neighbouring township from forgoing worship to meet in the church's cavernous driving shed and pass around a bottle. Once it was drained, they stumbled to their rigs to begin the trip home—just as church let out. As the *Spectator* reported, "There were democrats and broughams and drays and nifty rubber-tired buggies in the parade homeward after the final 'amen,' and naturally traffic was stalled many times." One of the worshippers was none other than Clare Laking, who had driven down from the family farm northeast of the township. But in the post-service crush, "Clare, driving a pestiferous, mean-dispositioned mare, was stalled. The ding-busted, dad-burned mare smelled oats at home and didn't relish the delay, so, naturally, she just tried to climb over everything in sight." What happened next was for the magistrate to sort out. Clare's buggy banged into Vic Weir's, leaving an ugly scratch down the side. Wellie McCoy, one of Vic's drinking buddies, responded by whipping Clare's mare, so Clare laid the whip on Vic. Eddie Wilder, the third of the trio, threw a few punches and took a few punches, coming out roughly even. Before things could degenerate into a general brawl, Charles Mount, a prosperous Mountsberg farmer who acted as constable whenever the law had to be laid down (outside of Halloween hijinks, he rarely had much to do as constable), appeared on the scene and laid charges. In the 3rd Division Court in the Bell House a few days later, Eddie Wilder insisted that he had joined in the tussle because Clare had thrown a few curses his way, but Clare denied that: "Never cussed in my life, and I defy any man in the world to say I did. I'm not prosecuting these roughs because I'm vindictive, but I feel that I wouldn't be doing my duty towards human-ity if I didn't thresh it out. I'd be ashamed to look respectable people in the face." After ninety minutes of witness testimony, the magistrate fined McCoy, Wilder, and Weir ten dollars each plus costs, and advised Mount to do a better job of curbing rowdyism in Carlisle. The constable, however, laid the blame on the Dundas magistrates: "I've been bringing my prisoners to Dundas, but every time I charge a man with being drunk he brings all the drunks in the village to prove he wasn't."[26]

The magistrates were used to dealing with young roisterers who had over-indulged and clearly the weight of the war hadn't galvanized the entire nation into good behaviour. But there was no question that things were changing. No matter how hard they tried, people couldn't pretend that everything was normal. More and more, the war started to creep into the everyday, often in an unexpected way. One shop owner, upon unpacking a shipment of new picture postcards to sell, found that a third of the new postcards featured vessels of the German navy. "Needless to say, they are going back with the remark 'Try Germany.' At a time like the present," he informed readers of the *Spectator*, "it's more than I can stand to sell them. Yours, An Englishman."[27] The Kirk Hotel and the American Hotel in Waterdown (the latter, in operation since 1824, was then run by Mary Cook, described as "a lady of culture and refined tastes" who succeeded in making it "the abode of cheer and hospitality that it is") still served Dawes Königsbier, but in the advertisements, the old name was crossed out and replaced with Kingsbeer. "Are You Doing Your Duty As a Canadian?" was the pointed question. "If you're not going to the front, at least be loyal to Canada. And show your loyalty by patronizing Canadian products. If all Canadians would do this and keep their money circulating in Canada, they would be doing more than anything else to help the Empire and their country. When you drink lager, ask for Kingsbeer—a Canadian product, made by Canadians for Canadians."[28] For people who found the new lexicon of war confusing, the *Spectator* offered a phonetic pronunciation guide of "jaw-breakers and tongue-twisters," from Mawng dee di ay (Montdidier) and San kon tan (St Quentin) to Psham e sel (Prszemsyl) and Sar a yav o (Sarajevo)—complete with accented syllables and nasal sounds identified.[29]

But the biggest changes weren't in the shops, the bars, and the newspapers; they were in the social life of the township. Rural life had always been animated by relentless sociability and a strong drive towards mutual aid, but often the latter had been a pretext for the former. There was a kind of false solemnity behind meetings of groups such as the Society for the Recovery of Stolen Horses, which met frequently, invariably agreed on the same report ("No horses were stolen during the past year"), and then got down to the feasting and entertainment.[30] Now, a genuine sense of purpose took over the communal life of East Flamborough. Everyone could join the war effort. While the young men, and eventually the young women, were enlisting, those who stayed behind were mobilizing their fundraising ideas and handicraft skills. They would fight the war with knitting needles and loose change.

Community patriotic groups were up and running even before the 1st Contingent left Valcartier. To the north, the Township of Puslinch had already established a Farmers' Patriotic Fund, "for the collection of oats and cash from the rural districts, for National Aid and Relief in the present war crisis."[31] In Campbellville, at the north end of Halton County, forty charter members had signed up to establish the Women's Patriotic Society.[32] Such things spurred the people of East Flamborough; it was no time to be left behind by their neighbours. The Wentworth Patriotic Association had been established early in the war, and in October 1914 meetings were held to inaugurate branches in Waterdown and Freelton.[33] The East Flamborough Red Cross quickly created a war services committee and a local branch of the Belgian relief fund, part of an international effort to assist civilians displaced by the German invasion of Belgium. Villagers in Waterdown set up the Women's Patriotic League and the Patriotic War Fund; doubters who pointed out that the membership rolls for the two organizations were virtually identical were shushed into silence.

But the first fundraising experience wasn't a happy one. At the beginning of the war, the Imperial Order Daughters of the Empire had offered to the British government a hospital ship, to be paid for by the women of Canada; eventually, a central committee representing more than a dozen of the nation's leading women's organizations pledged to raise at least $100,000 in just two weeks. The campaign succeeded beyond all expectations, raising more than $280,000 that went, at Britain's request, not to a hospital ship but to expand the naval hospital at Haslar, near Portsmouth. The Waterdown

Women's Institute had jumped into the fray and, with a flurry of box socials, tag days, and door-to-door canvasses, quickly raised the not inconsiderable sum of $140—almost as much as the village clerk was paid in an entire year. And then to suffer the indignity of rejection: a polite but firm letter from the central committee saying that, because the fund had already been oversubscribed, the help of Waterdown's women was not required. A crushing blow, delivered so graciously and tactfully, but a crushing blow nevertheless. The WI regrouped at its October meeting and decided to send seventy-five dollars to the Red Cross, and hold the rest as a wartime emergency fund. Then, after agreeing to host the Carlisle and Millgrove WIs for a guest speaker on the war, sent by head office, the women got down to what they did best: "Mrs Blagden gave us an ideal Paper on Our flag, and what it stands for and left us with some beautiful thoughts," followed by Miss Robson's paper entitled "Simple meals, well cooked and nicely served. The Refining Influence." Mrs. Davidson demonstrated the proper way to ice a cake, and the meeting ended, as it always did, with the singing of "God Save the King."[34]

Slowly but surely, the war took over East Flamborough's community groups. The Anglican Young People's Association (AYPA), whose usual fare involved musical selections and members' talks on subjects such as adventure novelist G. A. Henty, explorer David Livingstone, and the poetic genius of The Khan (a.k.a. Robert Kernighan), received an offer from a Toronto gentleman to visit with a lantern slide lecture on the war. The members decided that such an event "would not be suitable for our entertainment," and resolved instead to put on a patriotic concert or play. At the November meeting of the Waterdown Women's Institute, the president "presented to the meeting the question of helping the Belgians and told of the Committee which had already been formed in the village and were doing good work." The decision was made to raid the branch's emergency fund and transfer ten dollars to the Patriotic War Fund and twenty dollars to the Women's Patriotic League. And then, Edith Stock "gave a valuable paper entitled the 'Twentieth Century Girl.' She showed how the French mothers deal with their daughters which proved their wise judgement. Canadian mothers are too lax in dealing with them."[35] It was another expression of the common view that the war's benefits were many and varied, and that it might improve standards of conduct and deportment, which, many thought, had been slipping a bit in recent years.

The war bought Waterdown's drill shed a stay of execution, Militia and Defence deciding in August that "this matter could very well stand for a month of two, until the Department is relieved of the present pressure of work."[36] Two months had passed since the matter was first raised, and there now seemed to be a good chance that the shed might actually be put to its intended use. The German advance into Belgium in August had been stoutly resisted but the weight of numbers told, and within ten days German troops were pouring over the border into France. It had taken them much longer to get through Belgium than expected; the goal of enveloping Paris, which would knock France out of the war, counted on timing, and soon the offensive was behind schedule. A British Expeditionary Force (BEF) of four infantry divisions and one cavalry brigade had been despatched to the continent in August, taking up positions east of the city of Cambrai, in northern France. On the 22nd, British and Germany cavalry patrols clashed south of Mons, Belgium, the BEF's first engagement of the war, and the following day British divisions along the Mons canal found themselves outnumbered by more than two to one as a massive German offensive struck. British riflemen inflicted punishing losses on the attackers, but eventually had to give ground as the German armies swept south towards Paris in a great counter-clockwise arc. The Entente armies were not out of it yet, however, and along the Marne River, French and British divisions stood their ground, pushed back where they could, and forced the invading Germans to abandon the idea of conquering Paris. But what the Allies celebrated as a great victory in September 1914 condemned the world to a long, brutal war. The opposing sides were now roughly equal in numbers, an advantage in one place balanced by a weakness somewhere else. After the Marne battle, a series of offensives extended the front lines to the Swiss border in the southeast and to the English Channel in the northwest. In a bitter fight in October and November, the Germans tried to push the Entente out of the last corner of Belgium that was still free. At the coast, the Belgians broke their dykes and flooded the land rather than see it fall to German troops. Inland, the ancient cloth-trading city of Ypres faced furious German attacks that were beaten back by a much smaller force of British defenders. For the moment, a small corner of Belgium would remain unconquered.

"Over by Christmas" was by now consigned to the past, a symbol of the naïveté of August 1914. On all sides, casualties had been terrifying. The French had lost as many as 850,000 men, including some 2,200 killed for each day the country had been at war. Germany lost roughly 750,000 and Belgium 50,000. The BEF had lost nearly 100,000 men, the end of the superbly trained

professional army of the Edwardian era. Canada's volunteers had despaired
that the war might end before they got into the thick of it; they were now
guaranteed a place in the fight. The federal government had already opted to
double Canada's commitment; a second contingent would be raised, to follow
the first overseas as soon as possible, and 50,000 men would be kept continu-
ously in training in Canada. Prime Minister Robert Borden declined to say how
many men the nation might be prepared to mobilize. Was it 50,000? Or even
100,000? "I prefer to name no figure," Borden responded. "If the preservation
of our Empire demands twice or thrice that number, we shall ask for them."

The asking began on 20 October, when the *Spectator* announced that
recruiting for another fourteen infantry battalions, some 16,000 men, would
begin immediately; cavalry, artillery, and other units would begin accepting
volunteers shortly. Once again, the 13th, 77th, and 91st Regiments began to
enrol volunteers, single men first and then married men, with or without children. Any man under the age of twenty-one had to present the written consent of his parents, as did a man of any age whose parents were dependent on
him. Married men had to provide the written consent of their wives.[37] This
had less to do with consideration for the sanctity of the family than with
hard-headed pragmatism; no one wanted soldiers' dependants to become a
charge on the state. Even with such inconveniences, the response was swift.
Thousands of men had been turned away from local armouries in August and
were keen for another chance; thousands more, having witnessed the cheering
crowds at railway stations, decided to get in on the fun. Across Canada, units
filled even more quickly than they had in August. Within a few weeks, most
of them had reached their authorized strength.

In East Flamborough, the announcement of a second contingent sent the
township's military apparatus into action. The 77th Regiment in Dundas had
already beefed up its officer corps, adding sixteen new subalterns in September, but more volunteers were needed for Waterdown's company, which had
taken over the roller rink a couple of nights a week for training while the drill
shed was put into shape. The 77th had also been given the task of providing
volunteers to protect one of the region's strategic assets and had despatched
more than 100 men to the task, including a handful of men from Waterdown.
Not for them the furious tilt against the Hun on Flanders' fields. Their job
was to keep an eye on the Welland Canal, to guard against enemy saboteurs
while avoiding the greatest risk before the force: falling in the water. But some
of the guards wanted to go overseas with the new contingent, and it was up to

regimental headquarters to find replacements. The pay was $7.70 a week, plus board, and Militia and Defence did its best to make the assignment sound like a plum: "authorized to offer any present or new member of your company the privilege of nominating one Niagara guard for every five residents of your township. He enrols in your company provided he is sober, well behaved and a fit young man, and joins your company before the second overseas contingent is mobilized. Any resident of your township hereafter volunteering for overseas, and who is accepted, shall have the privilege of nominating one Niagara guard."[38] Deep into a long, cold night spent pacing along the banks of the canal, many a volunteer might have wondered if the job was as desirable as it had been made out to be.

Within two weeks, the next lot of volunteers to the 13th and 91st Regiments was ready to depart. The scene in Hamilton that brisk November morning was not very different from what the first volunteers experienced in September. The troops marched from the armouries along streets packed with people. "Here and there," observed the *Spectator*, "the tears were seen to start from the eyes of sweethearts, wives and mothers who were watching their loved ones leave Hamilton, perhaps many of them never to return." A little after 11 a.m., as the bands of the 13th and 91st Regiments played "Tipperary," the men climbed aboard four carriages. A few minutes later, the express from St. Catharines pulled in bearing more men; a yard engine hooked up the Hamilton carriages and soon they were on their way, the words of a specially written ditty ringing in their ears: "Get out your new Ross rifle and put a trusty bayonet on it, / And we'll meet Der Kaiser at the war: / Then we'll send him to Dover, to think the matter over, / While we pile up his navy on the shore."[39]

But they wouldn't experience the joys of Valcartier. It had been good enough for a fall mobilization, but not even Sam Hughes saw the camp as suitable for lodging and training troops over the winter. Instead, units would be concentrated regionally. For new volunteers from the 13th and 91st Regiments, that meant Toronto's Exhibition Grounds. Along with men from Toronto's Queen's Own Rifles and Royal Grenadiers and a contingent from a regiment in Sault Ste. Marie, they would become the 19th (Central Ontario) Battalion. It would be quartered in the Government Building (rather inappropriately, the men's mess was in the Women's Christian Temperance Union Dining Room), with headquarters and the sergeants' mess in the Women's Building, officers' quarters in the Fine Arts Building, and officers' mess in the Administration Building. Men from the 77th Regiment of Dundas became part of the

20th (Central Ontario) Battalion, and were put in the Horticulture Building; their mess was in Bird's Restaurant, behind the main grandstand, while their officers and sergeants were housed with those of the 19th Battalion.

It was dormitory living for the men. The buildings' great exhibition halls were filled with large bed frames, each about fourteen feet long and eight feet wide, which served as bunks for eight men. Each was issued a straw-filled mattress, a pillow, and two blankets; their rifles were stored in racks attached to the frames, and hooks were provided at the end of each bunk for all their worldly possessions. But they didn't spend much time in the barracks, for the training week was long and arduous. It began early—before the sun was up in the winter months—usually with a thirty-minute run and calisthenics before going into squad drill, small groups of men learning to work together, in concert, so that their movements became automatic. As they grew more comfortable with the routine, they began to work in platoons, then companies, and finally entire battalions. It wasn't the most exciting of experiences, but periodic route marches through the city provided a welcome diversion, in addition to teaching the mysteries of marching in order. Rifle practice took place under the grandstand in the winter months; in the spring, they started making the seven-mile march to the rifle ranges at Long Branch, west of Toronto, for firing. They practised digging trenches around Stanley Barracks, and occasionally went out for larger manoeuvres so their officers could learn the art of moving large bodies of men quickly and with a minimum of confusion. Those routines were considerably less popular with the men, for they invariably involved long periods of waiting for something to happen. As they tramped around Cedarvale on a bitterly cold day or waited for orders in High Park through a pitch-black night, they might well have seen themselves as so many chess pieces being manipulated by grand masters.

But if the surviving photos are any indication, they were having a grand time. They mug for the camera with broad smiles and bright eyes, their horseplay giving no hint of the deadly task for which they were preparing. Their neat serge uniforms and peak caps give them a look of distinction that is enhanced by the moustaches—so many moustaches! At least one battalion commander announced that, in the interests of promoting their marksmanship, his men must not shave their upper lips. This, reported the *Spectator*, was "based solely upon the scientific principle that scraping the upper lip affected nerves which influenced the eye."[40] Perhaps the First World War really was the war of the scientists.

October brought the first snow flurries to the township, and high winds in November sent temperatures plunging. Delicate blooms of ice fringed Grindstone Creek and frozen baubles already dangled from branches below the Great Falls, where the water splashed up from the rocks. A sheen of hoarfrost blanketed the pastures most mornings, and old-timers confidently promised that a heavy snowfall was only days away. It came in mid-December, with gusty west winds carrying in the first of what would amount to two feet of snow for the month, just as the township was preparing for Christmas. The season was less commercial than it would be a century later, but if there was less gift-giving, people more than made up for it with their relentless socializing. Every organization had to have a Christmas social, and every church and home had to be decked out for the season.

The AYPA set about decorating Grace Church with masses of sweet-smelling evergreen boughs that Rob Buchan brought from his yard. The members were deep into rehearsals for their contributions to the church Sunday school's entertainment—"A Slight Mistake," a fluffy romance involving a mix-up between an heiress and an actress, and "Dad Says So, Anyhow," about a tongue-tied bumpkin trying to woo a farmer's daughter.[41] Neither of them had anything to do with Christmas, but they were fun. At the roller rink on the 11th of December, the children of the Waterdown schools gave their annual Christmas concert, featuring songs, club drills, and a short play. And what Christmas concert would be complete without an address on "The Causes of the Great War" by James Gibson Hume, a philosophy professor at the University of Toronto, with Waterdown's schoolmaster, a forty-year teaching veteran with the Dickensian name Ebenezer Rufus Witherill, in the chair? Never given to excessive praise, the *Spectator* applauded the evening as "pleasing" and "most acceptable."[42] It was ice-skating season, and Will Reid could sharpen as many pairs of skates as he had a mind to—or as many as he needed to restock his supply of photographic plates. He always did a good trade at that time of year, as locals asked for photos to send to distant relatives. Will has happy to oblige, and had them printed on postcard stock for ten cents apiece.

It was the first real wartime Christmas that anyone had experienced, and already it was clear that the war was casting a shadow over daily life. Over in England, at least a dozen men with East Flamborough connections were serving with the 1st Contingent—some were residents or former residents, others had parents or siblings in the township. Because of the deplorable conditions on Salisbury Plain, the authorities had been generous with leave passes, allowing them to spend the holidays with family or friends, rather than in the dismal tent city. The Princess Patricias were already in France, and Tom Flintoft was spending his first Christmas at war. The unit reached its first front-line billets, in the tiny French village of Blaringhem, on Christmas Eve, and the men spent the next morning sorting out their equipment. "Unfortunately," reported the unit's war diarist sourly, "Christmas comforts not available."[43] Across Canada, another dozen men with ties to the township had already enlisted with the 2nd Contingent—but they at least had a better chance of getting home for the holidays. Edwardian families were used to being separated, even at Christmas, by work, marriage, or circumstance, but this was different. Behind the cheery letters home and the smiling faces in snapshots, behind the conviction in the rightness of the cause and the necessity of defending a way of life, there must have been uncertainty. What would it cost? How long would it take? How many wartime Christmases lay ahead?

3

1915

A brand new year in East Flamborough. Crisp, clean snow blankets everything—soon there will be up to two feet in places, enough to collapse the roof of Burlington's new skating rink.[1] On another of his seemingly endless errands, Will Reid clops along the concession road on his rig, then pauses to survey his world. He hears the trees creak and watches a solitary crow skim from fence to fence over corn stubble that sticks through the snow, making the field look like an unshaven chin. Off in the distance, two skaters chase each other around a frozen pond as a herd of cattle watch fixedly, wreaths of steam surrounding their heads as they breathe deeply. Will likes what he sees.

A brand new year on Salisbury Plain, according to a member of the 1st Contingent: "We sit, a dismal wet circle, around a creaking tent-pole, listening to the 'pat-pat' of the infernal rain on the dripping canvas overhead ... there is no attempt at cracking feeble jokes. We have got beyond that stage of misery. And so the morning drags on! There is nothing to do—no place where one might go to spend a dry hour. Clothes, blankets, bedding—all are sodden."[2]

The diarist wisely decided against recording just what he thought about military authorities, but the new year found the army clattering along in the attempt to make the 1st Division ready for war. The desperate effort to outfit everyone at Valcartier hadn't gone as planned; the division was still short of most things, and much of what it possessed had to be replaced. Canadian boots came apart as the stitching rotted under the assault by English damp. Web equipment was uncomfortable to wear, couldn't hold enough bullets, and wouldn't accommodate a knapsack. Field shovels, pierced by two holes through which a rifleman could fire, were good neither for digging nor for shooting. Motor trucks, heavy wagons, harnesses—almost everything had to be replaced from British stocks. Battalion organization went from eight companies to four and back again to eight before the War Office finally decided that all British and Empire battalions would be organized into four companies. The canny soldier guessed that the feverish activity was leading to something, but it was the formal inspection on 4 February that offered proof. The appearance of King George V and Queen Mary, accompanied by Lord Kitchener, the dynamic War Minister whose stern face gazed from countless recruiting posters, to inspect the division was a sure sign that it would be leaving soon. "I am well aware of the discomforts that you have experienced from the inclement weather and abnormal rain," read the King's message, "and I admire the cheerful spirit displayed by all ranks in facing and overcoming all difficulties. From all I have heard, and what I have been able to see at today's inspection and march-past, I am satisfied that you have made good use of your time spent on Salisbury Plain."

On the 7th of February, the men of the 1st Division began to march away from their camps—in a drenching rain, which seemed entirely fitting. Because of German submarine activity in the English Channel, they had to take the roundabout way to the front, not straight across, but from Avonmouth to St. Nazaire. This meant a long, stomach-churning voyage through the Bay of Biscay, with men constantly on guard duty to watch the grey, ominous waves for enemy U-boats. As one fellow of the 3rd Battalion recalled, the "stern of the boat was going up and down, and I'm watching the waves to see if I can see a periscope bob up, but all I can see is the roast pork we had for dinner." St. Nazaire had limited port facilities, so unloading was a slow process—some units spent as long as five days on board their transports—and then they had to do their own stevedoring. A painting of the division's arrival in France shows a pipe band marching past the smartly clad soldiers, their officers watching admiringly and local children gazing in awe. In reality, it was a scraggly group of soldiers, exhausted, green at the gills, and grumbling, that filed through St. Nazaire to the railway station, to find that the best the army had to carry them into battle was cattle cars.

It was a slow journey to the front but after being cramped in the transports for days, the men revelled in the fresh air. They left open the big sliding doors of the cattle cars and sat dangling their legs over the ledge, as children might have done. But high spirits bred carelessness, and on the evening of 13 February, after they had been on the trains for about twenty-four hours, bugles blew frantically and the train carrying the 4th Battalion shuddered to a halt near the French village of Darnetal. One platoon reported that Fred Norris, an English immigrant to Peel County, had been hanging his legs out the open door when a sudden lurch of the train pitched him off. He fell awkwardly and was caught up in the train's running gear; pulled under the wheels, he died instantly. The train couldn't be delayed, so the battalion's medical officer and two orderlies were left behind to deal with the body. While the rest of the 1st Division carried on to join the 2nd Army near Armentières, west of the gritty French mining city of Lille, Norris was buried in St. Sever Cemetery in Rouen. He was just nineteen years old.

If the War Office had its wish, the Canadians wouldn't have lingered at Armentières, but would have gone into the line piecemeal, to stiffen British formations wherever they were needed. But the Borden government was adamant: the Canadian division would not be broken up. So, beginning on 17 February, individual units were sent into the lines to shadow British units and familiarize themselves with trench routine. Three weeks later, on 3 March, the 1st Division was pronounced ready to take over its own sector south of Fleurbaix, 6,400 yards of front-line trenches that snaked through sodden fields, farm hedges, and rows of pollard willows.

They had so much to learn, but proved themselves to be remarkably adaptable. After just a week in the trenches, one Halton County soldier of the 4th Battalion wrote home to describe the experience:

> We are still doing our turn in the trenches. When the weather is good it is not bad at all, but when it is wet and cold, it is horrid. Our feet are wet all the time. They have places there to rest; they call them dugouts. They are in the earth dug out in the sides of the trenches. You lie down in them at night, fully dressed, with all your ammunition on, while there is a sentry placed on duty. If there is anything wrong, he gives the order to stand to, and everyone jumps to his post at a moment's notice.
> ... we are all first-class cooks. We turn out some of the finest dishes you could wish for. I suppose it's the mud that falls in it that makes the

flavor. Everybody is getting their hair clipped off short in our company. The Germans will wonder what is coming at them when we make a charge.

The damage some of the shells have done around here is horrible, whole villages are ... ruins. One place we were in the Germans started to shell and all the people were seen to leave their houses with bundles and make for the next town. One of our guns started sending souvenirs over to the Germans, and the French people, hearing the firing, jumped out of their houses. One of the civilians had an alarm clock, another had a glass and everyone had something different. They made one leap across the road like so many rabbits, and dived headfirst into the cellars of a big building opposite.

All over the country you will see little wooden crosses which mark the place of soldiers' graves—of our own soldiers. On some of the crosses you will see hung the soldier's cap. Some of the English soldiers told me of a certain place where such a lot of Germans were killed they didn't have time to bury them properly, and often when you are walking along you will see an arm or a leg, and sometimes a head sticking up out of the ground. The first time we entered the trenches we were just in time to see them carrying out two poor fellows who had been hit by rifle grenades. It was an appalling sight in the moonlight.

Sincerely, your son.

Tom[3]

The 4th Battalion's familiarization routine was interrupted by an outbreak of scarlet fever—showing its usual unintentional sense of humour, the army moved them to billets in an unfinished hospital building, "which was found to be very draughty owing to scarcity of windows and doors," noted the unit's diarist.[4] Like the rest of the Canadian battalions, the 4th moved in and out of the trenches on a routine basis, repairing trench works, training when they could (the war diary for a typical day records "trench attack practice—running across ploughed field"),[5] enduring inspections by senior officers, testing their skill at estimating distance. Some of it was fun, some simply tedious. But it wasn't always safe, and there was a small but steady toll from stray shells or bullets, accidents, illness—"normal wastage," the army called it.

Tom Flintoft was one such casualty. The Princess Patricias weren't part of the 1st Division—they had joined a British division and were coming to the end of another familiarization tour in the trenches near St. Eloi. On the day they were due to be relieved, a flurry of trench mortar shells rained down on one of the forward companies. Four of the men were hit, including Tom, who took a piece of shrapnel in the wrist. As the rest of the battalion marched back to their rear-area billets, the four Patricias were sent to the nearest casualty clearing station. Tom ended up in Versailles—not at the palace, but in #4 General Hospital.[6] The wound wasn't serious, but it kept him away from the unit for almost a month.

In its trenches south of Fleurbaix, the 1st Division had been put on readiness to support the BEF's attack on Neuve Chapelle on 10 March. In the event of success, the Canadian battalions would be called up to exploit the gains and push deeper into enemy-held territory. But it was a sad truth of the time that a division held back to exploit success was rarely called upon, and so it was at Neuve Chapelle. The British lost nearly 13,000 casualties, for no appreciable gain. The 1st Division lost about one hundred men—typical for a spell in the trenches. It was also a sad truth that a failed offensive was followed by soul-searching and finger-pointing—whether it was to learn lessons or shift blame wasn't entirely clear. This time, the post-mortem led to a redistribution of the Allied front. For some time, the French had been pushing the British to take over more of the trenches, and in early April 1915 the 1st Division became part of this reorganization. Along with two British divisions it went north, to the Ypres Salient, to replace three French divisions. The sector had been relatively quiet since the fighting of October 1914, but it remained a vulnerable spot in the Allied line. It was a huge bulge into enemy-held territory, some two miles deep and four miles across, into which the enemy could pour fire from three sides. A rational tactician would have abandoned the salient, withdrawing to the southwest of Ypres and reducing the front line from about seventeen miles of trench to perhaps ten, and freeing up thousands of troops in the process. But the rational argument didn't always carry the day. Ypres was the last Belgian city in Allied hands, a centre of Flemish culture, and for centuries the heart of the region's cloth trade. To surrender it, even on sound tactical principles, was unthinkable. Hadn't tens of thousands of Belgian, French, and British soldiers already died defending it? No, Ypres would not be given away cheaply.

Still, it was a tricky tactical situation. The northern shoulder of the salient was in the hands of two French divisions while the southern shoulder was held by two British divisions, one of which included the Princess Patricias. Those were the most vulnerable points—any attack aimed at cutting off the salient would come on one of the shoulders. The safest place, or so it seemed, was in the central sector, at the far end of the salient. And that's where the 1st Division was sent. Its frontage, about 4,500 yards across, roughly followed a shallow stream called the Stroombeek and was held by the 2nd Brigade on the left and the 3rd Brigade on the right. The farmland was flat and low-lying, broken only by a few gentle ridges—Gravenstafel, Zonnebeke, Frezenberg, St. Jean, and Bellewaarde. Tiny hamlets dotted the landscape, most scarcely more than a scattering of farms and cottages, and here and there were tobacco-drying sheds and a few small factories that turned beets into sugar or alcohol. Occasionally a pungent smell wafted from the huge piles of beets, but for much of the year, a high water table cast a damp, peaty odour over the fields.

From the Canadian front lines, two roads ran to the southwest through the sector, converging on the village of Wieltje before continuing to Ypres. In the early spring of 1915, Ypres still showed glimmers of its past greatness. The city had been fortified as early as the fourteenth century and successive conquerors had added to the defences, but by 1914 it wore the patina of genteel yet fading prosperity. Its ramparts, moat, and defensive gates remained, but had long since lost any military purpose. The triangular bastions jutting out into the moat were now parks, and the moat itself had long since been conquered by lovers in rowboats and children with fishing gear. To the west, the Yser canal, linking the city to the English Channel, was a green and brackish reminder that Ypres's best days as an economic powerhouse were in the past.

The city centre was dominated by the magnificent Cloth Hall, still bearing witness to the basis for the region's early wealth, St. Martin's Cathedral, and the Grote Markt, where farmers gathered to sell their produce. After the fighting of November 1914, German artillery had targeted the Cloth Hall and the cathedral, but Yprians were trying very hard to carry on as normal. When the first Canadian units passed through in April, the worst of the damage had been cleaned up. Shops and cafes were opens, farmers trundled in with their crops, and civilians exchanged greetings and gossip between the gabled houses with their red-tiled roofs.[7]

A few miles east of Ypres was the village of Vlamertinghe, where late in the afternoon of the 20th of April, the 1st Brigade went into billets as army reserve. A British attack south of Ypres had severely drained their forces in the salient, and there was a chance that the Canadians would be sent forward to that sector, but for the moment they busied themselves with the monotonous routines of army life. Since the 19th, the enemy had been regularly shelling roads and bridges north and east of Ypres, so when the bombardment started again on the morning of the 22nd, no one gave it much thought. It was a brilliantly sunny Flanders morning, the kind of day when even the dullest training routines or trench repairs was bearable. After lunch, the quartermaster in the rear area responded promptly to an urgent request from 3rd Brigade Headquarters: there were no playing cards available, but if a runner made his way back, he could collect 100 harmonicas to distribute to the men.[8] There followed an unexpected lull in the shelling; even though they had spent only a few weeks in the front line, many of the Canadians had grown accustomed to the sound of frequent explosions. The muffled roars picked up again around 4 p.m., but they were no longer intermittent; now, an intense and angry thunder came from the French lines.

On the other side of no man's land, German engineers had been working feverishly through the night on hundreds of steel cylinders that had been brought up to the front lines and hidden beneath sandbags. Wearing naval breathing masks that made them look like steampunk insects, they began to move the sandbags aside and screw long metal tubes onto the valves. The tubes, nearly 6,000 of them, were threaded through the parapet and reached out into no man's land like venomous tendrils. The engineers had been waiting for hours to take the last step, but delay compounded delay and it was late in the afternoon before the order was given. A little after 5 p.m., engineers along four miles of trench began opening the cylinder valves, releasing 160 tons of chlorine gas into a light northeast wind. Operation Disinfection had begun.

A torrent of small-arms fire swept the northern edge of the salient as hideous yellow-green clouds of gas rolled over the battlefield. Behind them came the German assault troops, wearing the same modified breathing masks, a modernist nightmare come to life. The villages of Pilckem and Langemarck were overwhelmed, and still they came on. The French defences melted away, and soon, terrified survivors began streaming south. Some were merely panicked but others clawed at their throats and gasped for air as they staggered towards the rear areas. There seemed to be nothing to prevent the German units from slicing straight south towards Ypres, cutting off at least three divisions and threatening the last free city in Belgium.

It was a desperate situation. Almost immediately, the 1st Canadian Brigade was released from army reserve and the 1st and 4th Battalions moved eastwards, across the Yser Canal, to take up positions east of the Pilckem Road. At the north end of the salient, the 2nd and 3rd Canadian Brigades realized that the immediate threat came, not from in front of them, beyond their heavily defended front line, but from their left, which was now completely open. On that flank, where the German advance was the deepest, there was only chaos. The most pressing need was to close the gap. Elements of a dozen British battalions were moved up, supported by scratch units of Algerian and Senegalese stragglers, and orders went out along the line to attack, to regain lost ground and create a defensible position.

Closer to the apex, the 10th and 16th Battalions were given the task of clearing a small stand of trees known as Kitcheners' Wood, between Mauser Ridge and the village of St. Julien. An enemy-held trench south of the trees would have to be cleared first, before the Canadians could push through and capture the entire wood. The 10th Battalion's four companies would take the lead, followed thirty yards back by two companies of the 16th Battalion and another twenty yards back by the other two companies of the 16th, eight lines of attackers in total. For a short time, there was confusion over how they should be armed. The first order, to leave behind their packs but wear their greatcoats, was quickly followed by an order to remove their greatcoats and fix bayonets. Then, the men were told to unfix bayonets and, a few minutes later, to fix them again. When they finally moved off, it was in a disorderly mix of tunics and greatcoats, some with packs and bayonets, some without. It was a calm, clear night and in the starlight, they could just make out their objective as a dark blur ahead in the distance. At 11:45 p.m. the men began moving up from their positions around Mouse Trap Farm, making their way over ditches and through gaps in hedges, until they finally reached the open field, bare and devoid of any cover, they would have to cross.

Marcus Mackay of Waterdown was in the last of the advancing lines, and had a fine view of everything. He could easily pick out the different coloured kilts of the 16th Battalion men in front of him, and in the distance the khaki tunics of the 10th Battalion men, silhouetted against the dark blur that was Kitcheners' Wood. Marcus was struck by how quiet it was now that the attackers had reached the open field. Then flares went up from the German trench; suddenly the battlefield was bathed in light and the fires of hell erupted. Flashes of flame danced along the dark blur ahead as the defenders of Kitcheners' Wood opened fire. Bullets cracked and zipped all around as Marcus watched the lead waves wilt under the fire, then firm up and begin pushing forward again. About forty yards from the German trench, the gunfire abruptly ceased and an eerie quiet fell over the field. All at once, the leading waves rushed forward and into the trench, while sections from the rear waves fanned out to clear the wood itself of defenders. Buoyed by their success, the men tried to entrench in the rock-hard ground.

But the success wasn't all it seemed. The 10th and 16th Battalions had taken Kitcheners' Wood, but nothing else. To their left, the promised assault by an Algerian division never materialized—because the Algerian division had ceased to exist earlier that day. To their right, the situation was no more encouraging. The Canadians held the wood, but the Germans still controlled their flanks. Not even the arrival of the 2nd Battalion after midnight made an appreciable difference in the defensive position. As streaks of light began to appear in the east, the surviving officers met and decided they had no choice but to abandon their gains and pull back to the trench south of the trees, leaving only scattered outposts in the wood itself.

The 23rd was a trying day. It might have been the lines of Canadian dead, distinguishable by the colour of their kilts, littering the field, or the German bodies just over the parapet, right where the Canadians had heaved them to clear the trench. It might have been the fact that, here and there, a body stirred—but the survivors knew it was suicide to leave their positions to help. Perhaps it was the devastating artillery barrage that rained down on them at 5:30 a.m., or the ammunition dump that exploded a little later, showering the 10th and 16th with debris. Or maybe it was simply that nothing happened for the rest of the day, leaving the men in the hot Flanders sun with only their imaginations for company. Whatever the cause, an ominous tension fell over the field and fed the survivors' unease. They were grateful to see the dusk, for nightfall brought some freedom of movement—for stretcher bearers, for ration parties, for ammunition carriers, and for the infantrymen in the pits and trenches around Kitcheners' Wood.

Dawn on the 24th saw no change in the situation. Everyone expected an attack, but it never came, and eventually the men of the 10th and the 16th were relieved by the 2nd Battalion and could make their way back to relative safety. But after seeing him through the worst of the last thirty-six hours, Marcus Mackay's luck ran out. As he manoeuvred down a communications trench away from Kitcheners' Wood, a random bullet from the direction of St. Julien caught him in the left thigh, snapping his femur. A pal quickly located stretcher-bearers to carry him to the nearest dressing station, but the wound was severe and Marcus had already lost much blood.[9] Over the last two days, many men had succumbed to lesser wounds. Marcus Mackay was out of battle, and so too was the 16th Battalion. Not that the unit could do much else; it had sustained 439 casualties, including most of its officers. Never again would the 16th take such heavy losses in a single battle.

To the west, between Kitcheners' Wood and the French division on the other side of the Yser Canal, the job of creating a defensive line fell to the 1st and 4th Battalions, which were joined with four British battalions into the hastily organized Geddes Detachment, named after its British commander. They were to advance at first light on the 23rd. In the War Diary of the 4th Battalion, there is a hand-drawn map of the day's attack, done on a page from a standard military message pad. It shows the trenches from which the battalion attacked, and the ground they traversed—or attempted to traverse. One is immediately struck by how tidy it is. The lines are clear and crisp, the trenches appear as neat little crenellations, and tiny trees stretch in orderly rows across the page. How difficult can it have been, one might be tempted to wonder? It all seems so straightforward.

On the ground, it was anything but. Not until 3 a.m. on the 23rd did Colonel Geddes receive his orders to advance; forty-five minutes later, the 1st and 4th Battalions began moving forward in support. Things got off on the wrong foot right away. Geddes had no idea that the Canadians were to be moving with him until his units brushed up against the 1st Battalion on their left. He was expecting the French to attack, but of them there was no sign. The two Canadian battalions were closest to the French but they could see nothing either. Geddes and his battalion commanders waited, but as dawn broke they could wait no longer and the advance went forward. Assuming that the French attack was hidden by hedgerows, the 4th Battalion began moving up at 5:25 a.m.; two companies of the 1st Battalion followed in support.

With three companies up and one in reserve, the 4th advanced along a 200-yard frontage into the shallowest of valleys towards the German positions to the north, on Mauser Ridge. To call it a ridge was misleading, for it was only the crest of a gentle slope, but it was enough to give the defenders a sweeping view of the men of the 4th Battalion as they moved forward, past Foch Farm, where the farmer's supper sat uneaten on the table and his cows stood unmilked by the barn. A line of cut willow trees marked the lowest point in the field and once the men passed those and cleared the stunted hedges that surrounded the farm, they came into full view of the defenders of Mauser Ridge. All at once, the machine-gun and artillery fire intensified, but the attackers held formation and moved forward in stages. Every twenty-five yards or so, they went to ground, and then rose up and carried on as soon as there was the slightest hint of a slackening of enemy fire. But each rush was a little more difficult than the last. On the right, the 1st Battalion and two British battalions had managed to get to Turco Farm, but were barely hanging on there. On the left, William Gillies of Flamboro Centre was with elements of the 4th Battalion as they struggled towards Mauser Ridge.[10] All around him, enemy fire was whittling down his company. On one side, a shell burst hurled an infantryman skyward like a rag doll, the body falling to the ground in pieces. A private on the other side was slowly moving forward, patiently, steadily, crouching in the teeth of the fire but eyes focused on the objective. Then a massive blast—a puff of smoke, a shower of earth, and he was gone. Looking back, he saw Will Humphreys of Aldershot heave himself to his feet and lope towards Mauser Ridge. A few steps, and then Gillies watched his legs crumple—Humphreys fell into a shell hole and was lost to sight.[11] Gillies turned and started back to help but had barely taken a step when a bullet slammed into his back and bowled him over.

With some companies down to half strength, the attack had clearly run out of steam. General Malcolm Mercer, the brigade commander, had seen enough; he ordered the 1st and 4th Battalions to dig in until reinforcements could be brought in for another push. That attack was to begin again at 3 p.m., but had to be pushed back as British and French units got badly jumbled. Unfortunately, no one told the artillery. Already limited to three rounds per gun per day (meaning that the entire divisional arsenal could be fired off in less than a minute), the gunners used what little ammunition they had at the original start time. When the infantry went forward, ninety minutes late, this time with the 1st and 4th in support, it was without artillery cover, and they paid the price. Gains were minimal, and many sections got completely turned around. They dug in, but at first light the next day, some discovered that they had entrenched facing the wrong direction. Their backs to Mauser Ridge, their rifles were trained on their own trenches.

The grim toll was soon evident. The Canadian battalions of the 1st Brigade had greeted the 22nd with about 1,100 all ranks each; on the 23rd, the 1st lost 404 men and the 4th 454, including its commanding officer, Colonel Arthur Birchall. At a shade over six feet four inches tall, Birchall had been an imposing figure since taking over the battalion from Labatt in January 1915. "To see him going ahead, waving his cane, and encouraging his men," wrote one of his NCOs after Birchall's death, "you would have thought he was on manoeuvres and not in a real battle." Also among the dead and missing were dozens of men who had left Hamilton on that wet day in September 1914. One of the survivors wrote home with the sad news: "There is not enough left of the original Fourth Battalion to be a backbone ... tell the Thirteenth mess that nearly all the Thirteenth bunch are gone."[12]

That left eight Canadian battalions strung out in a wide inverted V, sharing the front-line trenches with British units. The 1st, 4th, 10th, and 16th Battalions, after having been mauled at Mauser Ridge and Kitcheners' Wood, were deep in the salient, unfit for action for the time being. Before dawn on the 24th, a vicious ten-minute bombardment signalled another attack. As they had done on the first day, the Germans followed the barrage with gas, which smothered all of the 15th Battalion from Toronto and half of the 8th Battalion from Winnipeg. At 8:30 a.m., chlorine rolled over the battalions to the left of the apex, and later in the morning, German regiments began to push south, past Kitcheners' Wood and towards St. Julien. Outnumbered by more than three to one and with their hastily improvised gas masks providing little protection against the chlorine, the salient's defenders struggled mightily to stem the tide. They were also battling the most serious of their equipment deficiencies. The Ross rifle was a magnificent weapon for sniping or target practice, but it failed the test of battle. The grime of Flanders and the need for rapid fire conspired to cause frequent jams and many an infantryman, after hammering away at the bolt with whatever was handy, discarded the Ross for an abandoned British Lee-Enfield. That single image, of an infantryman struggling with a rifle that wouldn't fire and a gas mask that wouldn't keep out the gas, encapsulated the situation on the 24th.

They fought to defend clumps of trees, ruined farms, crossroads—anywhere they could make a stand to hold up the enemy. Companies, platoons, and sections were surrounded and overwhelmed. Riflemen in isolated outposts simply disappeared. Scratch units were rushed to wherever the need was greatest. Slowly the Allied line was pushed back as commanders sought positions they could defend with dwindling men and ammunition. By mid-afternoon, the Germans had reached St. Julien. But a series of local counterattacks by a handful of British battalions turned the tide; although they failed to retake any ground, they bloodied the attackers and chewed up precious reserves that the Germans hoped to use against St. Julien. More important, they allowed the Canadian battalions isolated at the tip of the salient to pull back before they were overwhelmed. They eventually withdrew to defensible positions near St. Jean, so that by the 26th, the Canadian sector had shrunk from about five miles to two, between Turco Farm and the Fortuin–St Julien road. Then they were withdrawn, leaving only the 1st Division's artillery engaged in the final stages of the battle. On the 28th, the 1st and 4th Battalions were pulled out of the salient and marched back to the billets at Vlamertinghe. When they had left the village less than a week earlier, it had been idyllic—trim brick cottages along tree-lined streets, a bustling mill with whitewashed walls that gleamed in the Flanders sunshine, a dignified school with a sweeping gravelled drive, an exuberant fairy-tale chateau with towers and turrets, the pastoral calm of a rural village.

In their absence, Vlamertinghe had been transformed into a massive, open-air hospital by the field ambulance units that had set up their tents there. Motor ambulances lined the streets, surrounded the mill, and clogged the circular drive of the school. On every open area were rows and rows of stretchers, and from the east, casualties continued to stream in—some on their own or supported by pals, even a few on all fours.[13] A small car belonging to the 3rd Canadian Field Ambulance had been turned into a makeshift ambulance after a sergeant offered to drive back and forth into the salient to collect more wounded. Three times, he pulled the Ford into the school's courtyard, each time with three wounded soldiers in the passenger seats, but he never returned from the fourth trip. A volunteer went out and eventually brought back the car, which he had found abandoned on the road. It was a horrific sight: "In the back seat was an officer sitting with his arms folded perfectly at ease, his head completely missing. In the front seat a soldier, sitting comfortably, with the whole of the face and two-thirds of the head missing. Our own poor Sergeant was brought in later, terribly mauled with shrapnel but with a chance for life. The other occupant of the car was thrown out by the force of the explosion and escaped with minor injuries. The car itself was riddled with shrapnel, but still going."[14]

A few weeks after the battle at Ypres, the Bishop of London, Arthur Winnington-Ingram, preached a memorial service at St. Paul's Cathedral in London in honour of the Canadian dead.[15] He described the five days of battle—the charge of the 10th and 16th Battalions on Kitcheners' Wood ("a most fierce struggle in the light of a misty moon"), the 1st and 4th Battalions advancing towards Mauser Ridge ("battalions whose names should live for ever in the memories of soldiers"), the 2,100 dead and missing whose bodies would, for decades to come, emerge from Flanders fields, the 1,900 wounded, blinded or limbless or lungs seared by chlorine, the 1,400 prisoners of war, condemned to an uncertain future behind German barbed wire. At Ypres, he said, Goliath met David, "the would-be overweening blustering bully of the world met Canada." And Winnington-Ingram read from Shakespeare's *Henry V*, as the young king addresses his English soldiers before meeting the French at the battle of Agincourt:

> This story shall the good man teach his son;
> And Crispin Crispian shall ne'er go by,
> From this day to the ending of the world,
> But we in it shall be remember'd;
> We few, we happy few, we band of brothers ...

On the evening of Wednesday, 28 April, as the last Canadian battalions were making their way from the Ypres salient back to their billets, Clara Salisbury Baker mounted the stage in Waterdown's roller rink. She had been married less than a year, and knew that her husband and two brothers might soon enlist. A leading light in the Waterdown Choral Society, she was about to begin the first of three recitations in the evening's Grand Patriotic Concert.[16] The applause for Lillian Vance's rendition of "The Magic Month of May" was still rippling through the audience, and there was some good-natured whispering and much rustling of programs. When Clara started to speak, her voice was low, barely above a whisper, and the folks in the back rows continued to chatter, unaware that the show had started up again. But as Clara's voice rose, a hush fell over the hall at the words that everyone had learned in school:

> We few, we happy few, we band of brothers;
> For he to-day that sheds his blood with me
> Shall be my brother; be he ne'er so vile,
> This day shall gentle his condition:
> And gentlemen in England now a-bed
> Shall think themselves accursed they were not here,
> And hold their manhoods cheap whiles any speaks
> That fought with us upon Saint Crispin's day.

The roller rink was not quite St. Paul's Cathedral, but the pride and reverence that the words evoked were the same. The earliest news reports had been sketchy, but it was becoming increasingly clear that the Canadian division had been involved in its own Saint Crispin's Day. On the 24th, newspapers had told of the asphyxiating gases used by the Germans and two days later of a "brilliant charge" by Canadian troops. On that day, the first list of Canadian casualties from the Ypres battle was released—only a few names at first, but the list would get longer every day. The *Globe* was optimistic, saying that the number of casualties in the ranks might be lower than expected and that many of the missing might be prisoners of war. The latter was true, the former, sadly, not. How many in the audience in the roller rink that night were now wondering if their boys would come home?

The people of East Flamborough hadn't really confronted that possibility yet. The new year had begun as the old year had ended—with fundraisers and send-offs, war lectures and patriotic gatherings. But none of it cut very close to home. Students at the high school sent $49.15 to the UEL Belgian Relief Fund and the village council responded to an appeal from the British Red Cross with a $200 donation.[17] Waterdown alone gave $909.65 to the Hamilton and Wentworth Patriotic Society, and there always seemed to be a box social, tag day, or collection tin for the Women's Patriotic League, the Willing Workers of the Methodist Church, or the Waterdown Belgian Relief Committee.[18] Still, since no one had ever met a real Belgian refugee, it all seemed a bit remote. Community meetings started to take up war topics. At April's WI meeting, members presented papers on Lord Roberts, Admiral Jellicoe, and General French before Gertrude Davidson sang "We Must Fight for our King and Country."[19] But they talked about the war as they had once talked about Byzantine art or the Dutch East Indies or Sir Walter Scott—as something that was interesting and important, but disconnected from their world. The women struck a subcommittee to organize the collection of newspapers and magazines to send to the front, and another subcommittee to keep scrapbooks of local news items for the township's soldiers. A meeting of the Anglican Young People's Association featured a reading of "a very interesting letter from a nurse in Belgium which was enjoyed by all." It might as well have been written by a member who was on holiday in Muskoka. Until April 1915, the closest that the township had come to the reality of war was the piece of shrapnel in Tom Flintoft's wrist—which moved the AYPA to send a cheery letter of support to its one-time member.[20]

WILLING WORKERS

The fate of nations may have hung in the balance, but in early 1915, local concerns still dominated life in East Flamborough. And there was always more that needed doing early in the year because spring was a mucky, dirty time in any rural township. The creeks, swollen with meltwater, carried along branches and undergrowth scoured from their banks. The roads were so full of ruts and potholes that wagon and buggy wheels slithered and lurched in the most alarming way. It was always an open question as to whether Waterdown's drill shed would survive another winter's ravages, but now the nearby school was starting to match it in decrepitude. With four primary classrooms on the ground floor and three secondary classrooms above, its seven wood-burning stoves couldn't keep up with the winter cold that blew in around the ill-fitting windows. Julia Crusoe (most of the children assumed she was well over a hundred years old, but she was only in her sixties) got the stoves lit every morning, then it was up to the students to keep them going through the school day. The outdoor toilets were positively toxic and a little too close for comfort to the school's drinking water supply. It was just as well that only about half of the fifty-odd registered students turned up on any given day. At best, the school was becoming inadequate, if not downright unsafe, and village council had passed a bylaw to raise funds for a proper high school. It was torpedoed by a ratepayer revolt, so councillors tried again, this time with the village and township councils acting together. Village council was in a bind—unwisely, it had already contracted to buy the land and was now on the hook to pay for it—but the Ontario Court of Appeal was unmoved and promptly disallowed the bylaw. High school students would have at least another dismal winter in the old building.

It would be up to the new township and village councils to set all this right. The first business day of a new year was always set aside for municipal elections. In Waterdown, John Vance became the new reeve, beating J. C. Langford by a margin of almost two to one, but Vance declined to stand

Facing page:

(Top): The Willing Workers of Waterdown Methodist Church, 1915. Eileen Richards, the sister of Charles and Harold, is standing at left. Stan Sawell's sister Velma is standing third from right. Photographer unknown. (Steven R. Sawell collection)

(Bottom): Waterdown's school, with primary grades on the ground floor, high school on the upper floor. Photo by Will Reid. (Author's collection)

for the warden of Wentworth County, a post he had held in 1913. For the reeveship of East Flamborough, a tough fight saw W. A. Emory of Aldershot emerge triumphant after championing the anti-high-school cause.[21] On the 11th of January, both councils met for the first time and got down to everything that would have to be done as soon as the snow melted.

Pressure on the city of Hamilton to repair the wharf at Wabasso Park had finally paid off, and the city committed to replacing the wharf in time for the summer ferry service to begin.[22] Vance was appointed to chair the village's Board of Health, his first order of business to instruct the sanitary inspector to survey all outhouses and backyards, and to see that they were cleaned up by 15 May. Council agreed to erect a fence on a dangerous part of Mill Street, with half the cost being billed to the property owner, and the village's billiard tables had their licences renewed (with some pointed advice on observing the bylaws). A report on the village's fire pumper, an elderly apparatus that took eight men with strong backs and arms to generate a steady stream of water, brought the unsettling news that the hose was fully iced up and couldn't be used. A couple of volunteers had cleaned it up and got it to what they thought was a working state, "at least as far as we are able to tell without a test with water." They recommended that the engine not be allowed out except for actual use or for training purposes (what else did they have in mind?), and suggested that someone be appointed to take charge of the equipment. Council might also want to buy some fire pails, they thought.

It was May before the Waterdown Fairgrounds was cleaned up and ready for use—just in time for yet another fundraiser. But this one had nothing to do with the war, at least not directly. One of the consequences of war had been a surge in usage at Canada's public libraries as readers tried to understand events in Europe. There was no shortage of books—publishers had been flooding the market with military and political titles—and the typical library had some catching up to do. Waterdown was no exception, and on the 22nd of May there was a field sports day to raise money to expand the library's collection. It was a nice little fundraiser. With the average book costing under a dollar, the librarian could look forward to adding dozens of volumes to the collection. He already had his want-list ready.

The library had come a long way in just a few years. Until 1905 it occupied a pokey little room at the front of a barbershop-cum-billiard hall. There wasn't a librarian—the high school principal took the role on a voluntary basis, in the hopes that he could intercept older boys on the way to the poolroom and turn their energies to reading instead. But in 1906 it had moved to one of the village's most impressive commercial buildings: Crooker's Hall, a grand brick edifice at the corner of Main and Dundas streets—fan-arch windows, elegantly turned finials on all of the gables, fancy brickwork, and the owner's name staring down from atop two sides of the corner tower. Billed as "the finest mercantile building in the village," it housed Whalley's general store and the post office on the ground floor and, above, a large hall for concerts and meetings, and the public library. There was plenty of space for all the new non-fiction that the librarian had already purchased in his imagination. As he watched the money being counted at the fairgrounds, he already knew where the books were going to be shelved.

That was on Saturday. Early on Tuesday morning, the fire broke out. It started somewhere in the back of Whalley's store—exactly where or how was never determined. There was plenty of flammable material scattered around, and before long the ground floor was fully engulfed. By the time the volunteer firemen arrived on the scene with Waterdown's dilapidated pumper, the fire had spread to the second floor. In the big meeting hall, flames licked along the floorboards and up the walls before spreading to the library in the next room to feed on the stacks of books and heavily varnished furniture. As the heat built up, the windows shattered and gouts of smoke belched out into the morning sky. The locals manning the pumper immediately realized that the job was beyond them and a call was put into Hamilton's fire department. The professionals arrived just as the building started to crumble; they could do nothing more than keep the flames from spreading. A wall collapsed onto Alton's barbershop, scattering bricks and charred timbers over the barber chairs. And then the corner tower keeled over, sending a shower of sparks towards the Kirk Hotel across the street. With that, the fire started to burn itself out. A few hours later, there was little to see but smouldering piles of brick. Amidst them, the cornice stone sat forlornly, the Crooker name stained with soot.

It took a few days for the village to realize what had been lost. No one would be getting a haircut in Alton's in the near future. The Kirk Hotel was badly scorched, its woodwork pitted by cinders and the paint bubbled from the heat. Whalley's store and its entire stock—gone. The post office and everything in it—destroyed. The library and all of its books, magazines, and newspapers—reduced to ashes.[23] The money raised at the sports day wouldn't go towards expanding the library collection, but to rebuilding it from scratch.

A few weeks later, after paying a few local men to keep watch on the site and clean bricks off the sidewalk, council members revisited the matter of the fire engine. The fire had been a wake-up call, as if the village needed one. Fire was a constant in early-twentieth-century village life because of the reliance on wood for fuel and building. Every block of the village was a blaze waiting to happen. The barrel factory yard on Franklin Street was packed with staves and headings drying in the sun and finished barrels waiting to be shipped out—at times so many that the manager stacked them in the street, for lack of anywhere else to put them. On Main Street North, a cordwood dealer kept his product on his front lawn; when that was full, he stacked it beside the street, the stack getting longer and longer as it crept along the edge of the fairgrounds and eventually reached the James house and the Anglican rectory a good 200 yards away. And the combination of wooden buildings and an imperfect understanding of safety when installing electrical systems meant that the township was dotted with death traps. Nevertheless, council was reluctant to spend money to fight fires, even after the heart of the village burned out. They agreed to send a note of thanks to Hamilton's firefighters, as well as a twenty-five-dollar donation to the Firemen's Benefit Fund—but only if the city of Hamilton didn't invoice Waterdown for the call. If it did, the twenty-five dollars would go to paying the bill. Then, firmly closing the stable door after the horse had bolted, councillors voted to buy a #7 Success Chemical Fire Extinguisher for $250. But even then, the parsimony of the rural mind reared its head. As a condition of the purchase, Council would ask for a 5 per cent discount on future orders. A 100-foot length of hose bought for sixty-five dollars was also returned ("we will not take the hose at that price"). Just to be on the safe side, councillors agreed to pay for repairs to the pumper, now back in its home in the Bell House.[24]

But on the 13th of July, hoses and pumpers were forgotten. As soon as the April patriotic concert had ended, the Daughters of the King began planning the next big fundraiser for Red Cross work. The setting would be Clunes, the McGregors' massive house in the centre of Waterdown. When I was a child in the 1960s, the house had long since lost its name and new building had started to encroach around the edges, but it was still a magical setting.

Facing page: Clunes, the McGregor family's residence. Photo by Will Reid. (Author's collection)

Later generations of McGregors had brought in two old railway carriages for storage, erected a couple of small cottages, and used skilful landscaping to turn the property into an oasis of calm. It was only a hundred yards from the centre of Waterdown, but it was so quiet and serene that it might as well have been a hundred miles away. In 1915 the property was much more open. There were two ponds fed by a stream that ran south before disappearing somewhere under the Kirk Hotel, but the only other dominant feature was the old Scotch church. It was a big weathered building that the doctor had turned into a barn when the Presbyterians built their new church on Mill Street. To affirm the transition from house of worship to oversized garden shed, Dr. McGregor hung an impressive rack of moose antlers over the main door.

Clunes sat on the largest property in the village, and it would need every bit of space on that July evening. The crowds started gathering late in the afternoon, not only from across the Flamboroughs, but with each train from Hamilton disgorging more and more people. By early evening, the grounds of Clunes were packed with as many as 3,000 visitors—more than three times

the population of Waterdown. They crowded the attractions—a fortune-telling booth, a fishpond, balloon displays—and enjoyed the strolling bagpiper. They sipped on lemon ices and munched peanuts and popcorn.[25] But as soon as the special guests came to the podium that had been set up on the veranda, all attention turned to the speeches. Acting as chair was the lieutenant-governor, Sir John Hendrie, a frequent visitor to the township, which was still home to his racing stable at Valley Farm. He spoke about the efforts of the St. John Ambulance Corps, and was followed by another local, former cabinet minister and Hendrie's predecessor as lieutenant-governor, Sir John Gibson, who gave an overview of the invaluable work of the Red Cross. But it was the next speaker that the crowds had really come to hear. Colonel James Ballantine of Georgetown was one of the originals.[26] He had taken a group of volunteers from Halton County to Valcartier in 1914, and had assumed command of A Company of the 4th Battalion. On board the *Tyrolia* on the voyage to England, he and Major Henry Belson, a fruit farmer from Port Dalhousie, Ontario, had entertained the troops with boxing matches. Ballantine had seen his company through the miseries of life on Salisbury Plain, and had taken them to France in February 1915. And he had been there when the storm swept over the Ypres salient in April. That was the story he told on that sunny evening in Waterdown.

Ballantine's company had been in reserve for the push against Mauser Ridge on 23 April, which explains why he was still alive the next day. On the 25th, he was just back from inspecting the battalion's new positions when a single enemy aircraft dropped a smoke bomb very near battalion headquarters. A collective gasp went up from the crowd at Clunes as he described how, within minutes of the smoke bomb landing, a rain of artillery shells fell on their positions. He talked about the shellburst that bowled him over and the rifle fire that struck him in the back and left arm. Before him on the lawns of Clunes, he had the crowds listening in rapt attention.

But it was a lovely evening, and Ballantine had no desire to dampen the mood with too-vivid descriptions of the horrors of war. So he talked about being loaded unceremoniously on to an old kitchen chair and carried back to the regimental aid post, where the battalion medical officer gave him first aid. "I told the Doc that I thought I was dying, but as I had never died before I wasn't quite sure," he quipped. He described being carried farther back, this time on a stretcher, through falling shells to a field behind the dressing station, where he joined dozens of other cases waiting to be evacuated by motor ambulance. He recalled noticing how stoic the Canadian wounded were, and that there was no whimpering or moaning—in contrast to the French and Algerian wounded, who "kept up a noise like one hears at a circus about five minutes before the animals are fed." An ambulance eventually took him to Poperinghe, where he was put on a hospital train for Boulogne and No. 7 Stationary Hospital. There, he met his old sparring partner, Major Belson, who had been shot in the stomach and who immediately invited Ballantine to go three rounds in the ring with him. The hospital ship *St. Andrew* took them both to Dover, where doctors removed two bullets from Ballantine's side. After all, he told the crowd at Clunes following a dramatic pause, "German bullets and Canadian blood don't get on well together." A month of convalescence, and then Ballantine had been granted leave to Canada. Since then, he had been making the rounds of events like Waterdown's garden party.

With Ballantine's appearance at Clunes, the war at last came home to the township. They had heard of it from an eyewitness, who described to them the hell that their boys had faced at Ypres. His account had breathed life into the often sterile newspaper stories and the sketchy reports that friends and relatives had sent in their letters home. He was a witness, and his words held special power now that the casualty lists, vague and incomplete in early May, were becoming longer and more specific. Now, the casualty was more than just a name in a newspaper column or a grainy photograph in a newspaper. Now, it was a name you knew and a face you recognized. He had worked on the next farm, or bought nails in your store. You had gone to school with him or seen him in church. He was one of you. Will Humphreys, originally posted as wounded, was listed as missing in action. William Gillies and Marcus Mackay were among the wounded, along with half a dozen other men from the township. The people of East Flamborough could now see the scope of their loss, and get a sense of what the future might hold.

Hard on the heels of the Ypres casualty rolls were reports, however scanty, of new Canadian attacks around Givenchy. In a rude introduction to alliance warfare, the division had been called back to the Armentières sector. The French were mounting an offensive against a little-known but tactically significant feature called Vimy Ridge, and they wanted the British to stage diversionary attacks to pin down German reinforcements. The British didn't like the place or the plan, but nevertheless launched an operation against Aubers Ridge. It was a catastrophic failure, but the French insisted on another effort. This time, there were early signs of success and the Canadian division was sent in to exploit the apparent breakthrough. But the success was a chimera. It's difficult to find anything that went right in the five separate attacks launched by Canadian battalions—gains were negligible, losses prodigious. And a few weeks later, they had to do it all again a few miles to the south. Three battalions were wrecked on German lines, achieving nothing in the process.

The losses had to be made good and in July, after the 2nd Contingent (including the 19th and other battalions that had trained at Toronto's CNE) had gone to Britain to become the 2nd Division, the Borden government announced that the authorized strength of the CEF would nearly double, to 150,000 men; in October, with a third division being assembled in England from Canadian units already there, he said that it would go up again, to 250,000. There was no hint that it would be difficult to find that many men, for enthusiasm still ran high. Over 7,000 volunteers came forward in April, and even more in May and June, despite the grim news from Ypres, Givenchy, and Aubers Ridge. For the last half of 1915, enlistment averaged over 16,000 a month. The first and second contingents had been dominated by the British-born but the mix was changing in new units, like Hamilton's 36th Battalion. It filled in a matter of weeks and included in its ranks eleven men from East Flamborough. Seven of them were friends from Aldershot who joined on the same day, 19 April 1915. John Filman, Frank Harrod, and Gordon Horne were all from old East Flamborough families, while George Flint and George Taylor were recent immigrants from Britain. So was Tom Humphreys, who joined in the hopes that he might see his brother Will overseas. Merv Hopkinson was from Grey County, Ontario, and worked with George Taylor, stringing line for the Bell Telephone company. A day later, two other Waterdown men joined the 36th. Clifford Nicholson enlisted because Rob Buchan was enlisting. Rob didn't really know why he was enlisting; it just seemed like a good idea at the time.

If the Aldershot lads were hoping for a quick trip to the war zone, they were in luck. Less than two months after they joined up, the unit was on its way to Britain. In John Filman's first letters home, there is an endearing mixture of gee-whiz enthusiasm, breathless bravado, and small-town camaraderie:

July 18, 1915
Folkestone

Dear Father,

I received the money all correct six pound three shillings two pence and was to get it as I needed it badly. I have been trying to get into the flying core but don't think there is much chance as apparantly I know nothing about machinery. The draft that was supposed to have went from here has been cancelled so that we do not know when we will be going now. Horne has joined the signallers and is working hard at it. He seems to like it allright to but I did not care for it or I should have joined them also. I am on guard tonight guarding the money our battalion is going to be paid with tomorrow. It is now about twelve o'clock at night and nobody has tried to steel the money yet and I guess they will not as we that is a corporal and I are both sitting here writing on the government paper and smoking away like good fellows. You ought to see the new rifles we are getting. They would be just the thing for hunting dear with they are so short and handy. They are only 8 feet and 1/4 inches long and weigh 8 pounds 10 and 1/2 ounces and hold eleven cartridges and if I ever come home I am going to bring one with me. They have come to the conclusion that the Ross rifle is of absolutely no use in the trenches as after about three of four shots they jam and cannot be knocked open with a rock. That would be a nice predickament to find yourself in with about a dozen Germans coming up on you wouldn't it? Well I guess this will be all for this time. Say have you received any of my assigned pay yet write and let me know.

From you loving son
John[27]

North Caesar Camp Folkestone
July 19 1915

Well I have decided to start over again. There was a big Zepplin Raid last night and nine of the 39th Batt were badly wounded and probably some of them dead by now as five of them were still unconsious this morning and a large transport was sunk and over a thousand British soldiers lost so you see the British are not having everything there own way but we will eventually win this fight if it takes a thousand years well I guess this is all so good bye for this time,

John

West Sandling
October 13th 1915

Dear Father, I am back to camp again but it seems quite different here as all the boys are away at the front and we are in huts here instead of being in tents and is a change for the better believe me. I was glad to get your letter as I was commencing to think you had forgotten me. My ankle is still swollen quite a bit and I am bathing it in hot water every hour so don't do much else. I am sorry to hear of the deaths of Mrs. King and Jim Ashball but that just goes to show that people will die when there time comes whether it be in war or at home. I suppose you have heard that Joe Harrod has gone to the front. He is with the first Battalion and two of Waterdown boys Bob Bucan and George Taylor are with the fifteenth Batt at the front. Tom Humphreys is a cook here now. This is going to be some war both Bulgaria and Greece are into it now and it looks like Romania is coming in to. I suppose there is not many young men around now. Everything will be different after the war over there. Gordon Horne is back again. He beat me getting better as he is out on parade now and I am in our hut writing a letter but I expect to be on duty in a week or so. You ought to [?] we heard the Doctor light into the seargent this morning. The doctor told me to do nothing and the Seargent took me out on parade and then brought me in for to sweep up floors and I went and asked the doctor if I had to work [?] send me back to

the hospital as my ankle would not stand for it. Just then the seargent came
in and the doctor told him off. Well I think this will be all for this time.

> From your loving son,
> John

West Sandling
October 29th 1915

Dear Mother,

I think I am off for the front at last. There is a draft going to the 19th
tomorrow and I am waiting man so if one of them happens to get drunk
tonight or doesn't happen to be there tomorrow why I will get away allright.
I have been issued with a new out fit all round and a new Ross rifle with a
sharpened bayonet and we are being issued with 120 rounds of ammunition
tonight so it commences to look like business. My ankle is pretty nearly
better or it is good enough to get past the doctor with although it is some
swollen and a little sore yet. We have had two kit inspections allready and
are having another in the morning by the Brigadier so we are having enough
inspections now but that is about all we appear to be here for or to march
past when some person comes here who happens to be somebody according
to military laws. It is possible that I may not go tommorrow and I hope I
don't as I want to go with the first Batt but if I did why I should worry as
one is just as good as the other but for just one thing and that is that the
nineteenth use Ross rifles and the first use Lenfields and all of us soldiers
would sooner use the Lenfield rifles.[28] Gordon tried to get on this draft but
he was on guard and when he came off they were filled up.

> Well this will be all for this time from your loving son,
> John W. Filman

PS my address will be the same untill you here from me again in fact
I would get all the mail that is sent to my old address.

Soon, the growing demand for men brought a new recruiting method. Militia units had done the job since August 1914, and had done it well, and it would have made sense to leave them to continue with the work of recruiting and preparing units for overseas service. But instead, the government went in the opposite direction, and threw it open to the community. For the federal government, this had many benefits. It was a way to capitalize on local enthusiasm and apply more direct (or less evident) forms of suasion on potential volunteers. This, in turn, would give local communities a greater stake in the war effort and, therefore, bolster their commitment. Now, each community that raised a unit would be inextricably linked to the war, for good or for ill. It was also cheaper, because it meant off-loading the substantial costs of recruiting on local committees. Beginning in the fall of 1915, any interested individual with the resources and connections could apply to raise an infantry battalion. The age of patriotic recruiting had begun.

So the Clunes garden party marked something of a turning point in East Flamborough's war. The fundraising events and information sessions would continue, but more and more the home front would focus on putting men in uniform. By the end of the year, eight infantry battalions had been authorized around Hamilton, quite apart from the artillery batteries, field ambulances, engineer companies, and other units that were looking for men. The new units had much more specific geographical affiliations (including boundaries between designated recruiting areas that were supposed to be strictly enforced) and more distinct identities. Although there was not yet any shortage of volunteers, the opportunity to join a hometown battalion might one day help to encourage waverers. And so on all sides of East Flamborough, units that traded on local identity began cropping up. Men from the north end of the township were likely to go to Guelph's 153rd (Wellington County) Battalion, while the 164th (Halton and Dufferin Counties) Battalion drew men from Aldershot and the eastern lots of East Flamborough. Closer to Hamilton, the potential volunteer was spoiled for choice. The 120th (City of Hamilton) Battalion billed itself as the first unit in the British Empire to be named after its community. The sporting types might prefer the 205th Battalion, the Tigers, informally known as the military wing of the Hamilton Amateur Athletic Association. For the man who favoured going to war in kilts, there was the 173rd Battalion, the Canadian Highlanders. The 86th Battalion offered something a little different: it was the region's only machine-gun unit. With every new unit authorized, a few more East Flamborough men joined up. With each new recruit from Waterdown, council voted to spend ten dollars on a watch, to be given at a farewell banquet as a token of the village's appreciation.

And then in November 1915, came word that many in people the township were waiting for: East Flamborough would get its own battalion, or rather part of a battalion. The Militia Council authorized Lieutenant-Colonel W. E. S. Knowles, a local lawyer who had been born in West Flamborough Township, to raise the 129th (Wentworth) Battalion.[29] It would be headquartered in Dundas, where Knowles had once served as mayor, but one company would be recruited, trained, and organized in East Flamborough. It was an announcement that would transform the township.

Knowles had first joined the 77th Regiment before many of his recruits were born, and became its commanding officer when some of them were still in short pants. He fully understood the challenges that lay ahead. Even though enthusiasm remained high, it wasn't as easy as hanging out a shingle and waiting for a stampede of volunteers to the 129th. So many units were recruiting that it was a seller's market—a prospective volunteer could be picky and wait for the right opportunity. Each unit had to aggressively seek out volunteers, rather than just wait for them to appear. Recruiting stations had to be set up across its region—maybe a half-dozen or more, in addition to battalion headquarters. They all required signs and banners, flags, perhaps even a mock dugout or trench—anything to attract the attention of passing men. Militia and Defence provided basic office supplies, but a successful battalion needed much more than the basics. It needed envelopes, postcards, and stamps for direct mailing, signs, posters, and billboards, and money for newspaper advertising. Transportation had to be available, preferably by automobile but streetcar or train fare at the very least. And there had to be events—band concerts (every battalion had to have a band), marches, socials, sports competitions—to bring out potential volunteers and their families.

Knowles set about all this with commendable energy, although his superiors were less enthused by some of his initiatives. Among the many letters Knowles despatched to Ottawa was a complaint that some fifty men had enlisted in Hamilton, perhaps attracted by streetcars that the 120th Battalion was using as mobile recruiting stations at major intersections in a city that he assumed was his designated recruiting area. "While I am firmly of the opinion that a man should be allowed to join any Battalion he chooses, still if my recruiting area is to be drawn on in this manner," he wrote in an offended tone, "I wish to point it out to you at this early date, so that I cannot in future be blamed for falling short in filling up the 129th (Wentworth) Battalion." Three days later came Ottawa's reply: the 129th recruiting area is Wentworth County, not the city of Hamilton.[30]

Next, Knowles unveiled to Militia Council his plan to place recruiters in Aldershot, Waterdown, Carlisle, Millgrove, Freelton, and the village of West Flamboro. All he needed were some automobiles to move recruits and recruiters around, because of the distances between the villages and the township's railway stations. No, replied the bureaucrats with an air of resignation, permission for such expenses could not be granted because there was no way to verify and control them.[31] Knowles then asked for a couple of returned 1st Contingent men to serve as instructors and recruiters. Not possible, came the reply, unless there was an official application for transfer. The 129th was free to use men who had already been discharged from the CEF, as long as they were medically fit, but they would have to do it out of the goodness of their hearts. Militia and Defence would not cover their pay, allowances, or expenses.[32]

The reality was that recruiting cost money, and it had to come from somewhere. At a meeting of Wentworth County Council, one councillor moved that $500 be placed at the disposal of the county recruiting league to help fill the 129th Battalion, and Councillor Vance moved that another $1,000 be granted for organizational purposes. That was a bit too much for some of the members. What would the money be spent on? If it was merely to stock the soldiers' canteen, argued one councillor, he couldn't support the motion. In any event, he thought, the town of Dundas got more benefit from the 129th because it was headquartered there. A battalion was big business. Most of its expenses were met locally, which meant a bonanza for merchants—printers, newspapers, dry goods stores, hotels and restaurants, food suppliers, hall owners, stables. Dundas council, clearly, should be paying most of the tab. Vance then moved that the money be placed in the hands of the county treasurer, who would pay bills after they had been approved by the finance committee; eligible expenses would include office equipment and the battalion band, but not a canteen. With that amendment, the motion passed.[33]

But the discussions about fairness didn't end there. Major Armand Smith, a Niagara fruit canner whose family name lives on in a line of preserves, complained on behalf of the 129th Battalion that a man who enlisted in a city battalion was paid more. Because country districts rarely had the facilities to house new recruits, they lived at home and received a subsistence allowance to pay for their meals, in addition to their regular pay; it added up to about $1.95 a day or $58.50 a month. A man who enlisted in Hamilton lived in barracks and got no subsistence allowance, just $1.10 a day or $33 a month; however, his wife would get a $20 separation allowance as well as $20 from the Canadian Patriotic Fund, or as much as $73 a month. One man pointed out that the country volunteer should be entitled to a payment from the patriotic fund, but observed diplomatically that, because "there is some difference of opinion between the battalion and the Hamilton and Wentworth Patriotic Society, some of the men run very short." 129th Battalion boosters tried to find the benefits of enlisting in a rural unit, but they were few. County men got free life insurance, underwritten by the County of Wentworth—city men had no such bonus. City units enforced curfews on their men; men in rural regiments who lived at home had no such restrictions and continued to enjoy the same sort of freedom they had before they joined up. It was a hard sell, the *Spectator* noting in January 1916 that "a great deal of criticism has been heard about the scarcity of recruits in the counties and that the cities are doing more than their share in the matter of producing fighters."[34]

East Flamborough was getting a crash course in the reality that, beneath the patriotic fervour, local issues were always at work—who would pay, who would profit, equality of opportunity, equity in treatment. But there was also pride on the line. No community wanted to be shown up by its neighbours, but neither would any community miss the opportunity to show up its neighbours. In mid-December, the recruiting league for Military District #2 met in Toronto and announced that, with a population of over 1.2 million, the district had enlisted some 35,000 men, or nearly 3 per cent of its population—better than MD #1 (headquartered in London) or #3 (Kingston). The signs were favourable, but there was no time for complacency. "Recruits have not been coming forward as rapidly as they should," Lieutenant-Colonel Herbert C. Gwyn, former Dundas mayor and long-time commander of the 77th Regiment, told a 129th Battalion recruiting meeting. "What is the reason? They should come forward and offer their services. This is Canada's war as much as anybody else's. No doubt when the young men get that fact into their heads they will come out and enlist. Australia and New Zealand men have come out in large numbers, and Canada should not be behind to help the mother country." On the 18th of December, Colonel Knowles reported that the 129th already had a strength of 271 all ranks, including sixty-one recruits enrolled between 12 and 17 December. But only six men came forward to volunteer on the 20th.[35]

That it was the holiday season hardly constituted an excuse, for Christmas and recruiting were inseparable in wartime Canada. In Wentworth County,

Christmas concerts were retooled into gatherings to promote the 129th Battalion. Every Sunday evening in December was given over to a recruiting meeting in Dundas. On the 18th, it was at the Music Hall, with Colonel Gwyn in the chair and the St. James Church choir and the band of the 77th Regiment providing musical accompaniment. On the platform, a Hamilton lawyer laid out the meaning of the evening: "It is a remarkable thing to see in Canada a meeting like this on a Sunday night. Had we said that such a meeting would be held two years ago people would think we were suffering from nightmare. Two years ago we were at peace with the world, advancing our country and attending to our regular duties, but there was another nation making strides commercially and for over forty years it was taught that Germany was the greatest country in the world, and this is the nation that we are now fighting." He went on to compare Germany to the Roman Empire, for they both worshipped a god of war. "While we might congratulate Germany on her commercialism and business," he proclaimed, "we could not congratulate her on her greed for war."[36]

It was like that throughout the area—war and Christmas intermingled, apparently quite comfortably, with one being used to explain and give meaning to the other. In Rockton, two young farmers stood under the mistletoe to be presented as the village's first volunteers for the county battalion.[37] Patriotic songs and Christmas carols were sung before the locals got down to discussing the most efficient way to recruit in Beverly Township, Wentworth County's most rural township. At the Carlisle Methodist Church Sunday School entertainment, there were carols and patriotic songs, a Christmas dialogue and a military oration, and an orange for every child. In Dundas, Colonel Knowles told crowds at the tree-lighting ceremony that Britain stood for the real spirit of Christmas. Rather than receiving presents as part of the ceremony, children had been asked to bring gifts for the men of the 129th, which Santa would distribute during his rounds. The collection brought in $150 in silver and a large assortment of socks, toques, scarves, and handkerchiefs.[38]

In the season of giving, it was the order of the day to remember the men who had volunteered for the county battalion. Lieutenant-Colonel James J. Grafton, a former officer of the 77th Regiment, one of the area's biggest merchants, and a generous benefactor to the town of Dundas, donated a pipe and tobacco to each man of 129th, while his daughter sent several cases of oranges. The John Bertram & Sons Company provided an assortment of games and other amusements for the unit and there was talk of buying it a top-of-the-line field kitchen. Grafton had also offered to buy machine guns, but the government insisted that it would pay for weapons. The caretaker of the Dundas armoury was looking for accommodation for soldiers in town, so they wouldn't have to travel from the far townships when winter weather blocked the roads. And talented performers were asked to volunteer their time to a series of entertainment nights being planned to raise funds for the 129th.

Christmas had always meant homecomings, but this year they were very different. Joe Eager came home for the holidays, which didn't happen very often. His family had operated Eager's General Store since 1873—other stores came and went, but the Eagers were always there. The family lived in a large and graceful house on the east bank of Grindstone Creek and the young Eagers, Joe and his twin sisters Agnes and Mary, had been trained in business at an early age. People got used to seeing little Joe out early in the morning, starting on the walk down Waterdown Road to Brown's Wharf, clutching a bag of gold and an order for sugar or molasses for one of the shippers. Even though he had gone away to university in Toronto to train as a doctor and then opened his own practice, to the older villagers he would always be little Joe, running errands for his father. And in their minds, it was little Joe who took himself to London on 28 December and joined No. 2 Field Ambulance Depot of the Canadian Army Medical Corps. For many young men, it was a time to set their affairs in order. A last Christmas with their families. Was their departure expected, or did they break the news over Christmas dinner? Did their families make a fuss? Were there tears or cheers, or did they leave for the army with as little ceremony as if they were leaving for school or work? On the 27th, Stan Sawell signed the forms to accept a commission in the 129th Battalion. Three days later, Roy Mount, of Mountsberg's founding family, enrolled in the 129th. On New Year's Eve, James Robertson enlisted in Parry Sound, where he was working, far from his wife, his four children, and his father Alex, the last owner of what had once been Waterdown's Torrid Zone mill. Dozens of other men had left the township earlier in December. From now on, there would be no more wristwatches, no more civic banquets from the municipal government—council simply couldn't afford the expense. Nor would there be long press accounts of farewell ceremonies of the sort that had filled newspapers earlier in the war. No more minute-by-minute narratives, no more heart-rending descriptions of tearful goodbyes—the kind of thing that historians rely on as raw materials. Departures became so frequent that they were almost—is it callous to say so?—commonplace.

4

1916

W hen Stan Sawell had pondered what life as a soldier might be like, he hadn't expected it to involve going door to door with a clipboard. And yet, there he was on his first official duty as an officer of the 129th Battalion, pounding the streets of East Flamborough in January 1916 to compile a military census. The federal government hadn't gotten around to that yet, so it was up to officers like Stan to record the names of potential volunteers in their designated recruiting areas, to see if they might be persuaded to join up. Stan's territory was everything in the township south of Dundas Street, and he was to visit every single house and list the men of military age.[1] Whether they were fit to serve in other ways was up to someone else to decide.

Almost everyone knew Stan. The Sawells were from Millgrove and Stan's mother was a Cummins, a family whose branches spread out across half a dozen counties in southern Ontario. Stan's father operated a shop on Dundas Street that sold painting and decorating supplies year-round and ice cream in the summer. Many small-town merchants were like that—there simply wasn't enough of a market to specialize too much, so they diversified. Stan found that being such a prominent local businessman was both a blessing and a curse in his military duties. He never had to introduce himself, and was usually invited in out of the cold to make his notes. But there was often a cup of coffee or a slice of pie on offer and Stan hated to say no, especially when the success of the 129th was at stake. He could have listed the men in any given house in a couple of minutes; instead, it might be an hour before he could excuse himself, after having been suitably refreshed. Army life was supposed to make a man lean and hard; a few more rounds of the south end of town, he thought ruefully, and he'd need to let out his uniform trousers.

That was Canada early in 1916, and East Flamborough was no different—it was all about recruiting. In cities and towns across the country, units were on the hunt for men, using all the tricks of the new science of advertising to catch their attention. Canada's streets were plastered with brightly coloured posters whose bold words and emotive images tugged at every imaginable heartstring. Cheery faces in khaki smiled down from billboards, asking men to fight for the Union Jack, the old country, their pals, their family, the people of Belgium and France—or all of the above. "The Happy Man Today is the Man at the Front," proclaimed a poster for one of Montreal's battalions. There were direct mail campaigns using specially printed postcards—"I thought you would like to know that I have enlisted in the [blank] Battalion. Wouldn't you like to join us? Drop me a line" or "I'm having the time of my life here at 176th Battalion C.E.F. Wish you were here too." Old soldiers from past wars were trotted out as examples for young men. Many units had mascots to act as ambassadors, and some had specially commissioned recruiting songs. There were pennants and tags, buttons and flags. War might have been hell, but it certainly was good for the printing industry.

In Wentworth County, half a dozen infantry battalions were looking for volunteers, so the 129th faced stiff competition, especially from the better-funded city units. The 86th Battalion commissioned moving pictures of its men doing manoeuvres and arranged to have them shown at local movie houses. In the window of a Hamilton department store, a patriotic tableau featured soldiers of the 120th and 173rd Battalions, surrounded by coloured recruiting posters. The Canadian Mounted Rifles were drawing big crowds with a trench-digging display on the grounds of their Hamilton barracks.[2] Visitors to the Dundas armoury might have thought that the 129th had followed suit, "for a war-like trench ran across the ground in front of the building." Alas, reported the *Dundas Star*, the reality was a little more prosaic; it wasn't actually a trench but a drainage ditch, put through "in an endeavor to remedy difficulties which had developed because of the lack of a town sewage system."[3]

That pretty much summed up the recruiting experience of the 129th. Other units had all the modern attractions—moving pictures, store windows, neatly constructed mock trenches—but Wentworth's Own had a drainage ditch. There were no sophisticated new gimmicks or advertising tricks to amaze and amuse the potential volunteer—just the old standbys. The Christmas recruiting concert became the New Year's recruiting concert, which eventually became the spring recruiting concert. They were held almost weekly, featuring local musicians and vocalists, and "picked talent" from the battalion, perhaps a juggler or a squad demonstrating physical drill. The battalion's buglers demonstrated bugle calls, and three privates performed a comedy sketch entitled "The Raw Recruit." There was a smoking concert—a roomful of potential recruits sitting around listening to gramophone records and enjoying cigars provided by a sergeant of the local home guard. A shooting match between a company of the 129th and a home guard unit was enough of an event to make the newspaper. An Irish Flag Day was held on St. Patrick's Day. And a popular draw was Private Charlie Chaplin, also known as Private Redman of the 86th Battalion, who had "an enviable reputation in Hamilton as an amateur entertainer and fun-maker."[4]

But whatever the event, there were speakers, always more than one. This was the age of the elocutionist, when public speaking was elevated to an art—a minor one, but an art nonetheless. Those who took the podium at 129th Battalion events gave full rein to their oratorical skills, for few subjects offered better scope for speechifying than a righteous fight against an evil enemy. "We are fighting for the principles of the Magna Carta," said the speaker at one recruiting meeting, and to save "women and children from the hands of the Huns." That was the crux of the matter. Yes, the war as about abstract ideas like Democracy and Freedom, but ultimately it was a war in defence of Canada. "If we don't go to meet the Germans, they will come here," said Hamilton businessman and historian W. F. Moore, who had a son with the 86th Battalion. "We don't want them over here. Go over there and fight him in his own backyard."[5] Any man who was hesitating should ponder "the terrible things done by the Huns in Belgium," and the atrocities in Ottawa and Hespeler for that matter—at the time, fires at the Parliament Buildings in Ottawa and the A. B. Jardine and Company munitions factory in Hespeler were being blamed on German sympathizers. This was our war as much as it was France's and Belgium's. Don't think of it as fighting for European farmers you've never met—think of it as protecting "the motherhood of our own country from suffering and death."[6]

That was all well and good, but would it sway the severely practical man? It's not that he was selfish, but he was looking for more immediate reasons to enlist. Much as he tried, he couldn't quite picture a troop of German cavalrymen trotting down Centre Road or zeppelins cruising over Aldershot. And when the Reverend Caleb Harris of Dundas said he would rather "see the Dominion barren, and the bones of her sons scattered across the waste, than have victory handed down to us by another's hands," our pragmatist struggled to see exactly how that was a point in favour of volunteering.[7] For minds like that, there were practical arguments. Enlistment meant opportunities for travel, not just to England, where many of the volunteers had been born, but to France and Belgium. It was a kind of holiday excursion, with genial sergeant majors acting as tour guides. The possibilities for broadening one's cultural horizons were boundless. And physical fitness—Colonel Grafton promised that the CEF would be something like a health club in khaki, turning the spindly, chinless man into a fearsome warrior. Perhaps there were some who wanted to learn a trade. The machine-gun section, while it offered no obvious postwar job benefits, might appeal to the mechanically minded. Even more attractive was a trade that was "conceded to be the most interesting branch of military work"—the signalling section. "When one considers the great advantage this training would be in after life, the signaling section should be a great attraction. When these men come back they will be in a position to accept positions paying very large money."[8]

All of this assumed that the decision to enlist was a rational one, the outcome of carefully weighing costs and benefits. In most cases, it was anything but. We are blessed with a wealth of personal accounts from soldiers—letters, diaries, memoirs—but they have surprisingly little to say on the fateful decision to enlist. Men offered a mixture of vague motives, from fervent patriotism to the desire for a steady job, but far more of them suggest that they were not really sure themselves why they joined up. We read of men who left home for work in the morning, with no thought of enlisting, but found themselves in khaki by dinner time. Men who admitted that they signed on because they were carried along by a crowd, and wondered how on earth they were going to explain things to their wife or mother. Men who claimed nothing more than that volunteering seemed like a good idea at the time.

Personal relationships mattered more than anything, especially in rural communities where everyone knew everyone else. When Stan Sawell came to the door, he wasn't just an officer of the county battalion but a man whom people knew and respected. Not because of his rank, which meant little in a community where militia service was a lark as much as anything. Not because he was a kind of local aristocrat; the social hierarchy of a rural community was much too flat for that. But because he was a friend and neighbour talking to men he knew, to families who had patronized his store, to farmers from whom he bought berries and tomatoes and beets. He was probably also a relative. In an era of large families when many people married close to home, after a few generations, any township's population became a collection of second and third cousins. Anyone who looks at the history of rural Canada a century ago quickly discovers that any community can be divided into three or four extended families. Most of East Flamborough could find a Cummins somewhere in their family tree—and an Eaton, a McMonies, a Mount, a Horning. Kinship networks mattered. They were expressed at christenings, weddings, reunions, and funerals, and especially in wartime. Over the course of the war, over 200 men and women left East Flamborough in uniform; nearly half of them were related, however distantly, to Stan Sawell.

In the last few days of January, Stan's hard work with his clipboard work paid off and nearly two dozen men were attested into the 129th in Waterdown. They were a cross-section of a typical rural community. A handful of farmers from Carlisle: Lewis Best, Lloyd Binkley, Ingle Bousfield, and Achilles Hearn—his older brother Arville had joined up in Toronto the week before, and his younger brother Austin would enlist in the 193rd Battalion in Hamilton in April. Maurice Scott, who worked on the family farm in Flamboro Centre. And from Waterdown, George Arnold the teamster, Fred Hayman the grocer, Robert Meader the farmer, Will Chisholm the clerk, Vern Willis the market gardener, and Richard James the blacksmith (his brother Fred would follow him into the 129th in March). Jim Simmons the bell-ringer enlisted as well. Ben Rayner, who left a wife and two small children in Waterdown, missed the enlistment drive in the village and went to Dundas to sign on. Soon after enlisting, fourteen of the new soldiers posed for photos with their officers, Stan Sawell and Cec Nicholson, beside Waterdown's hastily repaired drill shed. None of them had ever served in the militia, but they presented a fine appearance—everyone except Vern Willis, who hadn't yet been issued a uniform and was nattily dressed in a patterned cardigan, suit

The Waterdown platoon of the 129th Battalion, in front of the drill shed. Stan Sawell stands on the left, and Vern Willis is front and centre. Photographer unknown. (Steven R. Sawell collection)

jacket, and checkered cloth cap. But no one cared about such things. After all, Vern was one of them. It was, in fact, a decent cross section of the township, from members of the founding families to British migrants whose history in East Flamborough extended back just a few years. In their occupations, their ethnicity, their education, one sees a typical small town. The photo is at once intensely local and strikingly archetypal. It freezes the moment and suspends

those young men in time, before a shell burst at Arras tore apart Fred Hayman's foot. Before poison gas corrupted George Arnold's lungs. Before wounds sustained on the Vimy front took Achilles Hearn's life only a year after his wedding. Before everything changed.

On the fringes of the township, where the hamlets were smaller, the farms more distant and isolated, recruiting was much more difficult. For simple logistical reasons it took a much greater effort to reach fewer potential recruits, as another of those wonderfully wry articles in the *Spectator* made clear. One evening in February, four representatives of the 129th Battalion set out from Hamilton for faraway Freelton, where they were to speak at a recruiting meeting. As they drove north on Highway 6, they gradually left civilization behind them, the lights of the city giving way to the occasional glimmer flickering in a farmhouse window. Plowing north along the badly rutted road, they had to stop three times to repair the rear tire— the reporter wondered if it was enemy activity or the ample girth of Major McCullough that put undue stress on the car. But they made it to Freelton, where they were joined by three other 129th officers with long ties to West Flamborough, and began their assault on the local menfolk. The party "fired its heavy guns" in Freelton's town hall, but managed to capture only two men where Knowles had confidently predicted that they would get twenty-five. John Wilde was a Welshman who had come to Canada in 1911 and had a job stringing telephone lines. Stephen Duckhouse was from Birmingham and worked as a farm labourer in West Flamborough. He was another Home Child, and had come to Canada in 1910 with his younger brother. He had added two years to his age to get into the 129th. It was a disappointing result but "another effort to take the balance of the men prisoners will be made on Sunday next," concluded the reporter. The drive back to Hamilton was no less fraught with danger. At one point, the headlights shut off and nothing "could induce them to do duty." Reverend Shepherd uttered "Let there be light" on three different occasions, but the only light came from Major McCullough striking a match. Eventually, after removing the light from the rear bumper and attaching it to the front, they set out again and were making slow progress down the highway towards safety "when suddenly something like a six-inch gun was heard in the rear, only to find when the guard sprang from the car that one of the hind tires was flat." There being no spare, the party had to walk the last six miles back to Hamilton.[9]

Seven senior members of the battalion, twenty-two miles by car, six miles on foot, the better part of a day spent in travelling—all for two recruits. At that rate, it would take years to fill the ranks of the 129th. The story was the same all across the country; as the winter of 1916 reluctantly gave way to spring, the flood of volunteers dwindled to a trickle. There were just too many units chasing too few potential volunteers. Infantry recruiting, which had exceeded all expectations in late 1915 when the local battalions were authorized, was becoming especially difficult. The canny volunteer who saw himself in khaki was liable to opt for a branch of the service that didn't involve charging into enemy machine guns: the artillery, the engineers, or the service corps. One day's recruiting in Toronto, the largest city in Canada, yielded just eighteen recruits and only five of them were for the infantry; the others joined the artillery, the Service Corps, and the Military Police.[10] The fledgling Royal Flying Corps promised that volunteers could fight in the clouds—no muddy holes beside no man's land for new aviators—and the Royal Canadian Navy was continuing its tradition of drawing heavily from provinces far from the ocean coasts. British units had been given permission to enlist volunteers in Canada and were offering high rates of pay to men with specialized skills in mechanical or inland water transport. Doctors, medical students, and veterinarians were fast-tracked to commissions in the British Army. For the average infantry battalion, it became a tough sell.

And in some instances, the men the infantry got were not necessarily who they seemed to be. Max Buczeg, whose name appears on the Waterdown war memorial, had arrived in Canada in March 1913 with a large party of Home Children destined to be farm labourers. He was born in London to an English mother and a German father, and looked and sounded for all the world like a typical Cockney. When he enlisted in the 129th, he decided to use his mother's surname, Paul, to avoid getting caught up in anti-German hysteria. His Canadian guardian advised him to keep quiet about it, but someone ratted on him and Max was charged with false enlistment. It was a serious offence, but such was the need for men that Militia and Defence couldn't afford to take a hard line. Re-attest him under his real name, Colonel Knowles was told, as long as he was satisfied that Buczeg was actually a British subject.[11] Max was duly enrolled, although the army never did figure out his real name; his service file refers to him as either Max Arthur Buczeg or Arthur Ernest Buczeg-Paul.

But the county's honour depended on more than just filling the battalion with the right kind of volunteer. It had to be well equipped—everyone must see that Wentworth supported its boys in khaki, no matter what the cost. Colonel Grafton had already appealed to the citizens of the county with a laundry list of needs for the 129th—five field kitchens, five men's mess tents, orderly room and stores tents, wagons and harness, motor transport, musical instruments, sports equipment.[12] The regular weekly concerts had been a good source of money, the battalion expecting profits to top $900 by June, but it was the private donors who really came through. A Dundas businessman bought baseball equipment for the battalion. Dundas munitions manufacturer John Bertram & Sons donated a set of eight bugles, in addition to the eight the government supplied to the unit.[13] Wentworth County Council voted $1,000 for band instruments. Colonel Grafton pledged to buy the wagon transport and harness, in addition to the $1,200 he had already given. His mother sent a gift of $1,500. Even a rebuke from Militia and Defence that battalions shouldn't engage in such public appeals (because they implied the government wasn't able to equip battalions fully) fell on deaf ears.[14] All told, the 129th raised nearly $100,000 in current values from the local community, an impressive amount, given that most of the battalion's recruiting area consisted of traditionally cash-poor rural townships.

But generosity wasn't boundless. In 1915, in the wake of the Second Battle of Ypres, there had been a brief fad for raising money to buy machine guns. Responding to news account that Canadian units were under-equipped with machine guns, fundraising committees sprang up across the country to solicit donations so that all Canadian battalions arrived in England armed to the teeth with machine guns. Among the many thousands of donors was, in August 1915, East Flamborough Township Council, which sent $1,000 to the national machine-gun fund. But the campaign was fuelled by enthusiasm more than good sense. There weren't sufficient machine guns being manufactured to meet the demand from community groups, nor were there enough trained gunners, and the thought of looking to sewing circles and youth groups to pay for weapons didn't sit well with Militia and Defence. In 1916, Ottawa put a stop to the fundraising and notified donors that money subscribed wouldn't be needed. But East Flamborough had already paid, and in February 1916 the council wrote directly to Prime Minister Robert Borden asking for its $1,000 back. "This Council does not think it fair," wrote the clerk, "that their paid subscription be retained when other municipalities are allowed to withdraw theirs."[15] It's easy to excuse their ire. The donation represented nearly $20,000 in current values, rather more than the township spent on everything in a typical month.

Council was still waiting for its money by the spring, typically the most expensive time of the year for rural governments. The pinch caused by the shortfall was just one of the tiny dramas that made up the fabric of life in East Flamborough. An enormous crowd, estimated at 4,000 people, attended the garden party given by South Waterdown Women's Patriotic League (I don't know what surprises me more—that a small village raised, in a single day, the equivalent of over $30,000, or that Waterdown considered itself large enough to have more than one branch of the WPL).[16] Two freight trains collided head-on near Waterdown, blocking the main line of the Grand Trunk Railway.[17] The vestry of Grace Church agreed to pay for a telephone to be installed in the rectory.[18] Fifty Women's Institute members met at McGregor's Hall in Waterdown to listen to a paper entitled "The Up-to-Date Woman" and to debate the resolution that more crime was caused by wealth than by poverty.[19] Gladys Buchan was married in Aldershot, with her brother Stanley in attendance; older brother Rob was with the 15th Battalion in France. None of these episodes were earth-shattering, nor were they unusual—just part of the quotidian life of Canada. But their very banality threw into high relief the events in Europe that were never far from anyone's mind. Soon the township would be drawn in even more deeply, for it was evident that the 129th Battalion's time in Wentworth was coming to an end. It was near enough to its authorized strength that plans could be put in train for the move to Camp Borden, the first leg of the journey overseas. It was the time for banquets and send-offs, a prospect that, for some young men, was more alarming than facing German guns. Maurice Scott was the guest at a farewell dinner held in his honour in Flamboro Centre, and had to stand awkwardly beside the podium as an address was read:

We, a number of your friends at Flamboro Centre, desire to express to you our appreciation of the fact that you have heard the call of duty at this time of your country's need and peril. These are days when the best of our manhood is appealed to and when there is demanded of us an unparalleled sacrifice. We have known you both at work and at play and have found you to be a congenial companion in whatever capacity we have come into contact with you. We shall miss you in future days, but at the same time we rejoice that you are willing to go at the call of duty and try to do your bit for this fair land of Canada and for the Empire of which we form a part.

If it is your lot to go forth in the days to come to the forefront of the battle we hope and pray that you may come safely through the struggle and be one amongst those who will share in the victory which shall end this gigantic struggle. May you come back crowned with honour & victory. As a tangible expression of our appreciation & of our goodwill we ask you to accept the accompanying Wrist Watch, Safety Razor and New Testament, which are subscribed for by the many well-wishers with whom you have been associated in past days. May they constantly remind you during the days when you are absent from us of our loyalty to you and the Empire.

And when you return may they be constant souvenirs of the time when you did your duty and when your life was enriched by so doing. Also, of the great interest expressed by

Your Friends at Flamboro Centre.[20]

On the 1st of July, the battalion was notified that it would be moving; three days later, the men entrained at a railway siding west of Hamilton.

Their destination was Camp Borden, about 100 kilometres north of Toronto, a site that had been chosen in 1905 for a new military training base, to replace the aging and cramped space at Niagara-on-the-Lake. The project was shelved after civic leaders in Niagara got wind of the plans, but they were dusted off when the First World War began. Militia and Defence acquired over 127,000 acres and put a local infantry battalion to work building the camp. The area had once been thickly forested but aggressive logging and a series of burns had gotten rid of most of the vegetation, leaving a mix of sand and ashes that kicked up clouds of black dust at the slightest movement. "One day in this hole is enough for any man," wrote one disgruntled private. "We were a pretty sight when we got home just like a lot of threshers ... its awfully dirty here its just cleared from a pine bush the logs cut into lumber and the brush burned then they plant our tents on that when the wind blows it full of fine sand just like dust or quicksand when its dry ... Its a God forsaken place all around us ... the grass is all burned dry as a cinder and is nothing but sand, sand, sand." The only thing that seemed to grow well was the poison ivy. It was very difficult to pitch tents in the ground, and any truck that strayed off the road usually got stuck in the sand, necessitating the diversion of a whole platoon to haul it out. Transportation was poor because Borden was off the main railway line, so there were often shortages of supplies, even food and water. "We had pretty poor grub the first day and having to work so hard on it It makes you weak as a chicken," wrote one soldier.[21] This led to problems with discipline. Shortly before the 129th arrived, there had been a near-riot in the camp. A few days later, some soldiers stole a load of fruit and canned food. Small wonder that the men looked for any reason to get away, as one soldier wrote home to his mother: "I have good news to tell you orders came out last night that any man needed home for harvest can go for 1 month so if you need me or any body ... near home tell them to drop a letter to Major Heaman If you need me make it seem very pressing or if anybody else wants tell them to make it seem very hard to get men ... I would like to get clean once more this year and If I stay here I never will be."[22] One visitor cuttingly referred to Camp Borden as "a land of sand, sin and sorrow."[23]

Still, they did what they could to make it habitable: "Today we have all been busy fixing up our tents each bunch trying to have a nicer looking residence than the other and some of them are certainly well. Every tent here has a name. Ours is known as 'Burns' Cottage.' Some of the fellows have shown considerable wit too. For instance one tent has a nice little grave dug outside the door all nicely decorated and marked by a big white cross on which is painted in neat black letters 'Gone but not forgotten.' The grave contains an empty whisky flask. Nearly every tent has a rustic chair built out of twigs cut from the bush, just outside the door."[24]

The training day started with an hour of calisthenics, to loosen up the muscles and get the blood flowing. Then came an hour of bayonet fighting, with the trainees manfully driving their blades into suspended bags of straw, accompanied by suitably blood-curdling yells. Depending on the day, that would be followed by section, platoon, or extended order drill, the men learning through repetition how to move together as a unit. Before lunch there would be a lecture, and perhaps visual training (how far away is that flag—100 yards, or 150?) or instruction from one of the military manuals. The afternoon was usually given over to musketry training and, to end the day, another lecture. On Fridays the entire brigade was often brought together for a route march through the countryside around Borden, and on Saturday morning there was more drill at brigade or battalion level. Saturday afternoon was set aside for organized sports. Sunday, after church parade, was for the men to do with as they chose.

Every day, the battalion's adjutant detailed the mundane happenings of an infantry unit in training. There were the usual transfers, between companies or to different units, and promotions. Men went away to specialist training courses or came back from them. Every few days a new volunteer turned up to be attested into the unit but many more were discharged, and it was then that the overenthusiasm of the recruiters came back to haunt the battalion. Everyone who had been certified as physically fit upon attestation was re-examined by military doctors, who weren't invested in the honour of a local unit. In the process, every battalion that had proudly marched into Camp Borden at full strength found itself whittled down to three-quarters strength or less. The 129th Battalion was no exception.

The war had already revealed an alarmingly low level of general health and fitness in the country. Legend tells us that Canadian men were a race of giants—huge, strong, clean-limbed, their bodies perfected by the struggle for survival on the frontier. In uniform, they dwarfed their British comrades, whose bodies had been stunted by life in urban terraces and toil in dark Satanic mills. Doubtless there were some of those paragons of physical beauty in Canada, but recruiters soon found that they were the exception rather than the rule. Canadian men were small, averaging perhaps five feet six inches or five feet seven inches in height and weighing 130 or 140 pounds, with a litany of physical ailments. Bad teeth were epidemic, as were hernias and varicoceles (some surgically corrected, some not). Pigeon breasts and webbed hands and feet were common, and the word "underdeveloped" appears with dismal frequency on attestation forms. Their bodies testified to the prevalence of disease—rickets, rheumatism, smallpox—and to the hazards of the typical workplace—missing fingers and toes, traumatic cataracts and missing eyes, perforated eardrums. When Sir Robert Borden had blithely pledged to put 500,000 Canadians in uniform, he surely had little inkling of how few fine physical specimens the country could provide.

The heady days of August 1914, when only the best bodies would be accepted, were now far in the past. The physical requirements had been progressively relaxed to the point that by mid-1916, recruiters were willing to accept almost anyone—and even then, the number of rejections was dispiriting. On one day in Toronto, thirty-seven men came forward to serve, but only fourteen of them passed the medical inspection.[25] Even this dismal average was achieved only because doctors were liberal in their interpretation of "fit." Sign them in now, and let someone else down the line decide on their actual fitness. Ebon Church of Flamboro Centre was an epileptic.[26] Thomas Crysler of Aldershot had varicocele for which he refused surgery—and at any rate, his character was judged to be "not very good."[27] Freelton-born John Hunter could barely see the hand in front of his face.[28] William Embleton of Freelton claimed to be fifty-four when he enlisted; he was at least a couple of years older and had advanced arteriosclerosis.[29] Never mind—the CEF could do something with them, and so each was certified as physically fit and duly attested. And when the battalion reached Borden, all four of them were quickly discharged, along with many others. Thomas Cutts was sent back to his father's house in Waterdown. He had claimed to be almost eighteen years old when he joined the 129th, but in fact he was only fifteen. However, it was as much a severe hernia as his age that sunk his military ambitions.[30] Charles Bomford was old enough to serve, but his hernia was also bad enough to get him sent back to Waterdown.[31] William Clark had Graves' disease, and should never have been attested in the first place.[32] The same was true of John Emery. He had a lame back from tubercular bone disease and his groin and hips were covered with abscess scars, some of them quite recent.[33] Both men were sent packing from Borden, back to West Flamborough. Emery would die at home, less than a year after the war ended.

Even healthy and fit men were constantly leaving the battalion for hospital, mostly because of training accidents or minor ailments. But a good number were hospitalized for venereal disease. That, of course, was a military offence—it would cost them fifty cents a day and loss of field allowances while in treatment. Far more common were other kinds of disciplinary problems, resulting in a parade of soldiers coming before the battalion's court of enquiry. Most of them had been absent without leave or had overstayed a pass, but there was a smattering of other offences as well—drunkenness, refusing a command, insolence, being in civilian clothes. One stalwart soldier racked up seven offences before the 129th even left Borden.

And then there were the deserters. The adjutant dutifully recorded their absence, and after a certain period of time a battalion court of enquiry declared them Absent Without Leave and struck them from the rolls—twenty-five men from the 129th Battalion, not including a handful scooped up in a late-night raid on a Dundas pool hall who were deposited in the Hamilton jail overnight and sent to Borden on the first train the following morning.[34] There were likely as many reasons for deserting as there were for enlisting in the first place and we can't claim to understand why men took the step, because they may not have fully understood themselves. One young soldier's motives are easier to understand. Percy Bowman left Borden to go back to Waterdown to be with his ailing father, and then followed him to the grave a year later.[35] Percy's death went unreported and unregistered, and he was buried quietly in the family plot in the Union cemetery. Did the Bowmans fear the consequences if someone discovered that their son was a fugitive from the CEF?

If so, they probably needn't have worried. Desertion was endemic in Canada during the First World War (in August 1916 some 1,500 men were illegally absent from Camp Borden alone), to the point that in November 1916 Militia and Defence offered an amnesty to any man who was absent from his unit, provided he returned to the colours and promised not to desert again.[36] At the same time, prisoners who had been committed to penal institutions for such offences would be freed, if they returned to their units. But the problem stirred much more ire in Canada's cities than in rural areas. In cities, anonymous tips and police raids (typically on pool halls) were a regular occurrence, but not in the countryside; there were no raids on Alton's billiard parlour in Waterdown. In a close-knit rural community, to castigate the deserter would have meant naming names, not just calling up stereotypes. It was one thing to stop a stranger on a city street and accuse him of being a deserter; it was quite another to do it when the man was a friend, a neighbour, a customer, or even a relative. And there is nothing in the local records to suggest that there was much appetite for that, not even among the legal authorities. It was common knowledge that the military had a hard time mobilizing the rural justice system to deal with deserters because, in small towns or villages, magistrates often "had some sympathy for the accused," as the *Globe* put it. One rural magistrate near Camp Borden took the position that alleged deserters were outside his jurisdiction and asked pointedly why the army didn't try its own prisoners. If the men were indeed soldiers, they should be tried under military court martial; if they were not soldiers, then no offence had been committed.[37]

No compromise was found to the difference of opinion, but there was one thing that all sides could agree on: the longer a unit stayed at Borden, the greater was the temptation for its men to disappear.

As a result, the 129th's time at Borden was mercifully short—a little over a month—during which time it was inspected by a senior officer sent down from Ottawa. The results were mixed. On the positive side, the battalion was close to full strength at 1,003 men, including twenty who were confined to hospital. On the other side of the ledger, five men were in prison for various petty offences and another twenty were absent without leave. More alarming from the training standpoint was that only about 150 men had passed the standard rifle test.[38] But there was no time to put that right now. On the second weekend in August, the entire battalion, except for ten officers and sixty men, was given weekend leave and left Borden on a special train for Hamilton and Dundas; a few men who hadn't been given leave decided to take it all the same. For the people of Wentworth County, it was a last chance to see their soldier boys at home; "khaki was again to be seen everywhere around the streets," wrote the *Dundas Star*, "making the town look as it did before the boys left for camp."[39]

Most soldiers felt that their first steps on the road to war were taken when they departed for overseas. For the men of the 129th, that journey began on Friday, 18 August 1916, when they and two other battalions marched away from Borden. Their progress was marked by receptions and bands. It was a four-hour train trip to Toronto, where a regimental band and civic reception awaited them. The *Globe* was enthusiastic, calling them "representative of the best blood of rural Ontario" and offering a kind of backhanded praise for the men's "precision that at times might be considered depressing."[40] They reached Montreal at 7 a.m. the following day (another reception and more bands) and Moncton thirty-six hours later (still another reception, still more bands). On the morning of the 21st, after travelling all weekend, the train from Borden finally reached Halifax, where the men got a glimpse of their next temporary home. But this was no ordinary troopship. It was the White Star liner *Olympic*, the sister ship of the *Titanic* and one of the largest vessels afloat. There were four other infantry battalions on board as well as a hospital unit from Western University in London.

Also on board was a large group of unattached officers, including Stan Sawell. Stan never pretended that he was a natural soldier, but thought that what he lacked in military brilliance, he made up for in hard work. Colonel

Knowles didn't see it that way, and said so. In his view, Stan was inefficient and for that reason was declared surplus to the unit's establishment, meaning that he would not go overseas with the 129th. To add insult to injury, Stan didn't get leave when everyone else did and had to spend the holiday weekend making out military wills for the men in D Company. It was a bitter blow, and decades later Stan admitted that he was never quite able to forgive his Commanding Officer.[41] He and four other lieutenants declared supernumerary to the 129th would travel to England as unattached officers. Not until they boarded the *Olympic* did they know that they would be sailing with their old unit. To his great surprise, Stan was given a first-class stateroom to share, with no assigned duties, while the officers of the 129th made do with third-class cabins and a full slate of administrative tasks. Not that Stan was comparing ...

At least there were plenty of battalions that would be interested in his services, because the Canadian Corps was expanding, with a third division being assembled and a fourth on the drawing board. Eventually, this would give it forty-eight infantry battalions. The two divisions that were already in France spent the first months of the year holding six miles of front south of Ypres—from north of Kemmel to Ploegsteert. Theirs was a winter of water-logged trenches and bitterly cold winds during which they rotated through front-line, support, and reserve trenches every six days. They weren't involved in major operations but they did begin to experiment with trench raiding, a new tactic that saw a small group of attackers cross no man's land at night with very specific objectives (usually to destroy defensive positions and capture prisoners), and then return to their own trenches just as quickly. Trench raiding was an art at which Canadian soldiers excelled, but its costs mounted up. Over the first three months of 1916, the Canadian Corps took part in no major attacks but still sustained 2,760 casualties.

It was in the Ypres Salient that the BEF decided to open its campaigning season, with an assault in April at St. Eloi, where the enemy held a slight bulge into Allied lines. A number of huge mines were dug under German lines, on the assumption that the explosions would so shock the defenders that they would be too stunned to offer resistance. The mines were blown as planned, but instead of a walkover, it inaugurated a two-week slugging match over seven large and fourteen smaller craters. The pointless battle cost 10,000 casualties, including 1,400 men of the 2nd Division, and left tattered reputations and hard feelings in its wake. The designated sacrificial lamb was the Canadian Corps commander, Sir Edwin Alderson. Genial and popular with the men, Alderson was no match for the political intriguers in Canada's halls of power. He was promoted to a relatively harmless (and meaningless) position in England, to be replaced by Julian Byng.

Conventional wisdom has it that cavalry generals were unsuited to command armies in modern war, but Byng was an exception. He had distinguished himself in the early battles in 1914 and was responsible for almost the only successful part of the Dardanelles expedition, the withdrawal. He was a rising star in the British Army and probably regarded his promotion to command the Canadian Corps, rather than one of the marquee formations, as a kind of punishment. But if he was disappointed with the assignment, he gave little indication of it. First World War generals tend to be easy targets, but not Byng. He was the personification of a host of admirable qualities—open-minded, imaginative, of enormous and unquestioned integrity, completely lacking in personal ambition, obstinately unwilling to criticize others. He was invariably seen at the front wearing a rumpled tunic, scuffed boots, and a cap that looked like he had sat on it, perhaps a holdover from a childhood spent wearing hand-me-downs, the fate of the thirteenth and youngest child of an impoverished aristocrat. Completely free of airs and guile, his rapport with the men under his command was apparently effortless—a rapport that his successor, Sir Arthur Currie, would never achieve. In return, the men came to see Byng, not as a red hat from far behind the front lines, but as one of them, someone they respected and even loved. As one of Byng's biographers wrote, "nowhere in the world at war was there such a large formation in which the links between commander and soldiers was so strong."[42]

Byng set about reforming the Canadian Corps with zeal and without mercy. He found scattered throughout headquarters and the fighting formations far too many political appointees for his liking, officers who held their positions because of political influence rather than ability. Unlike Alderson, he was more than a match for them, and they were unceremoniously shunted out. In their place, Byng brought in men who had proven their worth, regardless of who they lunched with. And although he was sensitive to the Corps' nationalist imperative, he also knew that it had to succeed—if it didn't, it wouldn't matter if it was all-Canadian or not. And so he filled very important staff positions with experienced British officers, men who will never appear on a postage stamp or in a textbook but whose ability to get things done would be critical to the Corps' success.

But before Byng could make much headway with his reforms, the Canadian Corps again found itself on the receiving end of a pasting. It was still in the Ypres Salient, and in the aftermath of St. Eloi was holding the most vulnerable part of the line, between Hooge in the north and Mount Sorrel in the south. It was the easternmost projection of the salient into enemy-held territory and the only part of the Ypres ridge crest still in Allied hands. The Germans had been eyeing it for weeks. If they could take the three heights, Mount Sorrel, Hill 61, and Hill 62, they could overlook the entire salient and perhaps complete what they had begun a year earlier—the capture of the city of Ypres. Early on the morning of 2 June 1916, the blow fell on the 3rd Division. A vicious five-hour artillery barrage was followed by the detonation of four large mines and an assault by fresh German infantry. Blocking their path, at the very eastern end of the Allied front, holding a section of trench known as The Loop, was No. 1 Company of Princess Patricia's Canadian Light Infantry, and Tom Flintoft.

Since its mauling at Ypres the previous spring, the Patricias had been recast. In November 1915, it had left the British Army division with which it had always served and joined the 3rd Division of the Canadian Corps. More important, its makeup changed. Once a battalion of hardened old soldiers, primarily working-class and mostly born in Britain, it had been reinforced by hundreds of Canadian university students (recruited across the country into a series of University Companies). The newcomers were young, generally well-to-do, and mostly born in Canada. Effectively, the Patricias had exchanged one kind of elitism for another. Once again, Tom Flintoft didn't really seem to fit with the other soldiers in the regiment, but it didn't bother him. As one of the surviving Originals, he enjoyed a level of status.

The 1st of June was a beautiful summer day with fine visibility, and Tom might have looked up above no man's land to see German observation balloons bobbing lazily in the slight breeze. He wouldn't have been bothered by the desultory shelling that fell on the ironically named Lovers' Walk to their rear that evening and the following morning, because he was well used to that by now. "We had come," wrote one of Tom's comrades, "to look upon the German as a creature of habit with his little bursts of morning and evening hate."[43] But this was no usual morning hate. By 9 a.m. on 2 June, every German gun in the sector was ranged on the trenches held by the Patricias and the 4th Canadian Mounted Rifles. By the minute, the casualties mounted, especially among senior officers. Three battalions, as well as the 3rd Division and the 8th Brigade, lost their commanding officers that day. Entire units were wiped out, among them No. 1 Company of the Patricias. Spencer Symonds, a McGill University student, was one of the few survivors, a fact that was painfully obvious to him as he surveyed the shattered remains of The Loop:

> I appeared to be the lone survivor, though doubtless there were a few here and there who like myself in some inexplicable fashion had so far escaped. The trench mortar fire had eased up. I continued to go slowly along the trench. I came to a small dugout, or rather a shelter built into the parados. It was about five feet long, and in height about up to one's waist. I crawled into this protection and lay on my side looking out. A direct hit of mortar would demolish this shelter, but there was little chance of being trapped or buried alive. I had remained there for probably half an hour when it suddenly dawned on me that the bombardment had lifted. The rattling and tin can noise as it seemed to damaged eardrums had stopped. The quietness in comparison was striking. I began to wonder what was next.[44]

What was next was an advance by German soldiers armed with flamethrowers. They probably didn't expect to find many survivors in the front lines, and they were right. Roughly 130 Patricias had been defending The Loop that morning. When No. 1 Company was relieved at the end of the day, there were only sixteen men left. Most of the rest were dead; the lucky survivors were wounded or captured, or both. Exactly what happened to Tim Flintoft isn't known. The records simply state that he was killed in action, "vicinity Sanctuary Wood," sometime between the 2nd and 4th of June 1916.

Byng, in his first major operation in command of the Canadian Corps, decided that the most important job was to regain possession of Mount Sorrel and Hill 62. The job fell to the 1st Division, whose strongest battalions were put together into two composite brigades, one to attack Mont Sorrel and the other to go against Hill 62. BEF commander-in-chief Field Marshal Douglas Haig was reluctant to release more troops because he was preparing for the summer offensive to the south, and said that the Corps should rely on heavier artillery support but fewer men; this meant that Byng had a staggering 218 artillery pieces from British, Canadian, Indian, and South African sources. For ten hours on 12 June, they blasted away at German lines before the attack went in.

At the southern end of the front, four men from East Flamborough were with the 1st Battalion, which would support the 3rd Battalion's assault on Mount Sorrel. They were part of the group of six friends from Aldershot who had joined up together on the same day, 19 April 1915. Two of them had gone to different units: George Taylor to the 15th Battalion, and George Flint to the 18th. But Flint's war was already over. On 8 March 1916 he had taken a bullet in the abdomen while on a work party repairing trenches; four days later, he died at a casualty clearing station. That left four awaiting the attack on Mount Sorrel: John Filman, Frank Harrod, Mervyn Hopkinson, and Gordon Horne. Mervyn counted himself singularly unlucky. He had been wounded on 24 May and had returned to the battalion that morning, just in time to take part in the assault. In contrast, John Filman's war had been quite pleasant so far, as he told his father in his first letter home from France:

France
Feb 17/2/16

Dear Father:

This is a nice little town we are billeted in about the size of burlington and everywhere you go you see houses or churches in ruins. The Germans once occupied it and it certainly looks like it. There are a lot of big guns here and every time one goes off it pretty nearly shakes the billet down. We are out of the trenches for a rest now and are lying around doing nothing but smoke and tell stories. I was down to see Joe Harrod. he looks fine and is getting fat. The weather here is fine but chilly and we are kept busy keeping warm. The food here to is pretty fair but I am broke as usual. Money here is realy of no use anyway so I should worry. We are billeted in a brewary here and we have beer with our dinner instead of tea. For ten cents we can buy a big can we have here, full of beer so we aren't going dry. Tobacco is the hardest thing to get especialy macDonald chewing tobbaco in this country is rotten. Would like you to send some McDonald chewing if you will. Our address is, Pte. John Filman, 406713 1st BN Signals, 1st Canadian Div., B.E.F. France. To look at the country around here you would never imagine there was a war on here.

From your loving son,
John, somewhere in France

But there certainly was a war on and, as far as the men of the 1st were concerned, this particular part of it started badly. All of the companies were late getting to their assembly trenches, some nearly three hours behind schedule, because of deep mud and congestion in the communications trench; at least one company had to advance over open ground, hugging a shallow furrow for cover. The assembly trenches, once reached, were either full of water or full of 3rd Battalion men, forcing platoons of the 1st to dig themselves new positions in no man's land. But once the bombardment ceased and the assault went in around 1:50 a.m., behind a dense smoke screen and heavy rain, the pieces fell into place. The German defenders were stunned, or had been obliterated, and resistance was confined to a few pockets. There were hitches—half of all rifles were so clogged with mud that they couldn't be used, bags of grenades were too heavy for the men to carry in the conditions, and because there weren't enough stretchers, "wounded men had to be left where they fell for a considerable time, which has a demoralizing effect on all who see them."[45] Even so, in an hour it was over, with all of the objectives in Canadian hands; as the British official historian said, "The first Canadian deliberately planned attack in any force had resulted in an unqualified success."[46] But it had been a costly couple of weeks—more than 8,400 Canadians killed, wounded, or missing since the first attacks on 2 June. Among them were Frank Harrod, who died near Maple Copse as the attack went forward, and Gordon Horne, who took a sniper's bullet in his left thigh while repairing telephone lines between the front and reserve trenches. He lived, but never returned to the battalion. Like in all too many situations, it seemed to be for so little. The battle ended with both sides firmly entrenched roughly where they had been when it all began. Hooge remained under German control, and the British had no interest in trying to retake it. Their attention was firmly fixed on the south, where the summer's great offensive would take place, among the sleepy villages and verdant fields that lay astride the river Somme and its tributaries. Few people outside that part of France had ever heard of the region, at least until the summer of 1916.

Once again, it wasn't the offensive that the British wanted to launch. Haig wanted to attack at a different place, around Messines to the north, and a different time, in the middle of August, but the French insisted that they couldn't wait; unless German reserves could be drawn away from Verdun, the sector might fall, taking with it the French war effort. Against this apocalyptic prediction, Haig gave way: he would attack on the Somme on the 1st of July. But as planning went ahead, the balance of forces had to be recast. The French had originally pledged two armies to the British one, but losses at Verdun left the French fronts dangerously thin and they could no longer spare two armies. So the Somme became primarily a British operation, with the BEF putting in twenty-one divisions to the French eight. The honour of launching the offensive would fall on the New Army, the massive all-volunteer force that had been raised by Lord Kitchener late in 1914 and had been in training ever since. Britain had pioneered the practice of turning recruiting over to local civilian committees, the practice that Canada had later adopted and which brought forth the 129th Battalion and many others like it. In Britain, they were known as Pals' Battalions, units recruited from one city or neighbourhood, occupation, or inclination—the Grimsby Chums, the Accrington Pals, the Tyneside Irish, footballers, public school graduates, Public Works employees, stockbrokers, sportsmen, textile workers. It was the largest, best-trained, and best-equipped army that Britain had ever fielded, eighteen months in the making. And within a day, it had been gutted.

The Somme campaign remains mired in controversy, as much for the disastrous first day that saw the New Army sustain over 60,000 casualties, for no appreciable gain, as for Haig's determination to carry on despite shocking losses and limited success. By the end of August, new blood was needed on the Somme and the Canadian Corps was brought in to relieve the Anzacs around Pozières. The Corps had been advised that it would get a couple of weeks to settle in before being thrown into battle; while the 2nd and 3rd Divisions prepared for that attack, the 1st Division held the entire line—3,000 yards from west of Moquet Farm to the railway line east of Pozières.

History knows the Corps' first operation as the Battle of Flers-Courcelette, but it is known less for the name than for two innovations that it brought to the battlefield: the creeping barrage and the tank. The former had actually been dreamt up earlier in the war by the French, but couldn't be used because of ammunition shortages. By the summer of 1916, the British had stockpiled enough shells that they could experiment with the new tactic. It was quite simple. Instead of ceasing when the infantry began to go over the top, and thereby giving the defenders a chance to emerge from their deep dugouts, the artillery would continue firing throughout the attack, laying down a curtain of steel just ahead of the lead infantrymen. An artillery program was a carefully choreographed dance of death, the rain of shells advancing by a set distance every few minutes as the men moved forward. For the infantry, it was a nervy situation; they had to stay as close as possible to their own barrage, risking friendly-fire casualties as a trade-off for reaching the objective while the defenders were still reeling. Artillery was a tried-and-true way of achieving shock and awe. The tank was something brand new. Commissioned by the British government the previous year as a way to support infantry advances and return some mobility to the battlefield, tanks were an unknown commodity. Vast amounts of money and technical expertise had gone into their development, but would a forty-ton contraption crawling across the battlefield at three miles per hour be of any use whatsoever?

The objectives for the 2nd Division on 15 September were two trenches called Candy and Sugar, because of their proximity to what was known as the Sugar Factory, a refinery that had processed sugar beets before the war. It was now a jumble of ruined buildings honeycombed with defensive positions, a daunting challenge for the Canadians' initiation to the Somme. But unlike earlier pushes in the offensive, they would not attempt a single charge towards one objective. Instead, using a creeping barrage for cover, the attacking battalions would make a series of leaps through successive objectives—Candy Trench first, then Sugar Trench, and finally the factory itself—pausing each time to let the barrage move ahead. On the right, the troops had about a thousand yards in total to cover, but only about 400 on the left.

Of the tanks, the less said, the better. For its attack, the Canadian Corps had been allotted six of them, designated either male or female, depending on their armament. Only five of the six crossed the start line and only one reached its objective. The others broke down or bogged down, in the process becoming lovely targets for German artillery. The creeping barrage, however, worked splendidly. The 21st Battalion had one of the longest drives of the morning, with orders to take the Sugar Factory, and the War Diary reveals how effectively the new artillery technique worked: "At 6.20AM as laid down in the Operation Order, the barrage was laid 50 yds in front of Enemy front line. At 6.21AM it lifted to enemy front line, at 6.24 it lifted to 100 yds beyond and the Battalion then advanced."[47] The first objectives were taken with little difficulty, the first three battalions reaching their targets by 7 a.m.; thirty minutes later, the lead brigade reported that all units had achieved their goals. The second stage of the attack began at 6 p.m., launched in broad daylight and with no set jumping-off point, and encountered a few pockets of staunch resistance. But by nightfall, all of the objectives had been carried; the Sugar Factory, Candy and Sugar Trenches, the remains of Courcelette, and the Fabeck Graben were all in the hands of the Canadian Corps.

And so ended Canada's first day on the Somme. I was tempted to go on to the second and third day, and beyond, through the ensuing two months of fighting—attacks that were stunningly successful as well as those that were catastrophic failures. There were East Flamborough men in a dozen different units, infantry as well as every other arm, so the township had a stake in every advance mounted in that tortured landscape. But having read all of the battalion war diaries and countless other accounts, contemporary and after-the-fact, I know that there is a depressing sameness about these operations. Artillery barrage. Over the top. On a good day, clear the objective with bombs and bayonets. On a bad day, stagger back to the start line with nothing to show. Pause. Repeat.

The repetitive character of the operations has long been used as ammunition in the critique of First World War generalship. Repeating the same action and expecting a different outcome is, after all, one definition of insanity—or, in this context, of the absence of creativity. I've never felt comfortable about passing judgment on whether there was tactical bankruptcy at the top—especially not from a comfortable office chair a century later. Haig and his generals, after all, eventually won the war—that has to count for something. But I do believe that in the Canadian Corps, at battalion, brigade, and division level, officers went to tremendous lengths to learn from mistakes, try different approaches, tinker with tactics. If the plethora of after-action reports and other post-morta teaches us anything, it's that these were not cold-hearted donkeys blithely sending their men into the slaughter. On the contrary, I picture them as generally intelligent, decent officers who, faced with impossible orders from above, had the agonizing task of making the best of a bad job—not just once, but again and again. Headquarters decided what had to be done and it was up to them to do it, even if there were never enough men or artillery, even if the ground was impassable, even if the men were running on fumes. Reading the documents of those eight weeks of attacks, one realizes how much was beyond the field commanders' control and how earnestly they tried to fiddle with the minutiae to attain a favourable, or less unfavourable, result.

Rather than dissect those processes, we jump ahead almost exactly two months after Canada's first attack on the Somme, to its last. On the 18th of November, elements of eight battalions from the 4th Division attacked the inaptly named Desire Trench and its support trench. Dawn had broken with driving sleet that changed to rain as the morning wore on—ideal weather for the attackers. In the centre, twelve officers and 500 other ranks of the 54th Battalion clambered from their trenches and hugged the artillery barrage that jumped ahead fifty yards every two minutes. Right on schedule, they took their designated section of the Desire Support Trench and began to consolidate it. It was, as their brigade commander said, a "perfect operation," so there is more than a hint of pride in the unit's War Diary: "The operation was conducted with great precision and exactly in accordance with orders received, the men showing the greatest intelligence, endurance and courage."[48] For the 54th Battalion, the success capped six days in the line that had cost fifty-three killed, 202 wounded, and twenty-three missing.

One of the casualties was Bert Hunter, who had been raised in Carlisle but moved to British Columbia with his family before the war. His medical records detail the nature of his wounds—a mass of shell fragments in his thighs, buttocks, neck, and face. Stretcher-bearers struggled to manhandle him to the regimental aid post, where he was quickly patched up and sent back to a field ambulance. When the casualties were pouring in, doctors had just minutes to pick who was worth spending time on and who was already doomed. I could picture the orderlies bringing Bert to the triage area, and the doctor looking at the wound tag pinned to his tunic. He would have lifted up the bandages to look underneath and perhaps taken Bert's pulse. Had he lost too much blood already? Were his wounds hopelessly polluted with battlefield filth, carried deep into the body by metal fragments? Would he survive the next leg of the journey, or would a bone-jarring trip over pitted roads undo any good the doctors were able to do? A shake of the head and a nod towards an open area beside the CCS, where there were already a handful of other stretchers lined up on the wet ground, would seal Bert's fate. He would be given strong drugs and kept warm, but his wounds were too serious for the doctor's attention; in the time it would take to treat one soldier, the doctor might treat five other men who had better chances of surviving. That was the harsh calculus of the medical officer—some had to die so that others might live. Had the field ambulance been busier, Bert's journey might have ended there; instead, he was stabilized and sent back to No. 9 Casualty Clearing Station at Contay. But the doctors had bought him only a few hours. His wounds may have been more serious than they first appeared to be, or perhaps the journey was rougher than usual. Bert died two days later.[49]

On the 19th, a jump in the temperature melted the accumulated snow and turned the Somme battlefield into a swamp. In the words of the British official historian, the terrain was not fit for further operations: "in a wilderness of mud, holding water-logged trenches or shell-hole posts, accessible only by night, the infantry abode in conditions which might be likened to those of earth-worms rather than of human kind."[50] With that, the campaign mercifully stumbled to a halt. The line reached by the British and French armies in mid-November was the best they could hope for over the winter. The fact that it was not far off the first day's objective, back in July, passed without comment. To the optimists, chief among them Haig, the Somme campaign had done exactly what it was intended to do. It had drawn German reinforcements from Verdun and allowed the French army to survive the year. It had supported campaigns in other theatres by preventing the enemy from transferring divisions away from the Western Front. It had cost the Germans as many as 680,000 casualties, and therefore was critical in the wearing-out effort. But the cost to achieve those goals had been staggering—620,000 British, Empire, and French soldiers. Since 1916, historians have argued over the Somme—a painful yet essential campaign, or a shocking display of military incompetence? It may have been both, but the tens of thousands of headstones dotting the landscape mark it as a human tragedy of heartbreaking proportions.

For the Canadian Corps, the eight weeks spent on the Somme were costly. It had been fresh when it came to the campaign in September, but after taking a host of tough objectives, from the Sugar Factory and Courcelette to Regina and Desire Trenches, after having done everything it had been asked to do, it was fresh no longer. The year would close with the Corps needing to make good over 24,000 casualties lost in those two months on the Somme. The campaign was also East Flamborough's first experience with multiple casualties; tragic news from the front, infrequent so far, now came more often. In those deaths, one sees how cruel an overseer history can be. A century is barely the blink of an eye is cosmic terms, but a century is all it took for those lives, and deaths, to vanish from our ken. On 22 September, Mervyn Hopkinson, after surviving the counterattack at Sanctuary Wood, was killed assaulting the village of Courcelette.[51] On 8 October, in the second attempt to take Regina Trench, John Akam of Aldershot went missing while serving with the 58th Battalion and Charles Hendry of Waterdown was shot in the head as he went over the top at the start of the 4th Battalion's attack.[52] On 13 October, Colonel George Inksetter was touring positions at Tara Hill in preparation for taking over the Canadian divisional engineers when he was badly wounded by enemy gunfire; he died two days later.[53] We know when they died, and roughly where, but the circumstances of their deaths have not survived. Nor, sadly, the circumstances of their lives. Akam left a widow and young son. She died shortly after the war and their son would be killed in action during the Second World War; with him died the line, and any traces that survived the First World War. Charles Hendry is listed on Waterdown's war memorial but I could find little of his life. He appears in a group photo of the 76th Battalion, which he joined in July 1915, clean-shaven and looking all of his nineteen years. But his slim file yields more questions than answers. On his attestation form he gave his trade or calling as "Gentleman," yet he was charged twice with absence without leave before the unit left Canada and, shortly before he was killed, had been sentenced to ten days of Field Punishment No. 1 for insolence to a superior officer.[54] George Inksetter built a large house in Waterdown for his new bride when they married in 1911. I knew it well as a child because a school friend lived there—the only kid in our class who had a swimming pool. But although Inksetter was East Flamborough's highest-ranking soldier to lose his life, even his record is confined to a few newspaper clippings, yellowed and crumbling, kept by later generations. Everything else became a casualty of time, death, and divorce.

John Filman from Aldershot is one of the few to have left an archival record, to give us a window into his last days. Filman was a signaller with the 1st Battalion, and it was his job to maintain the lines of communication between the companies at the front and brigade headquarters in the rear. German shelling was heavy and constant, and the signallers had to track back along telephone wires, often over open ground, to locate the breaks. It was exhausting work, as a letter to his father said:

14/9-16

Dear Father:

Just a few lines to let you know I am still alive an kicking. We are having some busy time just now and I haven't time for more than a few lines but expect in a few days to be able to write a decent letter. I seen a couple of German prisoners, who came over and gave themselves up, the other day. One of them had an iron cross, and they were a poor looking pair of men.

If it wasn't for fritz artillery and machine guns this war would not last long as his men physically are no where near equal to ours and when we charge they simply throw up there hands and yell, 'comerade' in every attack fritz louses more men than we do, our artillery is far superior to his and when he tries to hit our front line all you can see is a procession of green lights going up from his trenches which means that his artillery are shelling his own trenches.

Well must cease for this time, with best love,
John

Then, on 24 September, a shell burst spattered shrapnel down John's left side. "Well fritz has got me at last," he wrote to his father. "And believe me I am feeling wrotten just at present ... I have not had all the shrapnel taken out yet and I guess they won't bother with the small pieces for a while yet. One of my legs is very painfull but the pain can't last for ever can it or that is the way I trie to cheer myself."[55] He was right on one account—the pain couldn't last forever. Gas gangrene and blood poisoning had set in and, in the pre-antibiotic era, his doctors could see only one option: his leg must be amputated. At first, he was able to muster a brave face in a letter to his pals in the 1st Battalion: "Dear Boys, I am still alive, altho' it is a wonder. I have only one leg now so do not expect to go up the line again. She was a nice cushy one, only for one piece which hit me in the knee. I have several other scars and my leg is damn sore. We are having some fine weather here now and are expecting more. How are all the boys? Old Borden is certainly a wise old nut, for if he had come up with me that night he would have been just as bad if not worse than I am, as I guess you would see for yourselves what was left of the dug out and equipment. Wishing you all the best of luck, I remain, Yours sincerely, John W. Filman. P.S. Please forward any mail that may have arrived for me on here."[56] A few days later, he was obviously starting to flag: "I have been in hospital now since Sept 24th and have had my left leg amputated, & feel pretty miserable ... I am getting on as well as possible—or so they tell me—though it isn't always easy to feel it." His condition was downgraded from seriously ill to dangerously ill, and on 8 October he could fight no more.[57] John Filman was buried in Étaples Military Cemetery. The number of dead on the Somme from East Flamborough hardly compared to the losses of cities like St. John's or Accrington, but for a small rural township half a dozen deaths constituted a profound shock.

Whatever misapprehensions about the reality of modern war had survived through 1915, they were snuffed out in 1916.

But Wentworth's own 129th Battalion would soon be ready to enter the fray, to avenge the losses and carry on the fight. Stan Sawell had quite enjoyed his journey over on the *Olympic*—it was just like a pleasure cruise because he had nothing to do but eat, sleep, read, stroll the deck (four and a half circuits equalled a mile), and chat with old friends. Only on a couple of days was it foggy, rainy, and rough. The rest of the time, it was clear enough to scan the horizon for other ships (including the ill-fated hospital ship *Britannic*, sister ship to *Olympic* and *Titanic*, which would be sunk by a mine off Greece in November 1916) or watch the whales and porpoises following in their wake. On 30 August, the *Olympic* drew into Liverpool; the unattached officers went in one direction, the 129th in another. Stan learned that his first duty upon entering the war zone was to go on leave in London. Again, it wasn't quite what he expected of military service—sight-seeing by day ("London is a very interesting place. It's just about the same as I always pictured it from stories. I have great difficulty in finding my way around as the streets are so crooked"), theatre-going by night. Then it was on to the 18th Class of the Canadian Military School for officer training, which struck Stan as odd because he had already been an officer for almost a year. He found the first few days dispiriting to say the least:

> Sept 11th—We started a course in squad drill today and I am thoroughly disgusted with it. An officer starting in on squad drill after 10 months training and to make it worse some staff Captain told me I needed a hair cut ... it was but a week ago. I will do something desperate if this keeps up.

> Sept 12th—Same old squad drill today. Got as far as form fours today (as if we did not know how to do it after 10 months). I got through inspection all right this morning. It was not noticed I missed two hairs shaving.

> Sept 13th—We progressed a little farther today. Squad drill in two ranks. If we keep at this rate, in about 100 years I think I will know enough to be Brig Gen.

As the trainees worked through squad drill, musketry, and entrenching, Stan worked through his frustrations in his diary—"Same as yesterday,"

"Nothing particular happened," "Same old routine again, nothing worth writing about."[58] He found the instructors, few of whom had actually been to the front, antagonistic, ineffective, or both, and the subject matter pointless, as he sarcastically wrote to his sister Velma: "We have been having a lovely time over here. Today they have some peculiar implements ... They call them picks and shovels ... you use them for digging holes in the ground ... My but they are cute little things!"[59] A lecture on gas and the proper use of gas masks was the "first thing of any use I've learned since I came here." But, as he reflected much later, "all things good and bad have an ending. So on Oct 18th, most of us were warned for duty in France with various units." On his last night in England, Stan decided to take in a show. I'm sure that its title appealed to him, given his experiences at the training school. It was called *Joyland*.[60]

While Stan headed for the Canadian Military School, the 129th entrained in Liverpool for its new home. The experience on Salisbury Plain in the winter of 1914–15 had soured the Canadian government, and Militia and Defence insisted that better training facilities be made available. From 1915, Canadian battalions newly arrived in Britain went to one of two areas: Shorncliffe and its many satellite camps ringing the Channel resort town of Folkestone; and a cluster of camps (Witley, Bramshott, and Bordon) in the British Army's heartland near Aldershot, west of London. The 129th was bound for Witley. By the time the battalion arrived, dozens of Canadian units had already passed through and the camp ran with commendable efficiency. For men accustomed to the bell tents and blowing black sand of Borden, Witley was a revelation. Dozens of wooden barrack huts were arrayed across the Common in tidy lines, all nestled among wooded hills. There was a movie theatre, a YMCA hut, and even a shopping street, known as the Tin Town, because some of the buildings were made from corrugated iron sheets. The bathhouse blocks were of brick and the men ate in large dining halls, their food prepared by soldier-cooks. Given what they had just come from, they had little to complain about.

Understanding the rhythms of life in a training camp like Witley is not unlike trying to understand the goings-on in a rural village like Waterdown— in sources written for members of a community, by members of a community, so much goes unsaid. Printed material tends to cast everything in an amusing light, as in the popular postcard that matched the events of the training day to well-known hymns. Postcards dashed off to loved ones at home say only so much, restrained as much by concerns over causing alarm or revealing sensitive information as by the two-inch-square space that was available for a message. Letters can be rich sources but they can also be all but unintelligible, thanks to a combination of obscure references and a grade-school education. Albert Sindall and Percy Thomas had both emigrated to Canada before the war, and both ended up working on farms near Millgrove. Albert had joined the Canadian Mounted Rifles in Hamilton in September 1916, and soon after arriving in Britain wrote to his pal back in Flamborough:

Dear Percy

am writing you again for to let you have something to read as I know you like to here from me as I like to here from you though I have not much to write about. I am work hard in bud these days it rains every day we went to the rainges yestoday and that was at Dover 9 miles from shorncliffe but we could much for their had been a big wind stome turned over every thing and it will cost 100es of pounds to fix it up it is interesting ofer here in the chanil we saw where a bout had been sunk by a sub and it was not deep so we could see the mast out of the water we hard the guns over in France last last night about 4 o'clock and air oplains over head all the time. I have not got my 6 day pass I will go to your Farthers then Tell the Boss Englands got the horses that would make your horses looke like rats longside them sheep cows and everything the same in the line of stock. I see lots of <u>chickens</u> over here such as they are and you see this boy keep away but their are sum smart fellowes.

Well this is all this time Picey.

Say there are about 24 MoR [Mounted Rifles] coming back under age this week so watch forn them and let me know all that goes on in Canada and we do not here as much about the war as you do over there.

So write soon, good buy
Your best Albert
11 reserve St martins plains
Shorncliff, England N226360
Or Army Post Office London

Thin gruel for the historian, even after the punctuation has been added and the spelling cleaned up—a big storm, the sound of the guns, a sunken ship, impressive livestock, and a final admission that Percy in Canada probably heard more news about the war than Albert did in England. But however unenlightening we find this letter a century later, it clearly meant something to Percy. Just a few days after receiving it in December 1916, he took himself to Toronto and enlisted in the Canadian Army Service Corps.

A better source is a battalion's Part II Orders, which acted as a kind of daily newspaper for the unit. But like a newspaper, it reported the unusual— special events and visitors, transfers in and out, disobedience. It is in those records of crime and punishment that we get the clearest sense of what went on in the average training camp, and it's not necessarily what we might imagine. Case in point, the bacon-for-beer racket.

Since joining the 86th Battalion in Hamilton in September 1915, Bill Scott of Aldershot had shown little aptitude for drill and weapons training, a failing that eventually saw him posted to the cookhouse of the Canadian Machine Gun Depot at Shorncliffe.[61] If there was one job in the army that generated more suspicion than any other, it was a spot in the cookhouse. Men who worked in the kitchens had access to all sorts of things that were rationed in Britain; soldiers assumed that their cooks kept the best of the army rations for themselves, filched the seconds to trade with civilians, and served them whatever remained. In most cases, such suspicions were unfounded; in Bill Scott's case, they were correct.

Bill could put his hands on foodstuffs that were difficult to obtain in wartime Britain, particularly bacon and sausages. And so was born the bacon-for-beer scam.[62] Scott and at least one other soldier in the cookhouse reached an arrangement with two civilians who worked in the camp canteen that sold extras to the soldiers at Shorncliffe. The civilians would provide the beer, and occasionally cash, and Scott and his co-conspirator would supply in return the bacon or sausages, sometimes as part of a meal, sometimes in bulk. They worked the scheme for a couple of months until the quartermaster, Captain W. J. Nicholson from Hamilton, noticed discrepancies in the accounts and began to suspect thievery in A Company's cookhouse. An investigation turned up nothing definite, leading Nicholson to conclude that "if there was any thieving going on, it was very petty." But he asked Sergeant-Major Hicks to keep a sharp lookout, and Hicks was a better sleuth than Nicholson. While watching the cookhouse area, Hicks saw Bill Scott go into the canteen building carrying a large parcel, and come out a few minutes later with a heavy jug. With that, the scheme came crashing down. Another sergeant questioned one of the civilians in the canteen, an angelic-looking man named Keeler, and asked if he had any army rations, which were not intended for civilian con-sumption. Keeler claimed that he didn't, but a search revealed the large parcel under the counter. Keeler insisted it was laundry, and continued to insist as much until Hicks opened the parcel—even Hicks' untrained eye could distin-guish between laundry and four pounds of bacon. Keeler admitted that Scott had provided it in exchange for sixpence and some beer. (Keeler's co-worker, Thomas Nash, later said that he had been working in the canteen for about two months and had eaten meals there almost every day, enjoying generous helpings of bacon, tomatoes, and sausages, which Scott provided in exchange for beer and sometimes a few coins.) The two sergeants went next to the cook-house, where they found Scott and two other soldiers drinking beer from large bowls. Scott was as bad a liar as Keeler. He first said that there was no more beer, but the sergeants quickly found an army water bottle filled with beer. Scott disavowed all knowledge of it—until Hicks showed him the bot-tom of the bottle, where Bill had carefully etched his service number. All of this came out at Bill Scott's court martial in August 1916, at which he pleaded guilty to the charge of theft but was found not guilty on a second charge, of conspiracy to commit theft. Bill then offered a curiously circular argu-ment in mitigation of his sentence: "If I had not been under the influence of liquor I never would have done it": in other words, if he hadn't been drinking, he wouldn't have stolen the bacon to trade for drink. The court martial was unmoved by this dubious logic, and handed Scott a sentence of five months in detention.

But when people back in East Flamborough were craving news of what their soldiers were doing for the war effort, the bacon-for-beer scheme wasn't exactly what they had in mind. They were more interested in reassurance than information, in knowing that all was well with the boys, no matter what the reality. Since the 129th left Camp Borden for England, local newspapers had keenly followed its fortunes, with regular updates and letters from members of the unit. For military historians, those letters aren't very revealing—not much about the things they like to analyse, such as the training regime or the men's morale. They rarely mention the soldiers' feelings towards their officers, or about the war as a whole. The sensibilities of their families at home, and of Canadian newspaper readers, demanded lighter fare, and the men of the 129th were happy to oblige.

A common theme was comparisons between England and Canada—the people, the food, the buildings, the weather, the transportation, and especially the class system. Most of the time, the old country came out on the short end of the stick, despite the fact that fewer than half of the battalion's volunteers had been born in Canada. "We were told that no officers could ride on a London 'bus—that plebeian mode of transit," wrote one soldier, "—and here in London we see Canadian officers atop of 'busses, we see them hobnobbing with privates. We see them piloting some privates through London Tower and the Zoo and then Westminster. What a jolt to dignified John Bull. Well, Young Canada does as he would in Canada and old corpulent John Bull will have to put up with it."[63]

There were also sentiments that few people expected to hear, like fond recollections of Camp Borden, that place of hateful memory, of black, blowing sand: "We are in huts at Witley Camp. They are very comfortable, but the board floors are not as elastic on our anatomy as Borden sand. I hear all the officers had to sleep on the hard, hard floors for two nights. How do you like it, Major Graham? And poor Capt. Pennington, with no surplus flesh for cushion, like Lieut. Lawson. Col. Knowles experimented in every conceivable position on the soft side of his plank and his legal mind concluded that there ain't no soft side to a plank, at least not the one he slept on."[64] The 129th always made good copy, so local newspapers were happy to give it lots of space. On 19 October the *Dundas Star* printed the lyrics to the battalion's unofficial song, set to the tune of "When You Wore a Tulip":

> I used to walk the sidewalks of dear old Hamilton town;
> One day a man came down,
> His face all bronzed and brown,
> He told us how the King had called
> Each man to do his share,
> And offered me a khaki suit to wear.
> He told me how the call had spread
> Far over land and sea,
> And when I heard him say that, then
> I said that must mean me.
>
> Now we wear the khaki,
> The King's own true khaki,
> And we wear it with pride and joy;
> That old advertiser, old moustache Kaiser,

Will hear from each Canadian boy.
Where troubles are brewing, our bit we'll be doing,
To hammer down old England's foes,
While the bugles are humming,
The 129th are coming
From the land where the maple leaf grows.

The editor declared proudly that the song showed "the fine spirit the boys are in, a spirit which they are going to take to the firing line."[65]

But just a day before the song was published, the axe had fallen. Rumours had been racing through Witley Camp for days. The battalion was going to Egypt or Salonika, or even Mesopotamia. It would move to Shorncliffe, and from there to France. And then came the bitter truth: the 129th Battalion was to be disbanded. It was nothing personal; it was simply policy. The Canadian Corps at the front needed reinforcements, not more units. It already had four divisions in the field, and there was no inclination to expand beyond that. But those four divisions needed a steady stream of replacements to keep them up to strength. And so most new units were to be dismantled—not just the 129th, but the 205th Hamilton Tigers, the 153rd Wellington County Battalion, the 173rd Canadian Highlanders, the 164th Dufferin and Halton Battalion, the City of Hamilton's 120th, units that had been the pride of their communities, full of men who had enlisted together so they could fight together. The turn of the 129th came on 18 October.

It was a difficult day. "Can I ever forget it?" one soldier wrote home. "We were to lose our officers whom we had learned to trust and respect, we were to go to strange units with strange officers and did not relish the hazard, but we obey orders as good soldiers should." The 129th Battalion had lived for less than a year, but its men were determined to go out with dignity. "It was a beautiful day, with bright sunshine and billowy clouds. On the parade ground we were lined up and were told that the canteen funds were to be divided and we would each receive about a pound. Then we were all presented with several cigars and several packages of cigarettes. Three cheers were given for the O.C. and the Majors and the Chaplain. Then we marched with full packs to our new camp ... We were parting with our friends."[66]

All that remained was to get rid of the battalion's remaining assets. Boosters had worked so hard to raise money for the battalion—so many dances and concerts, so many garden parties and tag days. It had been a point of pride that the 129th left Wentworth County as well equipped as any unit in the Dominion. Now it was all to be sold off for pennies on the dollar. The 77th Regiment had presented the battalion with two fine field kitchens; rather than ship them back to Canada, Militia and Defence opted to sell them for a song to His Majesty's Government, along with a $400 truck that Colonel Grafton had presented.[67] The sports equipment was picked over by other units, whose NCOs descended on Witley like bargain hunters at a garage sale. The band instruments were crated up and returned to Dundas; what happened to them from there remains a mystery. The musicians, the darlings of all those concerts and parades, went back to being lowly riflemen.

A unit's daily life was captured in its Part II Orders, the accounting of transfers in and out, temporary postings, awards and punishments.[68] As I sat in the reading room of Library and Archives Canada in Ottawa, scanning the long list of names of men who were transferred to other units on 18 October, I couldn't help but think of the effort that had gone into luring them into the 129th in the first place. My uncle Stan Sawell, going to every house with a clipboard to take the names of military-aged men. The recruiting party's assault on Freelton that yielded just two volunteers. Colonel Knowles' grand plans to blanket the community with battalion propaganda, plans that Militia and Defence so often declined to approve. The 129th hadn't quite managed to recruit to full strength, but it wasn't for want of trying. And then, with a few columns of names typed on foolscap, it was all over. Leafing through the folder of documents on the table in front of me, I came to the end of the 129th's official existence. It saddened me to see that, after the long list of transfers, the last few pages of its Part II Orders are handwritten. In its final days, the battalion was left without even a typewriter.

The men and junior officers would find places elsewhere in the CEF. The 123rd and 124th Battalions, to which the majority of the men were posted, may have been strange units with strange officers, but at least they were from southern Ontario; they had both been raised by Toronto militia units. Cec Nicholson transferred to the Canadian Army Dental Corps—it seemed a shame for a trained dentist to be wasted in the infantry. But the disbanding of dozens of battalions left a glut of colonels in Britain, many of them older and with no front-line experience. Almost all were sent home to Canada as surplus to requirements, including Colonel Knowles.

Back in Dundas within months of the unit's demise, he had the sad task of winding up the affairs of the 129th. Some matters were quickly resolved.

St. Andrew's Presbyterian Church in Ancaster had presented a bill for thirty dollars, which Knowles was happy to approve. A detachment of the 129th had billeted in the church hall throughout the winter of 1915–1916, and had used the Sunday School room for drill and lectures. The church asked only to be reimbursed for the actual cost of light and heat.[69] Other matters revealed the ugly side of local recruiting and the economic motives that often jostled with patriotism. One local business owner complained about officers of the 129th taking over his office on one of their sweeps for deserters. Knowles concluded that he was just looking for a payout; he had been quite happy to provide the space at the time.[70] A Dundas stableman demanded $9.50 for the use of a horse, which he claimed had been engaged by a battalion officer to round up deserters after the 129th had left the area for Camp Borden. When he wasn't paid, he launched a civil suit against Knowles and the unit. But since there was no proof that the expense had been authorized, the magistrate found in favour of the 129th. This brought a plea to the local MP from the Dundas lawyer who had argued the case for the plaintiff. He admitted that the stableman had no further legal recourse but asked that the amount be paid anyways, to avoid the bad feelings that resulted from a local tradesman feeling short-changed by the local unit. Knowles was unmoved. He said that the stableman had never presented a bill at all, and the officer might well have assumed that the horse was being provided gratis, out of patriotic goodwill. It was just one of many such bills that were now coming out of the woodwork, for goods or services that had never been authorized or even tendered. "Mr Shaver," wrote Colonel Knowles, "selected his forum, viz., the Division court and because he was beaten he squeals like a stuck pig. Having selected his forum and been beaten he now tries to get payment through political pull. A most manly proceeding on his part?" His response was the same when a Dundas hardware dealer claimed to have outstanding invoices from earlier in the year, and was demanding payment from Ottawa. Knowles would have none of it. The bills were not to be trusted, and neither was the merchant. "As to the strictures contained in Mr Wilson's letter," he wrote testily, "they come with a bad grace from a bachelor of Military age and physically fit who never subscribed a cent to the Battalion funds—never asked a man to serve His Majesty but in every way knocked recruiting and whenever a man in my battalion applied to him for his discharge, he procured it."[71] One can easily forgive his annoyance. For the last year, he had given all of his time and energy to the 129th, even to the point of lodging D Company on his farm. And his efforts were repaid with a quick trip home and immediate discharge as no longer useful to the Canadian government. It must have been deeply hurtful. Shortly after he got back to Dundas, Knowles moved to California, where he remained until his death in 1931.

As 1916 drew to a close, the soldiers continued to come home to East Flamborough—the wounded, the sick, the overage, the underage. They had been trickling in through the year. Marcus MacKay, his leg shattered at Ypres, had come home in February, his contingent of wounded heroes met by a large crowd and the brass band of Toronto's Royal Grenadiers. William Howison, who took a piece of shrapnel in his thigh on New Year's Eve 1915, returned in April, to be greeted warmly by the members of Waterdown's Anglican Young People's Association. William Bowden had been given leave for the 129th's last weekend before departing Borden and decided that he would rather stay home in Waterdown than return to soldiering. But then he tried again by joining the Canadian Mounted Rifles in Hamilton—perhaps hoping that his badly calloused feet, which had prevented him from completing a single route march while with the 129th, wouldn't be a problem if he went to war on horseback. A few days after Christmas, he was discharged a second time— the CMRs had no use for a fifty-year-old unskilled labourer with a systolic murmur, an enlarged heart, and a black mark on his file as an "intemperate."[72] Tom Humphreys returned to Aldershot after developing acute nephritis while in France. He had ignored the symptoms for weeks but when the shooting pains got the better of him, he reported to the 18th Battalion's doctor and was sent to England for treatment. The medical board that granted his discharge agreed that exposure to cold and wet in France had aggravated the effects of a childhood attack of scarlet fever and left him unfit for further military service—and that he was "prevented in the general labor market from engaging in any heavy work."[73] One son dead, another permanently incapacitated—that was the war for the Humphreys family of Aldershot. That was the war for thousands of Canadian families.

The end of 1916 brought some newcomers to the township as well—John and Annie Fleming, who came from Glasgow to take over the management of Hendrie's Valley Farm. The Flemings were a large family of nine children. Two of the boys were in the army in Scotland and three other children had good positions in and around Glasgow; only four of them made the journey to Aldershot with their parents. Elizabeth was the oldest at seventeen, a tall, stately young woman with a patrician air—the family called her Lizzie, but she always referred to herself as Elizabeth. Jim was twelve, with the fragile self-assurance of a lad who had made himself responsible for his sisters. Mary,

The Fleming family just before leaving for Canada: Mary, John, Annie, and Isabell, with Tom in the back.
Photographer unknown. (Author's collection)

nine years old, was darker and smaller than the others, and shy too, with a kind of furtive look that suggested she would be happy to hide behind her brother. The youngest was just seven years old—Isabel, my grandmother.

In family pictures taken at the time, little Isabel gazes directly at the camera, confident, forthright, unaffected. Her parents and siblings were all dark—Isabel alone was fair, with masses of wavy, golden hair that turned to a lustrous auburn as she got older. I try to reconcile the little girl in the pictures with the jumble of images that come to mind when I recall my grandmother later in life, before Alzheimer's attacked her mind: a patrician demeanour like her older sister Elizabeth, golf in Myrtle Beach, a bowl of plastic fruit, a beige living room full of uncomfortable furniture, a white Ford Thunderbird with suicide doors. At first, I can't put them together. But then I think of my grandmother laughing, her eyes sparkling as she threw back her head, and I can see in her the merest shadow of the girl in the photos.

My father and his sister remembered John and Annie Fleming with great affection, but a certain amount of trepidation. They both spoke with thick Scottish burrs that made them nearly impossible to understand. This was not so bad with Annie, for she was a typical Scottish grandmother of melt-in-your-mouth shortbread and bedtime songs softly sung. John was more alarming, thanks to the black leather glove he always wore to conceal a damaged hand. To his grandchildren, being approached by an old man with a black claw who spoke a language they couldn't understand was unnerving.

The Flemings had never been to Canada before, but their fortunes were already tied to the country. In the spring of 1913, their son Willie, then just nineteen, had boarded the Donaldson Line steamer *Saturnia* in Glasgow, bound for Quebec. The sailing records only hint at his motives. In neat columns, immigration officials listed the personal details of each newcomer, particularly their intentions once in Canada. Willie listed his destination as Winnipeg, Manitoba—the gateway to the west, the most ethnically diverse and vibrant city in Canada, and a magnet for young immigrants with a dream but not much else to their name. In answer to the question "What is your intended occupation in Canada?," he said "Anything." He was far from the only passenger arriving that May afternoon to declare as much, but Willie went a step further to ensure a favourable verdict from the immigration official. He took the precaution of adding two years to his age before tackling the question about his employability: "Have you ever worked as farmer, farm labourer, gardener, stableman, carter, Railway surfaceman, navvy or miner?" To this, Willie responded that he had seven years' experience as a miner, and had been going down in the pits since 1906.

Was he telling the truth? He was born and raised in Scotland's "Black Country," the rich coal seams of Lanarkshire, southeast of Glasgow, and Scottish lads could start working down below at the age of twelve. There's no indication that Willie was the rebellious type, but if he wanted to find work away from the farm, mining was an obvious place to start. It would also have given him good reason to emigrate, for mining was a dangerous and exploitive occupation, especially in Scotland. Unlike in England, Scottish miners were hired on "daily notices"; each morning, they had to go to the pits to see if they could work, and how much they might get paid. A bitter strike in 1912 failed to win them the minimum wage they demanded, and the mood among the miners was that they had been stitched up by their government and their unions. Scottish migrants had long shown a preference for Canada as a destination. Perhaps Willie joined the exodus that in 1911 and for the first time, saw more emigrants from the United Kingdom settle in Canada than in the United States. I don't know whether Willie had decided on his own to stake his future on a new country that had already drawn hundreds of thousands of Scots, or whether he was the advance guard, laying the groundwork for the rest of the family to follow at a later date. Maybe the Flemings had decided that the prospects of a long, healthy life in Glasgow were not good. In January 1913, twelve-year-old Nan Fleming died of diphtheria, which also put Willie, his mother, and his sisters Mary and Elizabeth in hospital. Canada, in contrast, was often advertised as a land of clean air, pure water, and healthy living.

But whatever plans Willie may have had, they were soon interrupted. When the war began in August 1914, he was in Manitoba, where he listed his trade not as a miner but as a draper. He was one of the very first to enlist. Two of his older brothers had been in the Territorial Army before the war—was Willie keen to follow in their footsteps? Was he looking for adventure, or a steady wage, or a free trip back to the old country? Did he see himself joining a crusade against the Hun? We shall never know—perhaps, like so many other eager volunteers, he didn't really know himself. Whatever his motivations, he signed on with the 99th Manitoba Rangers and went with them to Valcartier, to become part of the 8th Battalion, the Little Black Devils, of Winnipeg. He spent the winter on Salisbury Plain and in February 1915, went with the 1st Division to France, and eventually to Ypres.[74]

In April 1915 the men of the 8th Battalion were close to the apex of the Ypres Salient, their backs to the Stroombeek. The first German gas attack, on 22 April, had fallen far to their left but they knew full well that their time would come. Looking through the field of tall mustard plants beyond his trench on the morning of the 24th, Willie may even have seen the steampunk soldiers clamber from the German trenches, foul green clouds billowing around them. The 8th Battalion was struck only a glancing blow by the gas that morning, and all through the day and into the afternoon of the next, the men battled wave after wave of attackers, desperately trying to hold the apex. As the hours wore on, their ranks thinning, ammunition reserves running down, unaware of what was going on in the rest of the salient, Willie and the 8th grimly hung on, gaps in their lines plugged by stragglers from other units. Not until dusk on the 25th was it admitted that nothing could be gained by clinging to their positions. As dawn on the 26th broke over Flanders fields, Willie and the other survivors of his unit pulled back, leaving the new front lines to be held by fresher battalions.

But his parents and siblings knew little of this as they left Glasgow in November 1916 on the *Scotian*, bound for Saint John, New Brunswick. All they knew about his war was contained in an envelope of documents that had been carefully placed in the large, ornate family bible in one of their steamer trunks.[75] The first page was a letter from Willie, written shortly after the Ypres battle:

France, May 8th 1915

Dear Mother and Father,

Just a few lines to let you know that I am still alive & well, hoping this finds you all enjoying the same blessing. You will have heard of the grand fight we put up against the Huns we were very badly cut up. how I managed to escape without a scratch is a miracle to me. We are now having a rest behind the firing line & being reinforced by the second contingent. I am spending a couple of days in hospital having some teeth taken out, they had bothered me so much lately that there was nothing else to do but have them pulled. I will now close with best love to all, hoping to hear from you soon.

I remain,
Your sincere son,
Willie

The second letter was in a different hand—strong, educated, feminine. A nurse.

1 Ward
13 General Hospital
Boulogne Base
28 May 1915

My dear Father & Mother,

These few lines to let you know that I have been wounded. I have had my left thigh smashed with a bullet. I will very likely be in Scotland next week, I hope. Will you send a letter here as soon as you can, as I might get it before leaving here.

Your loving son,
William

No. 13 General Hospital was in the old Palais de Neptune, a large rococo building on the waterfront in Boulogne. A year earlier, it had been a casino, one of the jewels of the Channel coast, but now its ballrooms, gaming halls, and restaurants were filled with row upon row of hospital beds. Just before the Ypres battle, its terraces had been covered with ugly, utilitarian huts to accommodate even more beds. That's probably where Willie was.

After coming through the "grand fight" at Ypres without a scratch, his luck had run out. On the night of 25 May, Willie and his newly repaired teeth had been detailed to join a working party of 200 soldiers in support of an attack on Festubert. Another Canadian battalion had captured part of a German stronghold known as K5 and the hard-won ground had to be defended. It was up to the men of the 8th to dig new trenches linking K5 to Canadian lines. Few infantrymen enjoyed exchanging their rifles for shovels, but at least the work wasn't usually dangerous.[76] Only a handful of men were wounded by enemy fire that night, but Willie Fleming was one of them. A bullet snapped his left femur and he lost a lot of blood on the painful journey to the regimental aid post. But he never got back to Scotland; Willie died three days after the nurse wrote that last letter home. His name appeared on Ottawa's noon casualty list on 8 June, although the Flemings don't seem to have kept the fateful telegram announcing his death. The next letter in their meagre file is typewritten, severe, official. It indicated simply that "the deceased soldier marginally noted," no. 1102 Pte. W. Fleming, 8th Battalion, had been buried in Boulogne Eastern Cemetery and that "a small cross with number has been erected to his memory."

In 2011, I took my wife and children to the cemetery to pay our respects to Willie. It was July and Boulogne was doing what it does best—welcoming hordes of tourists to its seaside, its beaches, its pier, and its casino, a new steel and glass edifice on the site of the old Palais de Neptune, which burned to the ground in 1937. Tucked away in an urban neighbourhood far from the battlefields, Boulogne Eastern Cemetery doesn't draw many tourists; it lacks the allure of front-line cemeteries where the scars of war can still be seen. It's large, with nearly 6,000 burials arrayed in long lines on the western edge of the municipal cemetery, but it still wasn't large enough. Before the war ended, it was declared full to capacity and a new cemetery opened at Terlincthun, not far away. As we walk around, we see that Willie is in interesting company. There is the grave of Fred Campbell of Mount Forest, Ontario, who won the Victoria Cross at Givenchy in June 1915. The war poet Julian Grenfell is buried there—he died just a few days before Willie. In a separate section are the graves of 140 men of the Portuguese Expeditionary Force, which also had a hospital nearby.

Because the war cemeteries are superbly organized, it was easy to find Willie's grave—section VIII, row A, plot 60. The "small cross with number" had long since been replaced with a permanent headstone but, unlike most other Commonwealth War Graves Commission cemeteries, Boulogne's headstones lie flat, a consequence of the unstable sandy ground. It was a curious feeling to stand there with my wife and children. On the one hand, Willie was as much of a stranger to me as the thousands of others buried there. I never knew him—I'd never even seen a picture of him. At least I could visualize Fred Campbell and Julian Grenfell. But kinship exerts a powerful, perhaps irrational, pull. Here was my grandmother's brother. He would have seen her as a newborn, and perhaps watched as she took her first steps. Maybe it was his name that she first learned. Perhaps he walked her to school. I wondered if the Flemings were together at Christmas 1914—if they were, I'm glad that they didn't know it would be their last such Christmas.

Beneath the name, unit, date of death, and the maple leaf on the headstone, there was an inscription. Relatives could pick from a list of epitaphs provided by the War Graves Commission, or come up with their own. The Flemings had chosen one of the suggestions, a verse that was very popular in cemeteries of the time:

> We cannot Lord
> Thy purpose see
> But all is well
> That's done by thee.

As I read that, standing in Boulogne Eastern Cemetery on a gloriously sunny, and peaceful, day in July, I recalled the last letter in the folder that John and Annie Fleming brought to Canada at the end of 1916, and wondered if it offered them a measure of comfort:

YMCA
70 Bothwell St
Glasgow
1st July 1915

Dear Mrs Fleming,

I have just heard of the death of your son William while fighting with the Canadians in France & I offer you my sincere sympathy in your sad loss. It is very terrible that in this 20th century we should see such a slaughter of men to satisfy the lust of a few. Let us pray that this war may end war.

My excuse for writing is that your son came for a time to my Bible Class in the YMCA here before going to Canada & and I was sorry to hear of his death & hope that the knowledge of the sympathy of friends may help to ease your grief.

Believe me,
Yours faithfully
H. T. Galbraith

John XI verses 25 & 26

The large family bible that held their treasures would have gone to an honoured place in Valley Farm in Aldershot—perhaps on the mantelpiece. Since my childhood, I remember it sitting in my house in Waterdown, a typically massive book with an ornate cover. Most of the pages are quite clean. I don't know if the Flemings were regular churchgoers, but they don't appear to have consulted their bible frequently. That one page from the Book of John, however, is worn and soiled, as if fingers have run over those two verses again and again: "Jesus said unto her, I am the resurrection, and the life: he that believeth in me, though he were dead, yet shall he live: And whosoever liveth and believeth in me shall never die. Believest thou this?"

5

1917

Snapshots of innocence in a country slowly being hardened by war. The Bachelors of Waterdown held its fourth annual ball on a bitter January night in the roller rink. Cedar boughs and bunting had been nailed all over the walls to make it look a little less like what it actually was—a glorified barn—and the clatter of skates had given way to the sweet sounds of Lomas' Orchestra, one of Hamilton's most popular ensembles. The proceeds were to be donated to patriotic purposes and with a "gentleman's admission" ticket costing $1.50 (over $26 in current values) it looked to be a good fundraiser.[1] Was it naive to celebrate bachelorhood at a time when the unmarried man should really be in uniform?

Later in the year, the Women's Patriotic League's hosted its third annual garden party, featuring a palm reader, a tea-leaf reader, and the ever-popular Queen of the Carnival contest. This year it would be at the Fairgrounds, rather than at Clunes. The McGregors couldn't manage another big gathering, for they had had a difficult year. Of their seven children, four were now in uniform. Walker had enlisted in the 164th Battalion in March 1916 and Doug had joined the Royal Flying Corps in October. In the spring of 1917, Muriel and Flora had gone. Muriel went into the Canadian Army Medical Corps (CAMC) as a nursing sister, but Flora had married a major from Hamilton and the CAMC wouldn't accept married women—so she was on her way overseas as a nurse with the American Red Cross. The change in venue didn't hamper the event, however. The party pushed the WPL's receipts for the year to the equivalent of nearly $37,000 and spawned the formation of yet another patriotic organization, the Knotty Knitters' Klub. It started as a sock-making factory but eventually would branch out into mounting fundraising concerts and masquerades to purchase comforts for Waterdown boys overseas. For the rest of the war, soldiers would write back to the township, in blithe ignorance of the meaning of the initials, thanking the KKK for its kindness.

The AYPA held its regular meetings, passing motions, electing commit- tee chairs, debating resolutions, the war never far away. Members read letters from siblings in uniform. Cards are sent to wounded soldiers. And a letter of condolence is written to the family of Tom Flintoft, their former member. They vote to purchase the materials for an Honour Roll of church members who have enlisted, and are quick to offer support when the Flintofts donate a bell to the church. They pledge $60 to help with the cost of a belfry, and raise more than that within a couple of weeks—nearly $1,300 in current values, an impressive sum from a small-town church youth group in fourteen days. A member is thanked for letting the group borrow her picture of King George V. The decision is made to donate a ton of coal to the church. Essays are read on Sir Walter Scott and "Heathen Ways of Prayer." But occasionally there was a reminder that, no matter how much they acted like adults in time of crisis, they were still just teenagers. At one meeting, those teenagers decided that "the motion passed at the last meeting to take the picnic to Wabasso Park be rescinded, and that we go to the beach instead."[2]

Evelyn Galloway sent her first letter home after she and her sister Ruby sailed for England in June. Five years separated the Freelton-born sisters, but not much else did. They had both gone to New York to train as nurses, had joined the Canadian Army Medical Corps in Toronto on the same day in May 1917, and spent their entire military careers together—always transferred to the same hospital on the same day. They even arrived home on the same ship in August 1919.[3] I wonder how they were able to stay together. Their uncle, John M. Eaton, was an officer in the CAMC, but not high enough to exert any useful pull on their behalf. Their older brother Arch could have had nothing to do with it. He was a lowly gunner in the Canadian Field Artillery who was often on the wrong side of military law, once for telling his sergeant that he'd be fucked if he was going back to work.[4] In contrast, if Evelyn's letter is any indication, the sisters were the soul of decorum, the personification of innocent amusement:

We had the most delightful sea voyage that ever was. We were only sick a few hours, but I slept with my boots on for two nights, for the simple reason that I was afraid to stoop to take them off, for that seemed to make me sick quicker than anything. The first night we were nearly all sick before we were out two hours, all racing for the sides of the boat and some of us for bed, and slept with our clothes on and our hair not combed or anything, anything to get lying down. I stayed in bed till four o'clock next day. But after that I was fine and never expect to enjoy anything again like I did that sea voyage. We made some nice friends, including an Anglican chaplain who took a great notion to us Hamilton girls, so we played all kinds of games, especially quoits and shuffleboard, at which Ruby and I were champions of the boat. The chaplain and I always played on opposite sides and I would nearly always beat him.

We passed the Emerald Island and it is certainly beautiful. You can't imagine how green it is. We arrived at Liverpool (I can't tell you when) and missed the high tide, so we stayed on board a day longer than we would have. We got into the docks at night, with the twelve o'clock tide, and we stayed up to see them, or rather our old boat anchor after our wonderful trip absolutely in tears. I guess the prayers of those who know and who love us counted a great deal in our safety.

The chaplain and another officer showed us all over the boat and oh, it was wonderful. We stoked coal into the immense furnace, just to say we were stokers. Mother, stokers are the blackest creatures you ever had eyes on not niggers, though, if you could get far enough under to see the white just coal dust.

We left Liverpool Friday, about noon. We were on the boat ten days and certainly hated to leave it, and came through to London through the most beautiful country. No wonder Germany covets it. Really sometimes one would think it was the Garden of Eden, or at least what Eden must have been like. Its beauty is simply marvellous. We arrived in London at 5.30 p.m. and were driven in immense wagons, like band wagons, only to hold about thirty of us. Great big, fat horses (the horses here are wonderful, one never sees an old or skinny one) and away above is a silk-hatted driver, looking as if he were dressed for a ball. We did look nice, though, with our blue and red. People would stop and stare at us for blocks. I didn't tell you where they took us—just from one station to another, so they landed us on another train for Orpington, Kent. They have the funniest little trains here you ever saw, just about half as high as ours are at home, but they go like a streak of lightning and run very smoothly. The whistles on them sound like a peanut-stand whistle at home.

Well, we landed at Orpington, 60 of us, about 8 p.m. and were met by the Army Red Cross autos, those great, big ambulance things. Our trip certainly never got monotonous, for we had change enough, both in scenery and conveyances. Well, we were shown to our rooms, which were brand new ones and not finished yet, but even as they are, we love them, but we'll tell you about them later, when we get back there. We had lunch and, apart from the bread, there was very little appearance of famine. We stayed there overnight and next day took the 3.20 train for London once more. We are here at the Kingsley Hotel, where all the officers and nursing sisters room, at least most of them. There are three of us in a room, and we are very comfortable. Last night we took motor trucks, great, big twodecker things that sail around the streets, darting in and out like lightning. We sat away up at the top and nearly laughed our heads off. Everything seemed so funny to us. We got back around 9 p.m. and were certainly tired enough to go to bed, so we did and got up about 8.30 on Sunday morning, had our breakfast and started for St Paul's Cathedral and attended service there. Mother, of all the wonderful, wonderful buildings. We couldn't go through it to-day, so we have that pleasure ahead of us. We came home and had a rest till 5.30 p.m., then we hired a cab for 2½ hours and saw some of London. I'll tell you again about that drive, for it is nearly midnight.[5]

Was Evelyn simply writing what she thought her family wanted to hear? Were all of these people just pretending to be normal? We tend to assume that the matter-of-factness, the bravado, the gaiety, the resolve, must all have been a façade, and an incredibly fragile one at that. Looking back a century, can we see cracks? Or do we only think we see cracks because we assume they must have been there in this, the darkest year of the war? It's always important to read between the lines, but never at the expense of reading the lines. And in doing so, we find no hint of contrivance in Evelyn's letter, no sense of false genuineness in the AYPA records. Instead, an effortless breeziness hints at real candour. Some people really were having the time of their lives, at least for now.

———◆———

STREWN ACROSS A PITCH-BLACK FRENCH FIELD in the driving rain, the men of Stan Sawell's battalion made no pretence of cheerfulness. They were thoroughly miserable, and they took no pains to conceal the fact. And Stan was sympathetic—the situation was intolerable and should never have been allowed to occur. They had been relieved by another battalion on 24 March 1917 and went back to reserve positions behind the lines. There should have been accommodations for them—tents, or a few requisitioned farm build-ings—but there was nothing. They were left out in the open with only blan-kets and groundsheets to make into improvised shelters. The few men who tried to compare the situation to a childhood camping trip were silenced when the rain began. It came down in torrents and for hours, drenching the small piles of men huddled under groundsheets. Cooks moved around them with buckets of food, but it was nauseating stuff—the portable kitchens had been defeated by the downpour and the cooks had done little more than bring the food to lukewarm. Not until the following evening did sufficient tents arrive to get the men under cover, but even then it was too wet to do much more than sit and feel sorry for themselves.[6]

It wouldn't get any better soon. On 6 April, Stan and two platoons were sent forward for special duties with another battalion, but arrived to find that nothing had been prepared for them. He found shelter in Zivy Cave, a massive cavern cut deep into the chalk, but then had to go back out with a carrying party to bring in their rations. The slog through mud that was knee-deep in places took a lot out of Stan; once he got the men fed, he found himself a small bench and promptly fell asleep. But their carrying wasn't finished. At dawn, the men were back out moving supplies—after Stan had a pointed discussion with his superiors: "I had quite a difficult task convincing Brigade and 20th Bn headquarters how impossible it was to supply working parties totalling about 200 men out of 2 platoons numbering 80."[7] If there had been any doubts about what was in store for them, they were now dispelled. The training and constant movement of supplies could mean only that an attack was imminent.

The Canadian Corps had been out of action since Courcelette the pre-vious November, although hardly idle. There was always trench-raiding and the daily tossing of artillery shells back and forth across no man's land, wire to be strung and sandbags to be filled. There was always some kind of chore waiting. Soldiers were like children, thought the army—unless they were kept occupied, they would get into trouble. At least it wasn't just busy work. The new year had brought planning for another offensive, this time with a new man at the helm. Robert Nivelle had enjoyed a meteoric rise through the command of the French Army. He was the first general to employ the creeping barrage, and his successful use of it at Verdun had turned heads in the French government. To see him work a cocktail party was an education, for he always seemed to know the right things to say to the right people. The fact that his mother was English and he spoke the language fluently promised better understanding between the allies; that he was Protestant probably also helped to endear him to the British government. Support for Nivelle was by no means universal—Haig didn't trust him, so being a Protestant clearly wasn't enough—but Nivelle had enough backers to win the assignment. His big offensive on the Aisne River would involve 1.2 million French soldiers and a staggering 7,000 artillery pieces. To keep the Germans away from Nivelle's target, the BEF would launch a series of limited offensives in the north. The British 3rd Army would advance astride the river Scarpe, while the Canadian Corps would support that supporting attack by capturing Vimy Ridge. The highest part of a nine-mile ridge on the western edge of the Douai Plain, it was one of the most important features on the Western Front. It didn't look like much on a map, but from the top one could see to Lens in the north, Douai in the east, and Arras in the south. One Canadian commented that, standing atop Vimy Ridge, "more of the war could be seen than from any other place in France."[8]

Since taking over command in June 1916, Julian Byng had transformed the Canadian Corps from a promising formation hobbled by political appointees and inefficiencies, to one of the tightest ships on the Western Front. His plan for the attack on Vimy Ridge relied on all the factors that he had been drilling into his men for months—timing, coordination, artillery support, flexibility, decentralization. The four divisions would make a series of carefully timed assaults on four lines of objectives, identified by colour: Black, Red, Blue, and Brown. Everything, from the stages of the artillery barrage to the pauses between assaults, was laid out down to the minute. Rehearsals were done using scale models of the ridge or on fields that had been taped to represent the optimum routes for movement. Maps were distributed by the thousand, to all ranks of the Corps. Munitions and supplies were stockpiled. The Corps prided itself on attention to detail; nothing that could be foreseen was missed, and flexibility was built into the plan for things that couldn't be foreseen. When the guns opened up and the lead units clambered out of the jump-off trenches on the morning of 9 April, the men felt like they had already done it before. A harsh weekend of fighting lay ahead, but all the preparation and training paid off. The Corps took 10,000 casualties but captured the entire ridge, exactly as it had been asked to do.

Stan Sawell wrote a number of accounts of his experiences on Vimy Ridge that weekend. His diary, presumably written once the 21st had been relieved and had returned to billets after the battle, says almost nothing—he covers his weekend in three short sentences. Shortly after the battle, he wrote a long account in a letter to his father, but when the letter went astray in transit, he wrote another one a few weeks later, although he admitted that it was "probably not as good as the first one, as I wrote it while things were fresh in my mind." Fortunately, the second version reached Waterdown and became the basis for an article published in the *Hamilton Spectator*. That account can probably be credited to an imaginative journalist. Although it claims to give Stan's words and is presented in quotation marks, it bears little resemblance to the original letter that my cousin Steven has. Finally, in 1934, Stan wrote another, even longer account for his young son, supplementing his diary and letter with later reflections, in many cases to explain things (he added, for example, a section describing the workings of the Hales rifle grenade). By putting them all together, we have an unusually full account of that weekend through the eyes of a rural shop-clerk-turned-infantry-officer.

Stan began his 1934 account with a commentary that will be familiar to any Canadian who was paying attention during the centenary of the Battle of Vimy Ridge: "Canadian soldiers this day did more to give Canada a real standing among the nations of the world than any other previous single act in Canadian history. This was the first time that all the Canadian divisions now grouped together as the Canadian Army Corps under Sir Julian Byng had gone into action as The Canadian Corps and certainly we succeeded where others had failed."[9] There is no evidence that Stan was thinking in nation-building terms in April 1917, but he certainly was twenty years later.

He assured his father that he couldn't describe the battle as a whole— only his part in it, as commander of 13 Platoon, D Company of the 21st Battalion. D was the battalion's reserve company, and was to move up behind A Company on the right flank, watching for problems and being ready to move up quickly if the lead company ran into trouble. He admitted that the days of carrying supplies had taken a lot out of his troops, who were not in the best of shape as zero hour approached. By herding them into Zivy Cave, Stan was at least able to keep them dry before moving them out to their start position, Mill Street trench, at about 3 a.m. on the 9th of April. In 1934, he recalled that, "The suspense of waiting for zero hour was perhaps the most trying experience of the day. I feel quite certain the chill morning air had a great moral effect as one was not quite sure if the shivering of oneself or another was caused by cold, nervous strain or plain funk so everyone got the benefit of the doubt."[10] The last few minutes were the hardest. "I cannot quite explain my feelings as I waited there for zero minute," he wrote to his father in 1917. "Everyone talked of everything except the attack. I know I looked at my watch many times. The time seemed to pass so very slowly and I was keen for 5:30 to come. About 5AM I gave each man a ration of rum which increased the morale about 100%. About 5.25AM I took out my watch and did not take my eyes off it until the last second was up."[11]

He hardly needed his watch for, as he explained in his letter, "exactly on the minute, the sky was lit up by the simultaneous flashes of our guns opening up the barrage fire. We were off. The noise was stupendous! Thousands of guns of all calibres firing simultaneously. It sounded as if the whole universe had gone decidedly wrong!" But advancing was easier said than done. Stan had planned for his platoon to move up the Neuville–Les Tilleuls road, but he hadn't reckoned on how much the barrage would rearrange the landscape. He couldn't even find the road. As he told his father, "everything was in confusion and it seemed as if it would be impossible to get through the tangle of shell holes and wire. Before I had gone 15 yards I had lost my direction. Men of all battalions were mixed up."[12] But at that point, the endless training exercises kicked in. Assuming that the gunners would fire on the correct targets, his men simply moved towards the shell bursts, counting on the explosions to lead them in the right direction. It worked. In short order, Stan's platoon had reached its objective and could watch up ahead in the distance the advance on enemy lines.

Stan immediately recognized that A Company was being held up by two German machine-gun nests that had escaped the bombardment. Working together, the two guns had established an excellent field of fire, pinning down the lead company down and holding up the attack. This was just what 13 Platoon was waiting for. There is little difference between Stan's 1917 letter and his 1934 account, except that the former is slightly more detailed:

I moved up with what few men I had, thinking to be of some assistance. When I arrived at the Lens–Arras road which afforded some shelter on account of the high bank, I discovered that two of their [A Company's] officers had been killed and two seriously wounded with only a few NCOs left. I immediately took charge and organized three parties, each under one NCO. One was to work around each flank. I took charge of the third party which had for its object to keep the enemy engaged while the other parties worked to the flanks. Every opportunity I had when the firing stopped for a moment, I got the party forward by shell holes. By this time the left party had disposed of the one gun by dropping a Mills bomb through the loophole. But the other gun continued firing due (we afterwards found out) to an officer being present and forcing fresh men to replace casualties as they occurred. I had by this time got within 50 yards of the gun. The flank parties seem to have lost their direction or were making slow progress. I took advantage of short stops in the firing caused by the gunner being killed or reloading to rush the gun before they could get another man on the job. We were quite successful.

So successful, indeed, that Stan was awarded the Military Cross for organizing the destruction of the two machine-gun nests.

Stan's letter to his father is quite matter of fact, and in 1934 he added further details that, for him, captured the variety of the day. He was delighted to find confirmation that his unit had reached its objective in the form of a nicely hand-painted sign with the name of the trench they were to capture, Zwischen Stellung. He watched as a curious reinforcement tried to pull a rifle grenade from a sandbag but succeeded only in pulling the pin, killing himself and blinding his officer. His unit relieved a battalion of the King's Own Scottish Borderers, who had taken full advantage of the rum ration and were firing off ammunition so they didn't have to carry it back with them. Stan's company was led to its positions by a scout identified only as Doucette, "who was our guide and in the lead as was the common practise kept calling out when any obstruction was met such as wire or shell holes etc. Doucette who spoke typical French Canadian English would call out 'deys hole on de leff,' 'deys hole on de right.' Presently after calling 'deys hole on de leff' he eased over to the right and disappeared entirely. Then his voice came to us from the bottom of a deep shell hole into which he had fallen—'Chris', deys one on dey right too.'" And the sight of the enemy dead stayed with him: "One of these in particular lived on in my memory for a long time. Even yet the picture in my mind of that face is quite vivid. He lay on his back, a large hole in the forehead, instantly killed yet the mouth was moving open and closed in much the same manner as a fish just taken from the water. Strange to relate this continued for some time."[13]

Stan Sawell had been as close to the battle as one could possibly be. Joe Eager saw only its aftermath. His first year of war had been a whirlwind.[14] He had taken a commission in the CAMC in December 1915, and married a week later. By the end of January 1916 he was already in England, only to be hospitalized in February with influenza and in May with a broken arm. That at least got him a trip back to Canada on escort duties, acting as medical officer for a fresh battalion, the 104th from New Brunswick, on its voyage to England.[15] There were certainly worse assignments to be had—he too sailed aboard the *Olympic*, and while the conditions weren't quite what they had been in the glory days of peace, they were a good deal nicer than what Joe was used to in the army. By August 1916, he was back in England awaiting a posting. "We have had air raids nearly every night lately but the camp has not been touched," he wrote to his sister in Waterdown. "We could hear bombs exploding somewhere near a few nights ago. The gunfire has been almost constant day and night for the past two weeks, I did not think we could hear it from the front but don't know where it can be if not from there for it certainly is in that direction it is coming from ... My arm is just as good as ever now & perfectly straight."[16]

In September came a posting to No. 1 Canadian General Hospital at Étaples, a resort town on the Channel coast, although it wasn't all work:

No. 1 Canadian General Hospital
British Expeditionary Force
26/11/16

Dear Father

Have just come in from a long walk on the shore, the tide was out and the wet sand made good footing. The sunsets here are simply gorgeous, I thought they were exceptionally fine on the prairie but here they are much finer. About here is a favourite haunt of artists, although just now we do not see many. They say that the atmospheric conditions are just right for painting here.

I was walking through the little fishing village near here last night & looked in on an open door & saw a man standing on a pile of fish spreading salt on them & turning them over with a shovel, so went to watch him for a while, they were herring and they were salting them to pack in barrels like we get at home in the winter, I don't think I will eat any more herrings for a while.

One of the MOs here Capt. McGregor was up with the PBs (Permanent Base men) for some months and knew Tom Flintoft quite well but had not heard that he had been killed. He said he was in the bombing section when he left.

Received two mails yesterday. I think the papers do not get lost as often here as they did in England.

> Love to all
> Your aff. Son,
> Joe[17]

The new year saw the hospital expand to 2,230 beds, which generated a great deal of activity and, reported the war diary, "a general feeling that 'Something is going to happen' permeates the hospital."[18] For an infantry battalion, rehearsing and carrying were sure signs that a big push was in the offing. For a hospital, the clue was an increase in bed capacity. As the new beds were unloaded at Étaples, everyone assumed they would soon be filled. And so they were.

No. 1 Canadian General Hospital
British Expeditionary Force
10/4/17

Dear Agnes,

By the time this reaches you it will be near the 7th of May, let me wish you many happy returns. I posted a little birthday remembrance to you a few days ago. Hope it gets there all right. I have not received any mail from home for over two weeks, it seems to have been coming very irregularly lately.

We just got our first convoy of wounded from near Arras to-day, some are very badly shot up but all are cheerful and seem confident they can go through the Hun line where ever they like. They all say our artillery were simply magnificent and that the Hun had no chance at all against our guns. I suppose now that the advance has begun it will be kept up all summer. That means a lot of hard work for all the base hospitals but guess we can stand it all right.

We had quite a nice service here on Easter. I feel quite proud of myself, I was there twice, took communion at the morning service.

So Garth is still in England or has he been invalided to Canada?

Love to all
Your aff brother,
Joe[19]

At first glance, Joe's letter sounds a little like Evelyn Galloway's, all full of conventional phrases, reassurance, and good news. But is it too good to be true? Can the wounded really have been cheerful and confident, or is that just what Joe assumed his family wanted to hear? If that is indeed the case, what do we make of the hospital's war diary, which spoke in very similar terms: "the extraordinary spirits of the patients; optimism and cheerfulness radiate from faces that are flushed with victory, and even intense suffering from wounds received is temporarily forgotten as they speak of the 'great battle.'"[20] Was there a party line being followed, an unspoken agreement that the aftermath of the battle would be described in a certain way? Or, should we take the remarks at face value? Perhaps the wounded really did radiate optimism and cheerfulness.

No. 1 Canadian General Hospital
British Expeditionary Force
18/4/17

Dear Father

Received a letter from Agnes last night, written on Mar 15th and one from you several days ago written about the same time, it seems to take them a long time to come now.

Was glad the Choral concert was a success and that Agnes' song was so well received.

We have been very busy at the hospital during the past week, it was the biggest week they have had since the hospital was opened the operations varied from fifty-five to seventy daily and there were nearly 2200 patients in at one time, but to-day was much easier. We have had a few Canadians, one of them I was anaesthetizing yesterday happened to be from Hamilton and knew Waterdown very well. I noticed in the casualty list today the name of Capt. Campbell. He used to be a lawyer in Empress we used to knock about a good deal together when I was there, was very sorry to know that he had been killed. Major Greg[?], one of the men here, who used to be in Dundas got word that his brother had been killed.

Must close now two of the MOs have come in.

Your aff. Son,
Joe[21]

Joe's hospital saw hundreds of wounded from the Vimy fight—broken bodies, shredded flesh, blinded, limbless. Each generated a notification telegram and an entry on the official casualty list—Ottawa was releasing to the press two lists a day in busy times. Back in Canada, nerves must have been constantly on edge. Every letter seemed to bring bad news, every newspaper told of another family's loss. The Hunters lost their second son, Wray, and the Jameses their youngest, Richard. On another part of the front, Warren Cutter was killed with the Australians. As a young man, he had found East Flamborough too confining, as did his sisters Ethel and Maude. They both went to New York to train as nurses, but Warren's wanderlust was more severe. For a decade before the war, his name pops up on sailing lists around the Pacific—San Francisco, Honolulu, Sydney, Fremantle; sometime he was a crew member, sometimes a passenger. There is no indication of what he did in any of those places but August 1914 found him in Australia, working as a railway labourer. He enlisted in 1916 and soon got a trip to Europe. He went missing in action shortly after.[22]

The news only got worse in the weeks after Vimy.

No. 1 Canadian General Hospital
British Expeditionary Force
13/5/17

Dear Father

Was very sorry to learn from your letter that Colin Campbell was missing.
He is in the most dangerous branch of the service and I have been watching for his name in the casualty list, but missed it. I hope he will turn up
allright.

I received a pair of sox and some papers from the Waterdown school a
few days ago and wrote Miss Allen thanking her, in case she does not get
the letter, if you or Agnes see her, wish you would tell her I got it all right.

We are having great weather here now. On Sunday afternoon I went
out into the woods and basked in the sun for hours. We have not been very
busy lately and very often have two or three hours off in the afternoon.

I am enclosing a photo we had taken a short time ago, just before
Col. Hutchison went to England, I hope it gets there all right. We are not
supposed to send photos but one like this can't do any harm.

Love to all,
Your aff son,
Joe[23]

Colin Campbell had been raised in Waterdown, where he had attended public
school, before going on to Upper Canada College and McGill University to
study mechanical engineering. He left a position with a Toronto waterworks
engineering firm to join the Royal Flying Corps in the spring of 1915, and
went overseas in January 1916.[24] He was much more sanguine than Joe about
the dangers of his line of work, as he wrote to Agnes Eager in January 1917:

France
Jan 19/17

Dear Agnes:

Thank you very much for your thoughtful gift of the socks which you will be glad to know fit me like gloves.

Nice of you to congratulate me on my supposed success but I am really quite an ordinary individual still and just potter around the air dodging Huns or trying to bite their 'tails' off.

It has been snowing for the past few days so we are having a respite— the ground looks quite interesting from an aeroplane, under snow.

My very best to yourself and yours.
Sincerely,
Colin[25]

But Colin Campbell didn't turn up all right. During a reconnaissance mission over Tournai on 6 April, his formation was attacked by a much larger number of enemy scouts. In attempting evasive manoeuvres, two of the British planes collided and all four crew members were killed, including Campbell.[26] On 6 July, Eric Rowley of Aldershot died in a flying accident in France; six days later, Carlisle-born Basil Binkley was killed while flying on operations out of St. Omer. Roy Mount, a descendant of the family that founded Mountsberg, disappeared during an attack east of Arleux-en-Gohelle in May.[27] William Gillies, who had been one of the first from the township to enlist in 1914 and a veteran of 2nd Ypres and the Somme, was also killed in the trenches at Arleux.[28] Waterdown-born John Sills thought himself quite safe in his billet behind the lines—until an enemy shell burst beside him on 9 July, leaving him with wounds that claimed his life two weeks later.[29] There was no escaping it: 1917 was turning into a very bad year.

Any celebration of the capture of Vimy Ridge had to be tempered by the realization that it was virtually the only bright spot in a disappointing campaign. Nivelle's confidence hadn't been enough to make up for the tactical shortcomings in his plan, and almost everywhere his attacks were turned back with heavy casualties. Only on the British 1st and 3rd Army fronts was there success and, given the French failure, that success had little strategic importance. French losses in the Nivelle offensive had been so catastrophic that some units were in open revolt and dozens of others were simmering with discontent. Mutiny was in the air, and even the most optimistic realized that the French army would be unfit for major offensive operations for the foreseeable future. In Russia, there were signs that the creaky old czarist state was cracking under the strain of war. The capital, St. Petersburg, descended into rioting in March, with many local military units taking the side of the revolutionaries against the government. Few observers thought it would be an isolated incident. The United States had finally come into the war on the Entente side, but it would be months before the American Expeditionary Force was in the field in strength—and longer still, probably well into 1918, before it was ready to pull its weight on the Western Front.

But in Canada, it was the manpower situation that was most worrying. The capture of Vimy Ridge had been a great victory, but to lose 10,000 trained infantrymen over a weekend was a blow. At current rates, it would take more than two months to replace those men in uniform. The number of volunteers had briefly climbed in May but then went down again—in August, the number of new volunteers to the CEF dipped below 3,000 for the first time in the entire war. In rural areas, the impulse to volunteer was even more fragile. Going into the war, rural Canada had faced a shortage of agricultural labourers, a situation that had only deteriorated. The early recruitment drives had taken away a huge chunk of the itinerant labour force upon which farmers relied; the boom in wartime manufacturing, which promised higher wages and set hours, drew even more men from Canada's farms. Rural writers had long regarded leaving the farm as a misguided lifestyle choice; now, they could conjure up images of crops rotting in the fields for want of workers. That, combined with the unspoken suasion of a tight-knit rural community, clearly kept potential recruits on the farm. East Flamborough produced just thirteen volunteers in all of 1917; four of them were for the Royal Flying Corps and one was a nurse. Just three men chose the infantry.

It had come down to simple mathematics. Casualties were going up; enlistment was going down. Voluntarism had clearly run out of steam, as had the old-fashioned methods of mobilizing human resources. The public appeals and recruiting meetings, the colourful posters and marching bands, Stan Sawell going door to door with his clipboard—they were no longer enough. It was time for a more rational approach to securing reinforcements for the Canadian Corps at the front. Conscription had been discussed openly for months, but the Borden government was keen to explore every alternative before taking that step. The first mail of 1917 brought Canadian households an unwelcome surprise in the form of registration cards. All men between the ages of sixteen and sixty-five were asked to write down their personal information, physical condition, and willingness to undertake national service, either in uniform or in industry. This would tell Ottawa what it had been only guessing at since 1914: just how many men were available for military service, given physical standards and the demands of wartime production? By the time the results had been counted, some 1.5 million cards had been returned. After discounting men in essential occupations and those who were unsuitable for service for other reasons, there remained a pool of nearly half a million men who could be in uniform. The entire exercise was optional and Borden took pains to point out that registration wasn't a prelude to conscription, but how else might those 500,000 men be coaxed into the CEF?

If Borden's government wasn't yet ready for compulsion, it was prepared to extend its reach to see that the laws of the land were obeyed. Carrots were no longer working; it was time for sticks. Like clamping down on deserters. The 1916 law had given them amnesty if they returned to their units; the next step was to target their accomplices. Thomas Townsend of Aldershot was slapped with a $200 fine for harbouring a deserter, but eventually convinced the Department of Justice that it had been a misunderstanding. The man had sworn that he had been legally discharged, and Townsend wasn't to know that he was lying. In any case, he had a son in uniform with the Canadian Engineers and, reported the press, "he is a loyal Canadian, who has been a generous contributor to the Patriotic Fund."[30] But rooting out a handful of deserters and their accomplices wasn't going to help, not when the Canadian Corps' manpower deficit was into the thousands and growing every week.

In February 1917, Prime Minister Borden travelled to England to confer with the leaders of the imperial war effort. He fully expected a hard sell from British Prime Minister David Lloyd George, who was pushing for a greater commitment of men and wanted Canada to invoke conscription, as Britain had done in early 1916. In return, Lloyd George was prepared to offer the Dominions a greater voice in running the war; as a first step, he opened the company ledgers, so they knew where things really stood. Borden, for one, was alarmed at how dire the situation looked from London. France and Russia couldn't be relied upon for much, and the US entry was a double-edged sword; the Entente desperately needed American soldiers, but no one wanted the US to be able to claim that it had swooped in at the eleventh hour and won the war.

As unsettling as those revelations were, Borden was even more moved by his encounters with Canadian soldiers. On the weekend that Vimy Ridge was captured, he watched training exercises in England, and then travelled to France to visit with the wounded at #1 Canadian General Hospital, where Joe Eager was on staff.[31] Borden was a resolutely political animal, but there is no reason to doubt his claim that he was deeply moved by those meetings. To him, the manpower question was an abstraction; to the men lying in hospital beds, it was life and death. For Borden, it was numbers on a page; for the soldiers he met, it was about getting twenty reinforcements when you desperately needed a hundred, or trying to fight a battle with less than half the number of soldiers you should have. An under-strength unit takes heavier proportional casualties than one at full strength—was the failure to adopt compulsion needlessly costing Canadian lives? The prime minister was convinced. He returned to Canada on 5 May; just over a month later, the Military Service Bill was introduced into Parliament. On 29 August 1917, conscription was signed into law.

But it wasn't quite that simple. The last election had been in 1911, and Parliament had already been extended once. Borden tested the waters by asking about another extension, but the opposition from Laurier's Liberals was so strong that he decided not to pursue the matter. That condemned Canadians to an election before the year was out. But Borden had never intended conscription to be a partisan measure; it shouldn't be a Conservative policy, in his view, but a national policy. So he set about assembling a coalition, using every tool at his disposal to draw Liberals, from provincial as well as federal ranks, and others into his Union Government. By 12 October, he had a cabinet of thirteen Conservatives and twelve Liberals in place. His Unionists would go to the hustings to fight it out against Laurier Liberals, Labour candidates, and a handful of independents. Canadians would vote on 17 December 1917.[32]

Accounts of that election campaign are anything but inspiring. The rhetoric reeks of intolerance, ill will, and grievance, and the times brought out the worst in almost everyone who spoke publicly on the subject. The moral high ground in November and December 1917 was utterly deserted. It's a shame, then, that so little has survived about the campaign in East Flamborough, for it would certainly have produced some salty comments. The township was part of the constituency of Wentworth, which had undergone two rounds of redistribution since Confederation, although the riding remained Liberal by inclination. James McMonies was elected as a Liberal in 1867 and the party retained its hold until 1904, when the Conservatives won Wentworth by a mere ten votes. Waterdown merchant W. O. Sealey took the riding back for the Liberals in 1908, but it went Conservative again in 1911.

In 1917, it would be a three-man race. The Labour candidate was Hamilton metal worker Fred Flatman, who made the iron gates that graced the Hendrie estate in Aldershot. In fact, William Hendrie had helped to set Flatman up in business—was it inappropriate for a socialist labour activist to accept start-up money from a local aristocrat?

John Herbert Dickenson, the Laurier Liberal, was a young farmer from Glanford, south of Hamilton. The fact that he was from the other end of Wentworth County may have worked against him in East Flamborough, although he gamely made a campaign stop in Waterdown just two days before the vote. By then, he must have been feeling desperate. The day before, the *Globe* had hit him with a $25,000 slander lawsuit, alleging that he had repeatedly said "the *Globe* has been bought up by the Union government." This may explain his intemperate remarks to Waterdown voters, sentiments that Sir Wilfrid Laurier would surely have disavowed had he been aware of them. Dickenson began by claiming that in fact *he* was the man to defend soldiers and the war effort. All well and good. But he went on to draw a shameful contrast: real Canadian boys in uniform were fighting at $1 a day while "thousands of foreigners exempted from military service by this government are drawing $4.00 to $7.00 per day, and doing nothing to help win the war. If I am elected I will never close my lips till these foreigners are compelled to fight, pay or get out." And he cited a specific, if unidentified, case, castigating "A government that turns down a returned hero who loses one leg and a part of his hand, and places in the position held by his deceased father in the face of a petition asking for his appointment a wealthy brewer of German extraction."

Dickenson went on to argue that his Unionist opponent, Dundas hardware merchant Gordon Wilson, was no better. He claimed that Wilson, a military-age bachelor without children, had engineered an agreement with Arthur Rykert, the Conservative member of the provincial legislature for the riding. Despite the fact that Rykert was married with two children, Wilson somehow convinced him that he should enlist for military service, while Wilson stayed home to win the election.[33] Whether there was any substance to the accusation is unclear, but it doesn't quite match the facts: Rykert had been commissioned into the 176th Battalion in October 1916, long before the election was contemplated. And yet there may be something to Dickenson's evident distaste for his opponent, for we have met Wilson before. He was the very same man about whom Colonel Knowles had complained bitterly in 1916 for submitting questionable bills connected to the 129th Battalion. Knowles had described Wilson as "a bachelor of Military age and physically fit who never subscribed a cent to the Battalion funds—never asked a man to serve His Majesty but in every way knocked recruiting and whenever a man in my battalion applied to him for his discharge, he procured it." That man sounds an awful lot like the one Dickenson talked about.

Nevertheless, Wilson was clearly the man to beat. Elected provincially for the riding in 1908 and federally in 1911, he was a seasoned campaigner who spent a great deal of time in East Flamborough, including campaign events at the Orange Hall in Carlisle, The Plains in Aldershot, Waterdown's roller rink, McFarlane's Hall in Freelton, and the Millgrove Hall.[34] I could find no accounts of his speeches in the township, but it may be that the substance of his campaign didn't matter much anyways; people seem to have voted not for the man but for the war and for Unionism. As one of Hamilton's leading citizens was reputed to have said, "I would vote for a yellow dog if it was endorsed by the Union Government."

And so it went. The factors that drew East Flamborough towards the Unionists were probably similar to those that motivated rural voters everywhere in Canada: the effectiveness of Unionist propaganda, which made voting for Laurier akin to voting for the Kaiser, and Borden's pledge that the sons of farmers would be exempted from conscription—an admission that the skilled farmer was every bit as difficult to replace as the skilled tradesman (and also constituted a powerful voting block). Laurier had struggled to make the election about more than just manpower, and here and there he succeeded. But for most voters, it was a single-issue election, and the choice couldn't have been clearer. Would they say that enough was enough? Faced with mounting casualties through 1917, would they decide not to throw good money after bad, and instead turn off the manpower taps by rejecting conscription? Or would they conclude that to give up now was to render all the deaths meaningless? Would they accept that, having come this far, there was no turning back, and that they owed it to the men who had died, and those who fought on, to keep the Canadian Corps adequately reinforced through compulsion?

In an election that saw voter turnouts of 90 per cent in some ridings, they decided that there was no going back. The Unionists took 153 seats to Laurier's 82, the biggest majority in Canadian electoral history until 1957. The popular vote was much closer, and the Unionists' fiddling with the franchise undoubtedly helped their cause. In Wentworth, Flatman was never a factor, polling just eight votes in the entire Township of East Flamborough—although he took 11 per cent of the vote in the riding as a whole. After that, he backed away from labour politics and concentrated on his metal-working. Dickenson took 24 per cent of the vote in Wentworth, but 36 per cent in East Flamborough. Like Flatman, he never returned to politics and died during the 1918 influenza epidemic at age thirty-eight. Wilson won the riding handily, taking 65 per cent of the vote in Wentworth, with 62 per cent in East Flamborough.[35] He would remain the MP for the constituency until his death in 1937.

SNAPSHOTS OF EXPERIENCE in a country slowly being hardened by war. Ex-soldier Charlie Gray of Carlisle, on trial for stealing tires. He had joined up in Toronto in 1916, but was hardly a model soldier. Within two months he was hospitalized with syphilis, and the army also found him to be exceptionally nervous—the doctors thought that sunstroke he had suffered as a teenager had left him with neurasthenia. Whatever the reason, he was quite inept as a soldier: "When this man is given a command he becomes excited & either fails to carry it out or does the exact opposite. This has become progressively worse. He cannot keep up with the others on the march. Has dizzy spells. Sleeplessness." After just three months in uniform, the army discharged him as irredeemable.[36] The judge who presided over his theft trial was more sympathetic. Charlie had been only a passenger, he decided, and had no role in the crime. He was acquitted.

Charles Greenlee of Carlisle, also on trial, but for something more serious—intentionally shooting himself to avoid duty.[37] According to his testimony, he had been cleaning his rifle and had his hand over the muzzle when it went off. Friends of mine who are soldiers tell me that it's not the sort of thing that would happen accidentally. Even if you forgot there was a round in the breech, you would never put your hand over the muzzle while cleaning a rifle—it would be a very unnatural way to hold it. The army agreed and found Charles guilty of negligence causing a self-inflicted wound; the sentence was ninety days' Field Punishment #1. It probably didn't bother Charles very much, because he too was less than a model soldier. Even before leaving Canada with the 120th Battalion, he already had an impressive list of charges under his belt, mostly for absence without leave, suggesting that he didn't find army life particularly congenial. If he did indeed shoot himself intentionally to avoid duty (battle fatigue surely wasn't a factor—he had been at the front with the 19th Battalion for only two months, and hadn't yet been in action), it worked. The hand refused to heal and Charles was returned to Canada as unfit for further service. But rather than wait for officialdom to process his discharge, he deserted, wanting nothing further to do with the army. The feeling was surely mutual—on Charles' final form, the army indicated that his character was "Bad."[38]

A typical letter from another local soldier at the front—cheerful in a way, but also a little forlorn, even plaintive:

Somewhere in France
Oct 14, 1917

Dear Friend –

I received your welcome letter tonight and am answering by earliest opportunity. Our Battalion has made two trips to the line since I have been in France, and I myself have been on a part of the front line on listening post. I am always pleased to hear from you, no matter if it is only a line or two and I will try and send you some card scenes of France later. We are out on a kind of rest at present and do not know just how long we will be. I received a letter along with yours from Sister Alice (Calgary). She is well.

I cannot say as much as I would like about France, as you probably know; cannot give any dates or names of places, so you will understand how awkward it is to write a decent letter. I am glad to hear you are all well. I wish I had a fountain pen, it is to hard to write without ink, you will have to excuse this awful scribble.

My cousin, Ralph Breckon, has got a D.C.M. and corporals stripes since he has been in France. Big Will Uncle Watson's boy has also enlisted.

Quite a lot of Ontario boys in my own Battalion, but some from Waterdown
only Walker McGregor. I think he is in the Flying Corps.

I hope to hear from you again. Just think, it takes nearly two months
for a return mail from home, but I suppose we must be patient.

Will close now, with love to you. I remain your true friend
Pte W. J. Breckon[39]

Brothers Ralph and Big Will Breckon had moved from Waterdown to
Mawer, Saskatchewan, before the war. Ralph won the Military Medal (not
the Distinguished Conduct Medal) for laying communications wire under
heavy enemy fire near the end of the Somme offensive in 1916; he was back in
Mawer by February 1918, his war ended by shrapnel wounds in the chest.[40] Big
Will never got beyond England; he returned to Canada in 1919 with a British bride and a bad case of hemorrhoids.[41] Walker McGregor had joined the
164th, and ended the war with the Princess Patricias; it was his brother Doug
who had joined the Royal Flying Corps.[42] Like his cousins, Will Breckon had
also gone west before the war and ended up working as a bridge carpenter in
Nelson, British Columbia. He had enlisted in April 1916 and finally reached
the front in August 1917.[43] When he wrote the letter back to Waterdown, Will
Breckon had less than a month to live.

———————◆———————

WE SEE THE 2ND BATTLE OF YPRES through a sickly greenish-yellow cloud of
poison gas. The tragedy of the Somme comes to us through numbers—60,000
casualties on the first day, one for every eighteen inches of the sector's front
line. Passchendaele's horrors are manifest in images: a lone officer thread-
ing his way between water-filled shell holes; Canadian machine-gun teams,
almost invisible in a moonscape of slime; an artillery wagon covered in mud
that seems to reach up and pull it down into the muck.

It wasn't supposed to be that way. It had started promisingly at Messines
in June 1917, when dozens of explosives-filled mine galleries were detonated
beneath a ridge, literally blowing off the crest and allowing General Herbert Plumer's 3rd Army to capture the critical piece of high ground—now not

quite so high. Then, Haig planned to mount his major offensive near Ypres, clearing the Channel ports of Germans (and their U-boats) and rolling his cavalry eastwards through Belgium towards the Dutch frontier. But what had begun as a potentially promising solution to the stalemate of the Western Front had been transformed by accident, circumstance, and miscalculation into yet another attack of the kind that had been the stock in trade of all sides for over two years. The first day, 31 July 1917, went poorly, subsequent days not much better. By October, British units hadn't even reached their objectives of the first day, and the commanders were looking for decent ground on which to dig in for the winter. Their attention focused on the main Passchendaele–Wytschaete ridge line, behind the village of Passchendaele. To take it, they selected the Canadian Corps, which had not yet seen action in the offensive. Arthur Currie, Byng's replacement as corps commander, was less than enthusiastic. Currie's rise had been every bit as meteoric as Robert Nivelle's. He had been an obscure Victoria militia officer in 1914 with a cloud gathering over him because of funds missing from his regimental accounts. His handling of his brigade at 2nd Ypres had been sound, but he shone once he took over the 1st Division; his command had always been very good, and often brilliant—so much so that it would have been almost impossible *not* to appoint him to replace Byng at the head of the Corps. From the start, Currie didn't like the look of Passchendaele. In his view, nothing further could be achieved there and he had no desire to sacrifice his men in a lost cause. He drove a hard bargain with the British, demanding and getting extra artillery support and insisting on changes to the timetable. Currie couldn't refuse the order to take Passchendaele, but he could fight the battle on his terms. The Corps would mount four separate operations in October and November, each time jumping a little closer to its final objective. The conditions were appalling, the suffering Biblical, the endurance almost superhuman. But by the 11th of November, the Canadian Corps sat in possession of most of the Passchendaele–Wytschaete ridge line. It had cost some 16,000 casualties.

What was it all for? At the time, recalled Stan Sawell in 1934, he had no idea: "Many reasons have been given as to why this struggle was necessary at this time of the year. It certainly did not make sense to the average battalion officer at the time as the gain was so small in comparison with the losses sustained. We were told very little about what was going on in the adjacent sectors, or why this was to be conducted in this manner. I cannot see how a military commander could genuinely anticipate any type of success in the conditions that presented themselves over such a prolonged period at Pass-chendaele." Without understanding the point of it all, the conditions as Stan described them became even harder to bear:

> The ground conditions here for a battle were terrible beyond description ...
> Low-lying country where drainage was almost nil. A vast sea of mud was
> churned up by the fighting. The area had been so heavily pounded by artil-
> lery fire that few roads remained intact. There did not seem to be firm ground
> anywhere. Shell holes were so numerous that they overlapped, and were
> brim full of slimy, stinking water. The whole sector was littered with aban-
> doned equipment from both sides, tanks, limbers, artillery of all sizes, dead
> horses and mules, and of course, the corpses of dead soldiers. The nauseating
> stench of death permeated everything, everywhere. The horses and mules
> were used as pack animals to move supplies. Since movement of supplies had
> to be carried out under the cover of darkness, many of the beasts faltered off
> paths into mud up to their bellies. Once mired, they were almost impossible
> to get out. They were often shot as they panicked in their struggles against
> being trapped in the mud, as those struggles only served to make them more
> intractably stuck ... [the captured pill box] we now occupied was proving to
> be too heavy for the underlying (and now saturated) chalky soil. It had sunk
> to such an extent that only approximately one-third of its original height
> was above ground. Inside, someone had placed wooden support posts in
> the corners and constructed a floor of boards just above the water line. It
> reminded me somewhat of a beaver house—the outside entrance was ren-
> dered so low to the ground, one had to get on hands and knees to get in and
> there was barely any head room to even sit upright. Worse still was that the
> previous occupants had not bothered to venture outside when nature called,
> at least not when there were convenient cracks in the floor. When a shell
> would explode in the near vicinity, the force shook the ground and the water
> under the floorboards would ripple, followed by a gurgling and bubbling
> sound. Then up would come the most vile smelling stench. Still, this was
> better than taking one's chances outside.[44]

I imagine that when Richard James and Wray Hunter died at Vimy, their families were comforted by knowing that they gave their lives in a great vic-tory, manifest for all to see, and in the achievement of a Canadian nation. What comfort awaited the families of Passchendaele's dead? At least Leland

Dougherty was carrying the wounded to safety on 31 October when a shell dropped beside him, killing him instantly.[45] The relatives of Freelton-born Chester Maddaugh, who died the following day, would eventually learn that he was part of the 72nd Battalion's capture of Crest Farm.[46] But did that give his death any meaning to them? Will Breckon and Walter Emmons of the 7th Battalion simply disappeared on 10 November, joining the legions of men denied a known grave by the conditions of the battle. Walter was older than most, forty-five when he died, with a wife and five children in Carlisle. He had come back from New Jersey, where he was working as a railway station agent, to enlist in the 129th—and to vanish on a tortured battlefield an ocean away from home.[47] Donald Fraser has left a detailed account of the last moments of another East Flamborough man, an account that leaves one with a curious sense of emptiness:

> our transport went up the line and met with such opposition that a number were wounded and others so badly shaken and shell-shocked that they were either unfit or unwilling to proceed the following night. Our crew was, therefore, called upon for assistance ... For the first time we had each to lead up a horse to a forward dump carrying an assortment of goods. The transport men left behind soon had the horses loaded up and ready. Roughly there must have been something like 14 or 15 in our little convoy ... We started out and I found myself second last in the line. My horse was loaded up with cans of water, four on each side ... Up the road we went ... Shell holes were everywhere and most contained slimy, muddy water. The terrain was a wilderness of mud. Thank goodness, however, the road was fairly firm. We were warned to space out which caused quite a distance between the first and the last man ... The artillery was firing as we passed and Fritz was returning the fire. We soon saw that it would take practically a direct hit to do any damage. We watched the shells send up fountains of mud and water as they exploded. For quite a distance you could see eruptions taking place at various points resembling geysers or mud volcanoes ... Near the top, shells were falling beside the road ... Emerging from the hollow, we crept slowly up the ridge ... We were gradually getting through, when I sensed it was about time the next salvo was coming and with it trouble, and sure enough the shells came. I was thrown by the force of the explosion on to my face into the gutter at the side with the rest of me sprawled around the edge ... I was badly dazed and partially choked by mud and water ... my

mind quickly cleared and I looked around and saw my horse lying dead half over my right thigh and pinning me down. We were tossed from one side of the road to the other. Glancing ahead I observed the horse in front dead and its attendant also. He was Joe Bishop, a brother of Elmer who was killed several weeks before at Lens.[48] Joe was taken off the gun crew and given a supposedly safe job with transport. Ahead of him was Ladd. His horse was dead also and he, himself, was wounded and trying to rise. I turned around to see how the fellow behind me fared. I saw him and his horse motionless in death.[49]

The last man in line was Wurtz Edge of Waterdown.

And as if Passchendaele hadn't produced enough misery of its own, at the end of the campaign came chilling news from an earlier battle—the discovery of ten bodies of Canadians from the 87th Battalion, near Lens, all with their throats cut. All of them had originally enlisted with the 129th Battalion and two of them were from East Flamborough: Richard Fenning of Waterdown, an Irishman who had arrived in Canada in 1912; and Stephen Duckhouse, who had volunteered during the battalion's sweep through Freelton in 1916.[50] Newspapers reported that the men had been captured and killed, their bodies found in a later Canadian attack. There are no documents to support the press account and it may have been nothing more than a propagandized atrocity tale, but it stuck. The war memorial in West Flamborough, not far from the farm where he was placed as an eleven-year-old Home Child and where he lived happily until war intervened, reads: "Stephen Duckhouse—Murdered near Lens—Age 23."

As winter closed its grip on East Flamborough, a pall must have fallen over the township. So much had already been asked of them, and the asking would continue. Another Victory Loan was winding up and the township had again given far more than expected—$213,000 had been pledged, the equivalent of something like $3.6 million. Waterdown, with a population of just 750 people, had pledged an incredible $55,350, or nearly $950,000 in current values.[51] How could a small village afford so much—or could it? But it wasn't a question of fight or pay, as fundraising posters so often said—it was fight and pay. Everyone knew that the first conscripts would be called in the first week of January 1918, and the bad taste of the election remained in everyone's mouths. The campaign had been bitterly personal and brought out the worst in both sides; winners gloated, losers sulked, and no one was willing to offer apologies for hurtful things said. And the explosion that flattened Halifax on 6 December shocked the nation. The images of carnage and destruction could have come straight from the Western Front, bringing the war home in a new and disturbing way. Whether you believed it was an act of sabotage, a rebuke from God, or just an unfortunate accident, it was hard to shake the feeling that it was an evil omen. Bitter winter storms across the country strangled seasonal travel, devastated fruit farms, and forced the cancellation of holiday events. The 29th was the coldest December day in fifty years; coal stocks were rapidly running out, and even firewood was becoming hard to find.[52]

For once, Christmas at the front may have been more pleasant than Christmas at home. As Stan Sawell recalled, "we moved out to a small village—Auchy au Bois for a training and rest period. The conditions for training were far from ideal as the weather became quite cold with considerable snow—very much like a Canadian winter in Ontario. Billets for everyone were fairly comfortable so that we were able to spend Christmas and New Years away from the sound of battle ... Our Medical Officer Dr McCusker was called one night to attend a woman about to give birth to a child and no civilian doctor was available. He came back some hours later smiling and said it was a boy and the parents wished our Col to give him a name. St Pierre was the name of our first OC—it seemed very suitable and so he was named." In his diary for the 25th, Stan recorded, "It was more like X-mas Day this year. Six of us went for a ride this afternoon. It was a fine ride as the horses were feeling very good. We had our dinner in the school room tonight. It was a very nice dinner, although very quiet. We had a piano for the evening and had quite a lot of music afterwards."[53]

Or Joe Eager, spending his first Christmas at the front in the Avion sector as the Medical Officer of the 78th Battalion:

Xmas in a one-time German gun pit

Dear Father

My Xmas this year is somewhat different from last, but I am well off compared with a great many of the men and as happy as possible to be away from home. Myself and staff are sharing our aid post with the M.O. of another battalion and his staff but fortunately we are not very busy and have enough room. Just now we are back a good way from the front and very few shells get back this far and even if they did our dressing station is strong enough to stand a direct hit. The roof is made of concrete three feet thick. I am quite close to our mess and think we are going to have a real Xmas dinner tonight. A 15 lb. turkey came up last night.

In Agnes' last letter she said Mary was coming home for Xmas, I am very glad she was able to get down and hope Arthur was able to get down too.

I hope by this time next year the war will be over and we will all be together again.

Don't worry about me at all as I have everything I want & feel sure I won't get sick or hit.

Love to all
Your aff. Son,
Joe[54]

6
1918

◆

T he new year started just as the old one had ended—badly. The coal short-age was really starting to pinch, even though temperatures had climbed out of the depths of December. Many schools would remain closed until later in January to allow more time to stockpile enough coal to heat classrooms, and even hospitals were running out of the "black diamonds." There was talk of appointing a local coal controller to manage dwindling stocks in Wentworth County, and Hamilton council announced that it would suspend evening meetings so that city hall didn't have to be heated after business hours. In Waterdown, "coal and wood never were so scarce," reported the *Spectator*, "as they are this season. A large number of families have very little fuel."[1] When a Hamilton coal company announced that it had a small stock available for sale, hundreds of desperate householders converged on the office, followed by the police, who had been called to maintain order. And the gloom became more than just psychological when the government directed that all ornamental and advertising lighting be eliminated to save on hydroelectricity; many cities went a step further and turned off every second street light.

The institution of heatless days, sometimes as many as three a week, merely made the other shortages that much more painful. One amateur poet tried to put a cheery face on a situation that must have been deeply dispiriting:

My Tuesdays are meatless,
My Wednesdays are wheatless,
I'm getting more eatless each day;
My home it is heatless,
My bed it is sheetless,
They're all sent to the Y.M.C.A.;
The bar-rooms are treatless,
My coffee is sweetless,
Each day I get poorer and wiser;
My stockings are feetless,
My trousers are seatless,
By gosh—but I do hate the Kaiser.[2]

Then, in the middle of January, a massive winter storm walloped central Canada with heavy snow and high winds, sending temperatures plunging again. In southern Ontario, it would be the coldest January in more than sixty years. In cities, store windows were smashed and signs toppled by gusts; in the country, barns and sheds blew down. Roads drifted over and rail services were suspended, leaving farms and even whole communities entirely cut off. There were reports of people in isolated areas freezing to death in their own homes for want of fuel, their neighbours unable to reach them with aid.

We know now that 1918 was the last year of the war, but many Canadians found it difficult to greet the year with any sense of optimism. And in March, Germany mounted its spring offensive, which brought the Kaiser's armies closer to victory than at any time since 1914. At the time no one could imagine that it was Germany's last throw and that within six months the Allied armies would mount their own coordinated offensives that would carry them to victory. Viewed from a seat on the Waterdown-to-Hamilton train or from a pew in the Carlisle Methodist Church, 1918 wasn't the last year of the war. It was just one more year of the war.

ON MANY LEVELS, the township, like the rest of the country, had been transformed. Daylight savings time, income tax, censorship, national registration,
conscription, a new Unionist government that uneasily straddled party lines,
votes for women, and a whole host of other innovations, large and small, were
changing the way Canadians lived their lives. There were so many new things
in their world—Farmerettes and Soldiers of the Soil, Victory Bonds and war
savings stamps, all the "-less" days. What wasn't new was being changed—
iron railings into artillery shells, rags into bandages, razors into bayonets.
There seemed to be wounded soldiers everywhere and if you missed seeing
them, the *Spectator* drew your attention to them with large headlines like
"Pathetic Scene as Maimed Men Arrive: Nerve-Shattered, Shell-Shocked
Patients Now Quartered in Brant House," a luxury hotel in Burlington that
had been taken over to serve as a veterans hospital.[3]

But if the war had changed how people lived, it hadn't necessarily altered
how they thought. Even after four years of war, the continuities were profound. Consider this tribute to Waterdown high school's response to the war:

> During the year four of our boys have enlisted and more will do so when
> their tender years will permit. No class of citizens have acquitted themselves
> so well as the High School boys. They have learned that principles are before
> profits, and ideals before interests. They have not been permitted to vote, to
> determine the policy of government, and they have not waited to question
> the machinations of militarists, or autocrats, or diplomatists, but they have
> set their might against the corrupt current of domination that has come
> down from past ages with a truer instinct for the cause of right and freedom
> than any of our vaunted patriots or blustering statesmen have shown. With
> the ardor of boyhood, and the enthusiasm born of expanding ideals, they
> have barely stepped into the threshold of manhood when they are found
> with the weapons of war in their hand, bent on crushing the cursed cause
> that corrupts the Cross of Christ. If right and reform is to come out of this
> great struggle, and it will come, it will not be seen as a halo around the
> heads of ambitious generals, or manipulating politicians, but it will come as
> the roses bloom and the poppies glow upon the graves of the fallen youths

whose sacrifices shall not be vain, the incense of their efforts shall arise to heaven; their deeds shall be known but their names shall be forgotten.[4]

This passage wouldn't have been out of place in August 1914, but it was written in May 1918. Yet there is no sense of disillusionment or war-weariness, no hint that the "ardor of boyhood" had been smothered by the mud of Flanders or that "the incense of their efforts" might not be able to rise to heaven from a battlefield that was a loathsome stew of putrefying flesh, human waste, and toxic chemicals. The ground beneath them had shifted, dramatically and irrevocably, and it continued to shift. But in the placid rural mind, things were very much as they had always been.

Imagine you are at the Metzger house on a bright afternoon in May 1918. You have come for a send-off—Jack Kirk and Lloyd Henry will be leaving the next morning for Toronto, to join the 70th Battery of the Canadian Field Artillery. This is no small affair. It begins with a luncheon, instrumental and

The 1917–18 class at Waterdown high school. Photographer unknown. (Author's collection)

vocal selections, and presentations to the men before everyone retires to the
roller rink for dancing until the wee hours of the morning. But while the
guests are still fully attentive, the Presbyterian rector offers a short address to
the soon-to-be soldiers:

To John L. Kirk and Lloyd Henry:

There has gathered here this evening only a few of your many friends, to bid
you, our friends and comrades, adieu, and from each heart there is a sincere
expression that the God's speed we bid you is only for a short duration, and
that when the stress of war is o'er and the silver clouds of peace are shining,
you will be again with us.

We bid you adieu on the eve of your departure to join Canada's brave
sons in France to uphold the honor and emblem of your birthland, and also
the universal torch of freedom, and when upon France and Flanders fields
your thoughts will return to home and friends. We ask you to accept this
watch as remembrance of your friends and reminder that we are waiting and
praying for your return.[5]

A week later, you are invited to another gathering, this one for Frank Ward,
one of Waterdown's schoolteachers, on the eve of his departure to don the
khaki. Again, there are songs, recitations, and instrumental selections con-
tributed by members of the Choral Society and friends, and again there are
presentations to the new soldier and heartfelt words of farewell:

We, the members of the Silvia Club and of the Methodist Church Choir,
have assembled here this evening to express our appreciation of your good
fellowship, and of the valued assistance you have rendered us on many occasions. But more especially we have come together to wish you a soldier's
entrancing good fortune, service without sorrow, sacrifice which is gain,
battles without scars, and a safe return to our midst, when we may again
sing together the songs we have so often sung.

You have not given grudgingly of your time or talents when joy was to
be had or work was to be done. You have gone about your duties with the
buoyancy of youth, and it is our hope that you will carry that spirit into the
service of the King which you have shown in serving the community where
you have laboured for the past 15 months. We trust that the summer months

which you will spend in training may be pleasant and not fruitless, that they will teach the way of life with precision and decision. And when it is your good fortune to cross the seas and face the Hun, may you be supported by a strong arm and a gallant heart, and upheld by a faith that does not falter when the cause is right and the need supreme. Go forth knowing that death is on the threshold of life, and life beyond the gates of death, that the cause is greater than the sacrifice. Fear not, stand true, and the "well done" for service well performed awaits you, and our parting word shall be "Mizpah."[6]

These two addresses are remarkably like the one delivered to Maurice Scott two years earlier—it was almost as if the Somme and Passchendaele had never taken place. So much had happened, but in the way East Flamborough framed the war in public, so little had changed.

But there's something else that makes our farewell parties so remarkable: Jack Kirk and Lloyd Henry were volunteers, but not Frank Ward. Frank had gone before a judge when he was first conscripted in December 1917 and received an exemption because he was a teacher. But that exemption was cancelled in February 1918 and Frank was attested into the CEF. Yet there is nothing in the surviving documents to suggest that the three men were treated any differently because they took different paths into uniform.[7] And, if we are to believe Jack's letter home from training camp, it meant nothing that he and Lloyd had volunteered while their friend Frank had been compelled to serve:

Petawawa Camp, June 15

Hello Chas
Well, Chas, I was mighty glad to get your letter. Yes, we sure will have some Battery now. It is the only howitzer in the camp, so you see what good look-ing people will do for a Battery—Henry, Ward and myself.

Say, it is a shame that Henry wasn't put on the Signaling Corps; it sure saves us a lot of hard work, although we have to get up at 5 am.

Facing page: A proud soldier ... and a conscript. Lloyd Henry of Waterdown, photographed before leaving for the war in 1918. Photographer unknown. (Author's collection)

We quit work at 5 p.m. and were to have guns on a ride at 9:30 this morning, but today being the 15th, was pay day, so I decided to take my pay instead of riding. Yes, Chas, another $10, so you see I have little bit of money.

For heaven's sake Chas, don't give Foxy my baseball suit. You know what happened at Wabasso Park.

There are some great games here today. The 70th was to have played but the game was canceled. This sure is a peach of a day, just O.K. for motoring, but I am just sitting around like a bump on a log.

We bought a Kodak to-day, so look out for my mug around there in a week or so.

Some of the fellows are having a boat trip tomorrow up the Ottawa river, at 7 a.m. returning at 8 p.m. Ward, Henry and I are not in it.

We had a compliment paid to our Battery to-day. We had the cleanest lines in the Division; that is 16 Batteries. We have won this twice now. Some Battery! Yesterday the general alarm was sounds for fire. The CASC was on fire, but they had it out before we got there.

Well, Chas, you have asked me how I liked doing my "bit." In answer I may say I realize now that I am doing my bit for my King and Country, Canada the land we cherish, and any loyal Canadian who is not in Khaki should not be called a Canadian, and I am longing for our order when we will embark for France, where I trust I may do my duty to defeat that monster of Germany, the vile reptile. I hope I am to be the first to fire one of the guns of the famous 70th Battery and when the war is over and we will be returning to the land of our birth, it is then that I will be glad I am a Canadian.

Well this is all now. Oh yes, I received a box of eats today. Gee! they were good.

So long.
Jack[8]

How can this have been so? Kirk and Henry got the heroes' farewell that we expect, but Frank Ward should have slunk out of town in the dead of night, and then should have been frozen out by the volunteers in his midst. The debate over conscription had turned the 1917 election campaign into one of the bitterest in Canadian history, with respectable figures on both sides hurling insults and epithets. Historians have spilled much ink on conscription riots, on extrajudicial raids on dens of defaulters, on a wound in the body politic that would never heal. The lines drawn in the sand were clear and uncompromising: pro-conscriptionist, anti-conscriptionist; volunteer, draftee; freedom, compulsion; English Canada, French Canada. There is a cold tidiness to this—everyone on one side of the line or the other.

Except that it doesn't hold true everywhere, and certainly not in East Flamborough. Like the rest of English Canada, the township voted solidly in favour of conscription and, like the rest of Canada, many of its eligible men then lodged claims for exemption from the Military Service Act. But I can find no sign that conscription stirred much rancour or left many hard feelings in East Flamborough. Just like in 1916, when desertion from the 129th Battalion seems not to have disturbed anyone in the township, there were few grumblers about the man who had to be compelled to serve—nor about the man who tried everything, fair means and foul, to avoid service.

The Military Service Act had built into it grounds for exemption, but it was up to the individual to make a claim before a judge—and there was always a military officer in attendance to argue why the claim should be rejected. For farmers and their sons, it was easy, because the Unionists had guaranteed them exemptions. A business owner might claim that his firm wouldn't survive his departure—typically he would be given a few months to wind up his affairs before reporting for duty. Skilled workers, particularly those with the railways, might apply on those grounds; in such situations, the employer was often brought in to say that it would take too long to train a replacement. A man might claim that, as the sole supporter of his parents, his departure would cause real hardship. Medical and engineering students, teachers, government employees, munitions workers, and various other job categories would be judged on a case-by-case basis.

Sadly, few of the local tribunal records have survived so we have to rely on other accounts. Most newspapers published the decisions regularly, and not just for informational purposes. Publicity became a kind of moral suasion. Tribunal decisions were listed in the paper, but that was nothing new; the outcomes of legal proceedings, from murder to petty theft, had long been detailed by the press. What was new, though, was that newspapers like the *Spectator* promised not to print the names of draftees who reported on time "but the names of any who overlook the little obligation to don the King's clothes, will be published," so that their friends and acquaintances "will know just who the shirkers are, and so will notify the authorities where the 'soldiers' may be apprehended."[9]

Whether this worked in cities is not my concern, but it didn't seem to work in rural areas. I can find no evidence that anyone in East Flamborough cared who applied for exemption or whether they were successful. Wilf Langford of Waterdown sought an exemption because he was a druggist; he was turned down, but wasn't ostracized for having tried. Frank Ward in Waterdown and Erle Glennie in Mountsberg both applied for exemptions as teachers, but secured only temporary stays.[10] Yet there was no outcry from local parents about children being taught by men with no appreciation for their civic duty. Day after day, the *Spectator* listed the names of men who applied for exemption, as well as the decision in each case, and later the names of conscripts who had failed to report. Yet there is no hint of this causing any ripples in East Flamborough. Those who served would be lauded, but those who didn't serve or who tried to avoid serving should not be vilified. There were no shirkers; only men who were in uniform and men who weren't.

Instead of castigating the man who tried to avoid the draft, there was forbearance and tolerance. Evaders of the MSA are mentioned only infrequently,

and even then it is usually anonymously, as in one observation from a local newspaper correspondent that "One of our young men who has so far escaped the M.S. act is now making regular weekly visits to Waterdown." Or, there was good-natured ribbing. "We are pleased to see that Clare [Morden, a Carlisle-born farmer] is convalescing after his struggles with the M.S.A. authorities," it was reported. "He says the Waterdown hammocks look good to him."[11]

Even more striking is an article about the arrest of Lorne Carey of Millgrove. Lorne had gone before a judge in January 1918 to request an exemption, but he was refused and received his call-up notice on 3 July. He then requested, and was granted, a four-week extension, followed by another week's extension. But then, instead of reporting, he vanished and was at large until he was arrested in Armstrong, British Columbia, months later. At a court martial in the Hamilton armouries, Lorne was found guilty of desertion. The newspaper described in detail the sad sequel. With an entire battalion of soldiers drawn up in a square on the parade ground, Lorne Carey was marched in, bare-headed and in civilian clothes. As he stood alone, a senior officer read the verdict and the sentence: two years less a day at Burwash prison. With that, Lorne was marched away to incarceration.[12] It is a bit surprising that the article was published in the local paper at all, but even more surprising is that it is oddly flat, without any hint of judgment. It is not full of indignation that a local boy had been unfairly criminalized by the military, nor does it gloat over a local boy who shamefully failed to do his bit and eventually got his just reward. The story is told simply as another tragedy of war. It is neither good nor bad; it just is.

This, I think, is why conscription stirred so little rancour in East Flamborough, and perhaps in rural Canada generally. People there accepted, with a kind of resigned equanimity, that the war was a common affliction, a progenitor of many catastrophes, large and small. And though they clearly never lost faith in the rightness of the cause, they also had little appetite for demonizing those who had decided to stand aside. In a big city, you could easily rail against an anonymous shirker, confident in the knowledge that your paths had never crossed, and were unlikely to. But Lorne Carey was someone you knew. You

Facing page: The Careys in happier times, in front of their store in Millgrove. Lorne Carey is on the right and Roy on the left. Photographer unknown. (Author's collection)

had played baseball against him and shopped in his family's store in Mill-grove. You had gone to hear the Careys sing many times, proud that the township had produced such fine voices. He may even have been a distant relative of yours—his mother was a Cummins, and they were related to just about everyone in East Flamborough. And you knew that Lorne's twin brother had been killed in a car accident in April 1918, less than two months after getting married. All of that past didn't simply evaporate just because Lorne didn't want to wear the uniform. The community was too tightly knit for that.

And in 1918, the war truly became a community experience. It always had been, at least to some extent—the aggressive sociability of the rural world meant it could be nothing else. The sheer number of war organizations and events in the township, in any township, affirmed that the war was experienced collectively as much as individually. I couldn't find a single local patriotic organization that folded during the wars years. Lots of new groups were established, but they were always in addition to rather than in place of existing organizations. By 1918, East Flamborough had upwards of thirty separate organizations dedicated to furthering patriotic causes. At the same time, after three and a half years of voluntary enlistment and the advent of compulsory service, there was scarcely a family in the township that didn't have someone in uniform—and those that had suffered loss were a significant and ever-growing minority.

Equally important in making the war a shared experience was the appearance of the township's first newspaper, the *Waterdown Review*, which began publishing on 16 May 1918. Most of it was pre-prepared content—national advertising, human interest stories, generic war news—but the rest was unashamedly, relentlessly local. There were news items, obituaries, minutes of council meetings, birth and marriage announcements, and notices of visitors to the area. Most of East Flamborough's hamlets had correspondents sending in news items, as did villages beyond the township limits. The newspaper would be of little interest or value to anyone from outside the area, and even the passionate local historian in me struggles to make much of the content: "Archie Mullock has learned to ride a bicycle. Well done Archie!"; "One of our respected youths seems to find it necessary to obtain his slumbers by the roadside Monday mornings"; the Freelton Debating Society asks "'Has Waterdown any debaters? If so, Freelton would be glad to hear from them.' Now you Waterdown debaters go after them"; "A large percentage of the population have been viewing the GTR wreck near the Hamilton Y."

But it is in the letters from local men and women in uniform that we can see most clearly the transformation of the war into a collective experience. The *Review* allowed locals to see the war, not through the eyes of anonymous journalists, but through the letters of their own. To a certain extent this had always been true; since 1914, letters had occasionally been read out at meetings, to share the experiences of former members who were overseas. But printing them in the paper was altogether different. People had always had a stake in what was happening at the front, through their loved ones; now that stake could be shared. The private letter became the public statement. In those public statements, we can follow the war's last year as people in the township followed it—through familiar voices. We can see how much family and community meant to them, how deeply they appreciated reminders of the old township, either in the form of a local newspaper or a chance meeting with someone from home. We also see that whether a man was a volunteer or a conscript meant little.

By the summer of 1918, Rob Buchan of Waterdown was a grizzled old soldier. He had been posted to the 15th Battalion in France in October 1915, and had fought with the unit all through 1916. Taken sick right after Vimy, he returned to the unit, only to be caught in the arm by a stray chunk of shrapnel on 11 June 1917. He spent the rest of the war in Britain at training camps, regimental depots, and reserve battalions, getting new soldiers ready to move to the front—new soldiers like his kid brother Stanley, who was conscripted in May 1918 and reached Britain in June.[13] The *Review* printed letters from both of them, and it's clear that Rob intended to look out for the Waterdown boys, regardless of whether they were volunteers or conscripts—and that Stanley knew he could count on his brother to do just that.

> 12th Can. Res. Batt.
> Witley Camp
> Surrey 13-6-18
>
> Dear Sister,
>
> Just a line or so to say that I am well and that I received two of your most welcome letters to-day and was more than pleased to hear from you, one dated May 3rd, the other May 27th, so you see they have been a long time finding me. I might say that I had a letter from [sister] Beatrice on Monday

and that is the first mail that I had had for six weeks, and I couldn't understand what was the matter, but it is on account of me moving around so much. I will probably get my mail more regular now.

At any rate I got or I believe I got your letter before Stan arrived, for I have heard nothing of him as yet, but we are on the lookout for a big draft any day now and I expect that he will be on it. I will try and find out just as soon as I hear of their landing, and I will write and let you know. I daresay that it would upset you all, being that he was sent away so sudden. I know I kind of felt it myself, but not so much as you people would, and besides I will get over it sooner than you will, for I will be so pleased to see him, but I am very sorry that it was not me landing on the other side of the water, instead of him landing on this side. Well, I will try and put him on the right road when he gets here and I will try and look after him as much as I can. I don't like to tell you, but I think that it will be best in the long run, that is that they only get from ten to fourteen weeks in England and then they are shot across to France. Of course if things keep quiet over there why he may have longer to stop here, but you can never tell what's going to happen. They will be in segregation for a month after they land here, so it will be some time before he is able to see much of the country.

I will try and fix both him and Gordon Bowman[14] up for a leave as soon as it is possible, and find out where they want to go to, but I will not advise them to stop in London, for you can never tell when somebody is going to try to lead you astray up there, and besides it's not like it used to be, although there are lots of things to see there and wonderful things too. I would like to be able to go with them and it might happen so that I can, but I have just been a week back from Scotland. I had a very good time up there. I did not call on Jack Hutton's people, for I only stopped in Edinburgh about two hours and went on up to Aberdeen with a friend of mine, but that's where I should advise them to go, up North, for it is ever so much cheaper in the end, whereas in London you pull a pound out of your pocket and it's gone. I cannot bring Sgt Wheeler to my recollection, but I may know him all right, for I know so many people's faces and not their names and they all seem to know my name. I don't know how it is, though I keep meeting people every day, and I know their faces all right but I couldn't tell them their names.

Now don't keep troubling about sending me money. If I need it very bad, why I will send for it all right. I have never been broke since I have been in England, but no doubt I will be soon for I have all my credit used up and can only figure on half of my wages now. Of course the way I have kept going since I came to England is because I had a big credit when I left France ... didn't need it, for I never was much of a fellow for spending money and what I drawed after I got here kept me going nicely, so I was able to part with it. I told you that I would not be able to go to Scotland because I had no money but the paymaster gave me a big surprise when he told me that I had nine pound coming to me, for I thought I was overdrawn.

I received the snaps O.K. and they are very good, too. Of course I recognize a few of the faces, but very few. I dare say that there are lots of people over there that would know me and I would not know them.

I don't know as I have anything more to say this time, so hoping that these few lines find you all well, I will come to a close. Good-bye.

From Rob[15]

Mid Ocean, June 16th, 1918

Dear Sister,

Just a few lines to let you know I am getting along. Well, I am all right so far, but there has been a bunch of boys sick on the boat and the hospital is filled right up. I don't know where they put them now, but there are always some getting sick, but I haven't been sick yet; only the first day we were on the ocean, and I had a headache and got pretty dizzy, but I am not the only one, for there are over two thousand on the boat. We're put in there like a bunch of pigs. We sleep and eat in the same pen, and I have been sleeping on packs for two weeks in hammocks. Well, I guess I got to go to church now, so I will finish it again.

Well, Mattie, it has been fine weather on our trip so far, except one day and it rained, but not very hard. I tell you this trip makes you sleep and sleep, but there is something that I couldn't eat. One day we had eggs for breakfast and rabbit for dinner and fish for supper and I tell you I could not go much of that. I was peeling potatoes yesterday, but we don't see much of them. We get a little jam for supper, bread and butter, and peas and sometimes meat.

Say, did Mother get the picture from Mr. Bray yet! I guess you will find me all right, down in the bottom row. Have you heard how Gordon [Bowman] is getting along? I thought it was kind of funny taking all the boys out of the waiting draft but about thirty, and they went to Niagara, but one of the sergeants told me that they would soon be coming over, so I guess I will see them if we are not quarantined, for they have measles and mumps and fever. Some said that we would be kept in for about twenty-eight days, but I don't know. You hear so much you can't take much out of it, but we will know more about it when we get over there.

June 20

Well, I guess I will write some more. Well, it has been pretty rough this last three days, and the waves, you would think they were snowbanks when they go up. Well, I will tell you a little story. When we left Toronto there was a little dog wanted to go with us and he ran after the train and the train stopped, so one of the boys got off and got him in, and of the sergeants wanted to know what he was going to name him, and he said he had a name for him, and the sergeant said what was it, and he said, we will call him Sergeant, for he didn't do anything but walk around and growl all day. Well, we will get off the boat tomorrow, for we got a can of corn beef and some biscuits today, but they seem pretty hard, but I guess they will fill up the hole.

June 30

Well, we arrived here all right in London, at Tilbury, and then we took the train to Aldershot station and then we walked four miles to the camp and we were pretty tired. By the way the boys talk they feed us pretty good. We eat four times a day, so it might not be so bad. We will have two days rest before we do much. Well, I don't think I have much more to say. I will say good-bye for now. Write soon

I am about seven miles from Witley through fields, and twelve miles by road.

From your brother
Stanley[16]

Besides his older brother, Stanley would find other familiar faces at Witley. Austin Tudor, a Waterdown lad who had been in the first group of conscripts to be summoned, was another frequent contributor to the *Review*. As
in Stanley Buchan's letters, there is no obvious sense of grievance at being
compelled to serve—just the same boyish enthusiasm and desire to remain
connected with the township that was often satisfied by a chance meeting, on
the other side of the ocean, with someone who lived across the street:

Witley Camp, Surrey, England.
May 5th, 1918.

Dear Folks,

Have received your letter dated April 7th and was pleased to hear from you
again and to know that you were all well.

The boxes sent arrived safely and were very much appreciated by us. I
might say that there are about six of us who share all our boxes between us;
we hang together like glue and intend to try to do so.

I have received one paper up to date, dated March 30th, and it sure
does seem funny to be able to get a good old *Spectator* and to read all about
Hamilton and the surrounding district. We laugh when we see some of the
reports about the war, according to the Canadian papers, as I think the news
you get over there is about two weeks old and we get it here the next day
after it happens.

My old chum, Fred Hazel,[17] has been warned for draft to France, but is
not sure how soon he will be going, as they are taking drafts away all the time.

We are having better weather here now and it can keep on getting
better as we have been having awful foggy weather for the past three weeks,
but the last 3 days have been quite warm.

You should have seen us when we came in from parade last Friday. It
was very hot and the wind was blowing hard, it blew the sand across our
parade grounds, and as we were sweating good it stuck to us and we sure
were an awful sight. When we finished for the day we washed and had supper and then it was clean up our brass and rifle for Saturday's route march.
By the way we get a route march every Saturday with full marching order
and it certainly does harden a fellow.

I am none the worse off for all this hard work, as I weigh 162 lbs., "some man." My clothes are getting too small for me. I have gained 12 lbs. since coming to England, but I don't think I am getting any taller, so I must be putting it on like the mischief some place else.

I am getting to know all about a rifle. I took mine apart to-day and cleaned and oiled it. It took about three hours to clean my equipment and rifle, so you can imagine about what it is like; some job, believe me.

My platoon expect to start on musketry this week. We expected to start on it sooner, but there are some in the platoon who have not had their leave yet and that is the reason we have been kept back, but never the less we won't be long going through with it and then we will be able to go over the top, "hurrah!"

I wish some of you had been with me when I was on leave, as I have seen some great sights.

Well, mother, I am proud to say that I am coming home just the same as when I went away, and if I didn't think so much of you I wouldn't try and keep clean.

Well, mother, I have a lot more letters to write so I will close for this time, hoping you are all well, I am.

Your loving son
Austin[18]

London, July 8, 1918

Dear Mother, Father and Harold:

I haven't gone to France yet, and don't know when I will be going, as things over in France are beginning to look a lot better for the Allies than it ever did before, and I know that will be good news for you, as it sure looks good to me, and we get a lot more news than you folks do over home.

I am still looking forward to receive the first copy of that wonderful journal that is printed in Waterdown. I have been getting the Spectator pretty regularly, and am glad to get it, as we fellows over here like to read some of the reports that the Canadian papers get. Some of them are funny to what we get in Blighty.

I told you in my last letter about meeting Lieut. W. Attridge[19] on the Strand in London while I was on leave, and I was sure glad to meet him, and I guess he was glad to meet me, as I was the first fellow from home that he had met since he had been in Blighty.

We are having great weather now. It is just like summer time in Canada, only the twilight over here is so much longer than it is at home. Why, at 10 p.m. we can see to read in our huts without a light.

And mother, I'm going to ask you again not to worry, as I am O.K., and am having as good a time as the rest of the fellows, and they are not drilling us as hard now as what they used to, and when we do drill it is just a review of some of the drills we have had before, and I am at present on fatigue work down at what we call the railhead, and that is unloading cars, and believe me it is a cinch, as four of us only loaded seven loads all day to-day, and we quit work at 3 p.m. Not so bad a job, is it?

I have got word from Vern Willis and Roy Wilkinson,[20] and they are both well.

Well, mother, tell father that I was up around Buckingham Palace when I was in London, and it sure is some place, with all of its guards and policemen it is a sight worth seeing. I also went up and saw the Parliament buildings, Westminster Abbey, and some of the important places of old London. Gee, but they are old-fashioned; but I seen a sight worth seeing, and that was the Horse Guards at Whitehall. Say, but it is a nice sight. I had often read about them, but I am satisfied now, because I have seen them myself, and that is much better than reading about them.

Did you receive the brooch that I sent you. I just forget whether you told me or not. I sent it the same time as the money order. It is not a very good one, but I will send you a better one when I know which battalion I am going to in France.

Hope papa is well, also you and Harold, as this leaves me fine. I weigh 163 pounds.

I am, your son,
Austin Tudor[21]

Witley, July 13, 1918

Dear Mother,

Just a few lines to let you know that I have just come back to camp from a leave to London, and it sure is some place and I enjoyed my stay there very much.

I was staying at the Union Jack Club. It is a fine place, good beds and plenty to eat. It was at this club that I met sailors and soldiers from all parts of the world. New Zealanders, Australians, South Africans, American, English and Canadians, and they are very fine fellows.

I was going up the Strand one afternoon and I was lucky enough to meet an old Waterdown boy, Lieut. W. L. Attridge. He is a Lieut. in the Flying Corps and he had only been in Blighty two weeks and was spending a few days in London, and I was the first fellow he had met that he knew since he landed.

I was down Piccadilly and Leicester Square. The traffic on these streets is very heavy and all the street cars are double deckers and run on underground electric wires. Some differences to the ones on York Street, Hamilton. And then they have what they call the Tubes, it is an underground railway. It is run by electricity and I think it is the quickest way to get around London, as the cars can travel about 35 miles an hour. And then the motor busses they are double deckers also, and if a person wants to go sight-seeing, I think they are the best.

I went up to Madame Tussaud's Wax Works and believe me, I never thought that they could ever make such life-like figures with wax, but it is wonderful what they can do, and if a person ever goes into the "Chamber of Horrors" they never will forget it. I know I never will. I also saw Buckingham Palace, Parliament Buildings, Crystal Palace, Westminster Abbey, St. Paul's Cathedral, and they sure are old buildings, but the stone work on them is magnificent and then I saw the Horse Guards of Whitehall, which I think is grand, and there are several more places that I could mention, but will tell you about them later.

Hope you are all well at home, as this leaves me fine.

I am, your loving son,
Austin[22]

How much is the historian allowed to read into such letters? It's difficult to doubt Austin's touristy enthusiasm, or the declaration that he is obviously eating well in the army. The insistence that he is "having as good a time as the rest of the fellows" could be read various ways—is it damning with faint praise, or a sincere observation? And is the "hurrah" at the prospect of going over the top meant to be ironic? It would be easy to dismiss such letters on the basis that Austin was just telling his family what they wanted to hear. No need to alarm them, no need to tell them how miserable he really was, no need to write something that the censor would cut out anyways. And that might be true. But there is no evidence to suggest it is—only our assumption that a conscript *must* have been a disgruntled, embittered, unwilling soldier. And in the absence of such evidence, I prefer to take Austin at his word—that he was a young man making the best of an unusual situation.

As Austin discovered, one of the pleasures of service was getting to play the tourist. New arrivals enjoyed seeing the sights they had only read about, and often went through the ritual of returning to their old hometowns or, for the Canadian-born, looking up relatives that they knew only by name. Maintaining contact with East Flamborough was important, but so too was exploring their transatlantic links. When Muriel McGregor arrived in England, she used her first leave to trek north to Clunes, the Scottish village after which the family home in Waterdown was named. She wrote a long letter home to her mother describing a dizzying succession of visits to elderly friends and relatives, including an ancient clergyman who "remembered you and dad calling to see him, remembered Uncle Archie." She was shown homes in which various ancestors had been born, and "a road built by great great grandfather, at Lagan." Stan Sawell knew he had relatives in London but had lost the address. Fortunately, there was only one Sawell in the telephone directory and their home in Catford became his London headquarters on future leaves. Such anecdotes were popular with readers of the *Review*, as reminders of a world in which everyone knew everyone else.

———————•———————

BUT NOT ALL EXPERIENCES could find their way into the *Review*. The Doughertys weren't one of the original families of Mountsberg, but they married into most of them. And Nathan Dougherty wasn't the youngest boy in the family, but he was young enough that he still needed his father's permission to enlist in the 129th Battalion in March 1916—at an apparent age of sixteen years, eleven months. Even then, he had to add a year to his age to get into uniform; he was only fifteen years old when he joined up, and still wasn't old enough to go to the front in early 1918, when his world started to come apart. Among the many tragedies of East Flamborough's war, Nathan's is one of the most poignant. It is also one with as many questions as answers—only the bare facts and dates are confirmed in his personnel file.

Since early in the war, the CEF had been enlisting young men, some not even into their teens; many of them lied about their age but the army was quite willing to turn a blind eye for a big lad, or on a day when the numbers were down. But by 1917, the government had been forced to reconsider the wisdom of allowing teenagers into uniform. Many military men probably saw little wrong with the practice—the earlier a lad showed an appreciation for his civic duty, the better. But it didn't look so good when the newspaper reported the death in action of a sixteen-year-old. At the very least, it smacked of desperation—was Canada so short of manpower that it had to fill its army with teenagers? Caught in a tug-of-war between parents desperate to get their young sons home, battalion commanders anxious not to lose trained soldiers, and the soldiers themselves, who had gone to great lengths to get into the fight and didn't want to be denied, Militia and Defense came up with a compromise of sorts. Any soldier under seventeen and a half years old would be sent home, and the rest would be placed in a newly constituted Young Soldiers' Battalion until they reached the age of nineteen and could be posted to the trenches.

Nathan Dougherty would have known about the new policy, and must have been dreading a summons to see his commanding officer. It came in February 1918. An official communiqué had arrived in the Canadian Records Office in London confirming that Nathan was actually born in 1900—he was nearly eighteen years old, but perhaps a letter from his parents settled the issue. Did they write to Ottawa, as hundreds of parents did, mentioning the loss of their son Leland at Passchendaele and asking that Nathan be sent home to Mountsberg? Whatever happened, the army moved swiftly. Two days after that the letter was received, Nathan was examined by the medical officer at Witley and was determined to be "free from contagious, infectious and venereal diseases and fit to travel." A few weeks later, he was on his way to Buxton, in Derbyshire, to the Canadian Discharge Depot—the last step on the trip home to Canada. His orders had come through; on the 8th of April, he would leave Liverpool on the *Mauretania*, bound for Halifax. He never made it. On the 4th of May, a military court of enquiry declared him a deserter. Six days later, his body was found floating in a reservoir near Buxton.[23]

We'll never know what happened. There are no references to his death in the local newspapers, although British papers weren't shy about reporting on soldier suicides. If there was a coroner's inquest, the transcript was lost decades ago when the records of the office were destroyed. It's possible that he went on a bender and fell into the reservoir in a drunken haze, but that doesn't quite fit. Until February 1918, Nathan knew of nothing that would stop him from getting to the front to avenge the death of Leland in October 1917—surely it was only a matter of time before he was put on a draft for France. And then everything fell apart. Instead of doing his bit, like Leland had done, he faced the prospect of being sent home to Mountsberg like a child. Leaving the depot at Buxton was probably a rash, spur-of-the-moment decision but once taken, there was no going back. Nathan, the brother of a gallant fallen soldier, was now a deserter. The shame would have been more than he could bear. I expect that he saw no way out and took himself to Buxton reservoir to end his life. But the tragedy was compounded. On 30 July 1918, two-day-old Leland Ray Dougherty, the newborn nephew of Leland and Nathan, died because of an "imperfect heart." Never would he hear stories of his soldier uncles, and of the war that gutted his family.

———◆———

ANOTHER EXPERIENCE, this one more typical but also hardly suited to the pages of the *Review*. On the very morning the local constabulary pulled Nathan Dougherty's lifeless body from Buxton reservoir, George Arnold of Waterdown pulled himself from his bunk in his billet in France and decided, for the third morning in a row, that he needed a drink. He had been with the

27th Battalion just over a month when he and a group of soldiers decided to celebrate coming out of the front-line trenches by getting drunk. They had plenty of money—or rather, George did, for he had just received thirty-six dollars from home—so they went out and bought five bottles of wine, which they promptly polished off before stumbling back to their billets. They did the same thing the next day, and the next. On the morning of 10 May, after the battalion had been warned that it would soon move back to the front, George and his mates opted for a little more of the hair of the dog. They went to a village some distance away, bought a few more bottles, and quickly downed them. At that point, George's memory got a little fuzzy.

Eleven days later, perched on a wobbly old chair in the kitchen of a French farmhouse, George tried desperately to fill in the gaps in his memory as he faced a Field General Court Martial on a charge of desertion.[24] He wasn't the first man in the township to fall afoul of military law, but the stakes were much different. This wasn't simply a case of trading bacon for beer or shooting yourself in the hand to avoid service. Desertion was a capital offense and, if convicted, George could face a firing squad. He was on trial for his life. I wonder if George fully understood his predicament. He was able to sign his attestation form when he joined the 129th in January 1916, but the signature suggests that he wasn't far above illiteracy. At the very least, he would have found the atmosphere intimidating, facing five officers who would decide his fate. There was a sixth officer who would act as prosecutor and another, known as the Prisoner's Friend, to be a kind of defence attorney. The practice in British Army courts martial was that the accused would provide a written statement, but wouldn't speak on his own behalf—that was left to the better educated and more articulate Prisoner's Friend.

But all the fine words in the world couldn't make George's story sound anything but damaging. He remembered getting into the back of a truck, but the next thing he could call to mind was walking down a street in Doullens. At one point, he asked someone the way to Wailly, where the 27th Battalion was billeted, but he could recall little else until the evening of 17 May, when a sergeant of the military police, acting on a tip, went to a farm on the Route d'Albert in Doullens that was being used to billet French troops. He questioned George and another soldier of the 27th Battalion, Alf Clark, a Londoner who had emigrated to Brantford in 1910, and placed them both under arrest.[25] George had spent eight days in an alcoholic haze—although when he was arrested, he thought he had been absent for only three days. In his statement, he insisted that he always intended to return to his unit.

George's conduct wasn't exactly laudable, but did it make him a deserter? Alf Clark was court martialed the same day and the trial documents, not to mention Clark's long list of previous convictions, suggest that he was the ringleader—George was just a follower who happened to have a pocketful of money. But courts martial were self-contained; what happened in one had no impact on any other, even if they concerned the same events. What mattered was that the 27th Battalion had been told to stand ready to go into the trenches, and it was then that George left his billets to continue his boozing. Yes, he had remained in uniform and had left all of his kit at Wailly, which suggested that he had every intention of returning. But there was no getting away from the fact that George left at a time when the battalion was preparing to return to the front. That, according to the Army Act, was desertion, and the court martial agreed.

But he would not pay with his life. The court decided that a sentence of one year's hard labour would be more appropriate. And when the decision went up the chain of command to be confirmed, according to military practice, the brigade commander demurred and concluded that George was not in fact guilty of desertion. The battalion's schedule had been irregular over the past month, so George would not necessarily have known that it was time to move up. And although the order was certainly given, there was no evidence that George had actually heard it. Even the fact that George was drunk most of the time worked in his favour; the brigadier decided that his intent was not to avoid service, but to avoid sobriety. The finding of desertion was set aside, and George was convicted instead of absence without leave. A few days later, the sentence was suspended "in the interests of the service." That was the army's way of saying that George deserved another chance. So did hundreds of other convicted soldiers who returned to their units under the Suspension of Sentences Act. The Canadian Corps needed every man it could lay its hands on.

FOR NATHAN DOUGHERTY AND GEORGE ARNOLD, the spring of 1918 was when it all came apart. But for the majority of Canadian soldiers, those were pleasant days. Only the Canadian Cavalry Brigade and motor machine-gun units had been in the thick of the German spring offensive; the rest of the Canadian Corps had been holding a sector farther north or had been in reserve. The British grumbled at the fact that the Corps, with its four fully reinforced, fully rested divisions, was out of action for the entire emergency. But Arthur Currie, with the backing of his political masters, staunchly resisted all efforts to break up the Corps and use its divisions piecemeal. At the same time, he and his staff worked on reorganization. New machine-gun battalions were created with greater tactical independence and hitting power. Existing motor machine-gun units were combined into two motor machine-gun brigades, with their own mechanical support and therefore greater mobility. The engineers were restructured into battalions, bringing dramatic improvements in their efficiency.

All of that meant hard work for staff officers, but the soldiers too were busy. Training was intensive, for any reorganization meant that old habits had to be discarded and new ones learned. They trained with tanks, to make better use of the new weapon, and in small-unit tactics, what later soldiers would call fire-and-movement. They learned how to take better advantage of the indirect fire of their artillerymen and machine gunners. All of this would be critical on the battlefield in the coming months but didn't usually make it into soldiers' letters home. Soldiers knew that censors wouldn't allow such references—in any case, their wives, parents, and sweethearts had little interest in the finer points of new tactical doctrine for machine-gun battalions. Instead, the letters highlighted the other part of the experience of spring 1918 that soldiers would later look back on with fondness—the rest and recreation. The big event was the Canadian Corps sports championship, held on Dominion Day. Edgar Richards, a bookkeeper in Waterdown, was one of tens of thousands of Canadian soldiers who enjoyed the festivities:

July 6th, 1918

Well, here it is a fine and fairly cool summer evening and I have just come back from dinner and changed from puttees, breeches and heavy boots to a pair of slacks and canvas slippers and will now proceed to scribble to you folks.

Your letter of June 2nd c/o Surbiton arrived on Thursday and I was glad to get it. I have been amused at the experiences of my sister farmerettes and hope they have everything looking tres bonne.

I really think Dad and Mother ought to take a holiday and come over and visit us, for our chances of getting leave to Canada seem very slim. However, it will finish up some day and then we will go just as fast as they will let us.

I am glad that we went before they came for us. Going with a willing heart is much better in this game. I was down to see Harold this week and found him reading in his barn billet. He has just recovered from la grippe, but looks all O.K after being off duty a week. I am going over some day next week and bring him back with me and then get him a ride home. I took him your letter and we read it over and had some grins on the quiet. There is no more news of when we shall go to the line again, but neither of us are worrying. This rest stuff is O.K.

I suppose Dominion Day passed off all O.K. at home. The Canadian corps held a big sports day at a town about 12 miles from here. There were about ten lorry loads of us went down. I never saw such a crowd of soldiers in all my life. It reminded me of circus day at home, only all soldiers with a few nursing sisters added. It was a terrific hot day and the catering arrangements were rotten. I ran into Hart Allen and we lined up for twenty minutes to get a drink of lemonade and gave up all hope of dinner. We got back here at 9:30 and good old friend Hatch fried me some new potatoes and three eggs and so I soon felt relieved. I am enclosing program of events. The 1st Division carried off the championship with a score of 101 and the corps troops of which we are a part came next with 92. It seemed hard to realize that there was a war on within 15 miles of the place. We had the Duke of Connaught, Sir Robert Borden, Gen. Currie, American, French and Italian officers too. I didn't get time to speak to "Bob" to ask him how the folks were.

One of our corporals had his foot broken when the lorry he was sitting on backed up into another. He was sitting on the tail board and made England all right.

We had Heinie over visit us on Thursday night. He gave us an awful dose of his "eggs," but did no material damage. I am thinking of flying myself in bed though, as he rocks the whole house at times.

My present address is
B.Q.M.S. Richards
2nd Can. M.M. Gun. Brig.[26]

This period yielded from local soldiers just the kind of letters that the *Review* liked to publish—light and newsy, with lots of colour, not unlike a letter you might have written while on holiday before the war.

But they didn't shy away from the death and destruction or paint false pictures of comfort and ease. Evelyn Galloway's letter of 8 July 1918 is a case in point:

For the past couple of weeks I have expected to go on leave each day, and am happy to know I am going tomorrow and will mail you this letter from England. I saw Edgar a couple of weeks ago and he looks fine and I am sending him some things he requires from England when I get over. It is the first leave I've had, so really don't know how to act. Another nurse and I are going together, who trained in Hamilton, so I suppose if we don't have a good time, no one ever had.

We are going to Scotland, of course. There is a terrible epidemic of la grippe here and a great many children are developing bronchial pneumonia and dying. It is called "Spanish flue" here. We have had quite a time this spring at our hospital. We were frightfully bombed almost every night for three weeks. They seemed to be trying to wipe our hospitals off the earth. They succeeded in doing so to one. Our hospital got it so badly we were compelled to evacuate. The sisters are all scattered, but we will be starting again at a new point, beautifully situated on the bank of a river, and I will be glad to begin again, as I like it here very much, but hated some of the dirty surroundings we have had formerly. There are quite a number of Hamilton City Hospital graduates here, and four of us are class mates.

On May 19th Fritz came over our hospital with about thirty planes. They dropped 35 or 40 bombs on our hospital alone. One struck our quarters and killed three sisters. My pal and roommate died of wounds nine days later. After this raid and until we left, we sisters slept out in the woods, thinking they would not drop bombs on the trees. Some life. We just lay on the cold ground with a ground sheet for a mattress and a blanket over us, huddled together to keep warm, like cattle. Of course some sisters had to remain on duty.

I spent three months at Calais last winter. It was awful. I will never forget my sojourn there, but consider it a privilege to have had the time and experiences I had in that always interesting and historic city. It is a wonderful old place and although bombed so much very little damage has been done. They have wonderful barrage of anti-aircraft guns.

You will pardon this scrawl. I used to write at one time. I am writing in a marquee with my knee for a table. After the war is over, when I see a barn I'll say, "Oh, here is a nice hut, let's stay over night, for there is real hay to sleep on." Every comfort, eh!

This life is really not too bad. I like it, but all the fun we have we make it. I hook onto an ambulance in France and ride so far I have to climb on another one to get back. I cycle and do many things to see the country and am sometimes beaming with excitement.

Harold is fine and the English home hears from him every week.

With heaps of love and best luck to you all, yours
Evelyn[27]

The influenza outbreak, the bombing of her hospital, the casualties, the nurses taking refuge in the woods—she describes it all frankly, honestly, and without embellishment. At the same time, she hasn't been beaten down by the experience. I really can picture her on a bicycle, hanging on to the back of an ambulance as it drove the back roads of France—"beaming with excitement."

Another regular correspondent was Ollie Horning of Waterdown.[28] In an age when it was quite common to name children after politicians, he was born into a family that had great respect for Ontario premier Oliver Mowat—and so those became his Christian names. Ollie had joined the artillery in Guelph, following in the footsteps of his older brother Harry who, as a University of Toronto student, secured a commission in the British Royal Field

Ollie Horning before leaving for France. Photographer unknown. (Paul Kuzyk collection)

Artillery; he was there at the first day of the Somme, and would go on to fight in Salonica and Palestine. Firing an 18-pounder gun in Palestine wasn't much different than firing one in Flanders, but the scenery certainly was. Harry wrote of the Mount of Olives, date groves, the Holy Sepulchre, and the Garden of Gethsemane; Ollie's letters were a little less exotic—weather reports, references to friends from home, questions about relatives, and details on French agriculture.

55th Battery, C.F.A.
France, April 15, 1918.

Dear Friends,

Just a line to let you know all is well. Well, from all appearances Fritz is still the best man in this war game. We have been at war in earnest for the past three weeks. Have been in six different positions and are moving part of the battery again tonight.

Our position at present is at the highest point of Vimy Ridge, which the Canadians captured a year ago last week. We have been here two days now and are just beginning to feel at home. Have fine gun pits, but just shrapnel proof protection.

Can see the country around for miles and it is grand sight at night to see the guns flashing. Have two 8-inch guns about 20 yards from one dugout, which keeps things lively at night.

The weather has been fierce for the last two weeks; it rained steady for 10 days, and we were in an open position with nothing but an old trench for protection. The ground is sticky, clay, which just about pulls your boots off every time you step.

The night we pulled in here it was dark as pitch, and as we had been on the road since 3:30 that morning and were feeling pretty tired. One gun sunk in the mud and it took 12 horses and about 20 men to get it into position. It was 2:30 when we finally laid down under a piece of canvass, spread across the trench, for to get a few hours' sleep. Awoke next morning to find that the water had run in off the canvass and our blankets were mud and water about half way up and were every night for a week, so we were glad when we got up here on top of Vimy.

It has been cold, with a strong wind and overcast for the past three days. In fact have had more use for our overcoats the past two weeks than we have all winter.

Well, the 5th Division of Artillery have made a name for themselves since coming to France. We now have first place in field artillery. We were 25 per cent better in organization and firing, by Haig's report, than the "La Hore" batteries of Imperials, who formerly held first place and who were attached to the Canadians before we came over ...

General Currie was asked last week by the Imperials on our right and left to fall back from Vimy and Lens and straighten out the line, this he politely refused to do, saying it had cost too many lives to take to fall back now just to be in style with them. He said he would at least put up some kind of a fight first.

Well I guess I have said enough along that line, in fact too much if the censor happens to read it.

You will be into another summer's work by the time this reaches you. Do not work too hard, as the world was not made in a day. Drop a line when you have time, as the letters are very precious here. Well good luck and give my best to all.

As ever,
Ollie[29]

55th Battery, C.F.A. France.
April 22nd, 1918

Dear Dad,

Well here it is near the end of April, but the weather over here has not been much like spring. Had quite a snow storm the other night, and each morning the ground is frozen quite hard, and have had considerable rain and very little sunshine, but it looks clearer to-day.

We are at present near the highest point of Vimy Ridge. Have been here 10 days now and were certainly glad to get up here out of the mud below. We have a great view of the country for miles in all directions from here. Can see Arras on our right, several small towns in the rear and a great stretch of Heinie's land in front.

Four of our guns are going about a mile forward to-night and expect something to happen along this sector in the near future, as our heavies have been going day and night for the last two days.

We have had a deuce of a time getting enough to eat for the past two weeks, as the railroads behind the lines have been shelled so heavily since the drive started. Only had 13 loaves of bread for the whole battery (135 men) one day. The YMCA could get nothing up to the line and whenever they did there was always three or four hundred waiting in line to buy it.

Received a letter from [sister] Ell on Sunday but have had none from Waterdown for six weeks now. Had one from Harry two weeks ago.

We have good gun positions here, but of course just splinter proof. Have a deep dugout to get into in case he locates our position and have been digging a trench from it to the guns, 100 yards distant, for the past week.

Fritz sent us over a message last night by balloon saying the Canadian corps would be wiped out by noon to-day, but as it is two o'clock now he must have changed his mind for the present at least.

One of his aeroplanes came over last week and dropped us a note, saying he was out to revenge a comrade, and at once proceeded to do so by attacking our observation balloons. He attacked the first one and brought it down in flames, went on to the second one and done likewise, and on to the third and fourth and they suffered the same fate. It was the most daring piece of work and grandest night I have seen yet; had about a hundred aircraft guns firing at him and thousands of machine guns and a dozen of our planes chasing him.

These balloons are about twice the size of our lower barn, so you can imagine the blaze the gas in them would make. These balloons are all along the front, about five miles behind the line and two miles apart, and are used for directing the fire of the big guns and watching the enemy in general, mostly spotting his batteries, so you see the distance he had to cover to bring down four of them, and yet they tell us we have control of the air.

Well Dad you will be into the spring work once again by the time this reaches you. Do not work too hard, and here's hoping to be back with you before another spring. Give my best to all. Will say good-bye for now.

Your son,
Ollie[30]

55th Battery, C.F.A.
France, May 21, 1918

Friends,

For the past two weeks we have been out of the line on rest in a small town in the midst of a good farming district about six hours' march from the front line. Have our horse lines in an apple orchard, which were in full bloom when we arrived, but have fallen now. Am sitting under an old English cherry tree writing this, which is loaded with half grown cherries.

The inhabitants here are of a better class than we have been used to seeing in the forward areas, but they certainly treat us fine, far better than the English ever did. Of course there is only women and old men and kids left. The towns is all farm houses, as the farmers all live in villages in at least all of France that we have seen, and work the land for miles around. Have no fences except in towns.

The women, of course, do nearly all the work in the fields, and I guess did the most of it even when there were plenty of men about. It is certainly great to hear the cows and chickens in the mornings once again, and better still to get some milk and eggs to eat once again. They all milk their cows three times per day here, and we have a great time helping the Madam-elles milk the cows, as we are billeted in the different barns. But have been sleeping out under the trees for the past week, as it has been quite warm. There is a small lake near the town and we go out for a swim every night.

All the Canadians have been out of the line, really training for open fighting and storming troops. We are at it from five in the morning till four in the afternoon, taking our dinners with us, so that the work has been harder than we often get in the line.

Cecil Cummings[31] was down to see me last week. He is with the 4th Pioneers as batman to a Major.

Edgar Richards and Harold[32] are at present in towns about six miles from here, but have not had a chance to see them.

We are going back in the line to night or to-morrow. Have to be all packed ready to move by in night as I guess our rest is over for a time.

Have not heard from Harry for over a month now. Got a letter from Moll yesterday, and she has moved her abode in London, taking our kits with her.

Have been playing ball nearly every night with other batteries of the brigade. Have split about even in hard ball, but trimmed them all at indoor.

Well, [sister] Mary, this is about all to write about, so will ring off for now. Give my best regards to all and write when you can.

As ever, your brother.

Ollie[33]

May 27, 1918

Well, Mary, have not had a chance to post this, so will add a few lines. We have been in town for four days now. Were two days on the road. We have a very good position in a deep cutting not far from ———. We are supporting Scotch troops, the very best in the Imperial army.

I am down at the wagon lines for a change. Expect to be down for a couple of weeks unless some of the boys go west. It is a pretty good life at the wagon lines in the summer time. Get three half holidays per week, provided the horses, harness and wagons are kept in good shape.

Had rather a hard march up here, as it was so warm and dusty the first day, but it rained all the second day and we landed here pretty well all in.

Had a game of ball with the 4th Battalion this afternoon. Score 5–3 in their favor.

Well, will try and get this away this trip. Do not expect much doing unless the Germans start it, for some time yet. Of course, the guns on both sides keep pounding away, and the aeroplanes are making good use of the moonlight nights. Have two large naval guns right beside our horse lines, which keep pounding away all night.

With these few remarks will say good-night.

Ollie[34]

France
July 15, 1918

Dear Dad,

Just a line to let you know all's well. We are still occupying the same gun positions near Arras but have had to move our waggon lines, as Fritz got a line on us with his big gun. Did not get any of our battery, but killed two and wounded three of the 53 Bty., and killed and wounded several horses. It was lucky we moved out when we did for two days later he shelled it again, killing and wounding some 40 horses in the imperial Battery who were right along side of us, also landing several in our old stables and billets.

I was up at the guns for ten days, but came down to the waggon lines last night for another spell; it is the best place to be in the summer time as dugout life is no good in hot weather. We have only had about three real hot days as yet; has been raining for the past week.

The Scotch Divisions we were supporting have gone out of the line and the Canadian Infantry are in now.

Received two letters from Harry today, one written on June 16, the other July 2. He had been up to Jerusalem for a day and saw all the sights, and also had a seven days' leave to Alexandria; also received a letter from Mary saying you had been down to Toronto to visit and that Mrs. Breckonridge had died suddenly.[35]

I was back the other day to a town behind the lines. The grain that the French have planted is looking fine, the rye was cut and set up in stooks like corn; the women cut and bind it all by hand—they can certainly grow wheat here; never saw better, it is just beginning to ripen now.

Tell Jess I received the parcel of socks to-night. Well, Dad, it does not look much like the war was going to be over this year. We heard to-night that Fritz had started another drive in the south to-day, but do not know whether it is so or not.

Will have to ring off for now. Give my best to all and do not work too hard. Will say good night for now.

Ollie[36]

On the 7th of August, Ollie Horning sat down to write another letter to his father. He was exhausted. A week earlier, the 55th Battery had received orders to move about twelve kilometres closer to the front lines, to the village of Cachy. Such a long move was never easy, but three days of heavy rain had turned the roads to mud. That, and the fact that the whole area was clogged with troops—British, French, Canadian, Australian, Indian—sorely tried the men's patience. Having helped to haul up their guns, wagons, and 3,600 rounds of ammunition per battery, Ollie appreciated their new billets more than usual:

> Dear Dad,
>
> Just a line to let you know that all's well ... I am at present sleeping in a real bed; when you roll into it you sink out of sight in the feather mattress. We are in a small French town which the French vacated about a month ago, leaving everything behind them. The dishes were on the table just ready for a meal, so you have some idea how quickly they got out. It seems a shame to see the way these poor French have had to leave everything behind, but if all turns out per program it will be quite safe for them to return again before this reaches you.
>
> Since last writing Ell we have had a day's journey by train, and also two nights' march, and the rest of the nights packing ammunition on horse back from dusk till daylight, over roads which are at present knee deep in mud.
>
> Our gun positions are in a wheat field which is dead ripe, but too near the front line to be healthy. In fact our brigade had some 30 horses killed and wounded, and a dozen or so men last night ...
>
> Capt. Stan Sawell was over to see me Sunday afternoon; he was going into the support trenches that night. He was looking fine; said it was his company's turn to go over the top. Well, we all expect to go over the top this time. You will know where by the papers no doubt long before this reaches you. Will drop a card as often as possible. Give my love to all.
>
> Ollie[37]

At 4:20 the next morning, with the ground around Amiens blanketed in a heavy predawn fog, Ollie's gun team joined 900 other guns in blasting away at German lines as British, Australian, and Canadian troops swept out of their trenches. Finally, after the baseball games, watching observation balloons, and judging French farming techniques, this was what they had been training for.

————◆————

THE GERMAN OFFENSIVES that began in the spring of 1918 had been stunningly successful at first, but eventually came up against the law of diminishing returns. The more they attacked, the more modest were their gains, and the heavier the cost. By July, when the Germans launched their last offensive, the weight of numbers was starting to tell. They had lost a million men since March, casualties that could be replaced only over a matter of years. Germany had thrown the dice, and lost. Now it was the Entente's turn. The plan called for three major offensives to clear major French transportation hubs, followed by two more limited attacks aimed at liberating coal-mining and industrial areas. First, the French would attack near Soissons, east of Paris, followed by a joint French-American attack at St. Mihiel, towards the southern end of the front. Between the two, British, Canadian, and Australian units would launch themselves eastwards from Amiens. The Canadian Corps, with the 1st, 2nd, and 3rd Divisions at the front and the 4th Division in reserve, was allotted a part of the line in an apex created by two main roads heading out of Amiens. Ahead of them was the River Luce and, beyond that, the villages of Rosières and Chaulnes. To their left, the Australian and New Zealand Army Corps was to push towards and beyond the village of Villers-Bretonneux, and to their right, four British and one French corps were ready to carry the advance.

The Canadian Corps that awaited battle on that fine August night was the strongest, best-trained army that Canada had ever fielded. Aside from the reorganization of the machine-gun and engineer units, a host of other innovations had been brought in over the winter and spring, some of which had been gestating for months, some of them brand new. There would be no long preliminary barrage. Whatever good that did in softening up the objective, it certainly told the enemy you were on your way. Instead, the artillery would open up as the first wave left the trenches, and jump forward in stages as the infantry crossed no man's land and entered the German trenches. The attacking waves would travel light—no more would each rifleman have to haul sixty or seventy pounds of gear as he staggered over the top. Supplies would be brought up by later waves and by specially modified tanks. And each battalion had a limited objective that, once reached, ended its day. Following battalions, fresh and fully equipped, would move through them to carry on to the next objective. Much thought and training had been given to making the best use of tanks, with their significant technological limitations, and machine guns, whose potential was finally being fully exploited. Canada's gunners had honed their craft to become among the best artillery on the Western Front. They excelled at counter-battery fire, picking out and neutralizing enemy artillery positions from considerable distances, and at the creeping barrage. There would always be friendly-fire casualties, but now infantrymen could keep to within a few yards of the curtain of fire, confident that it wouldn't descend on them.

So well prepared for the attack were the Canadians that their accounts make it all sound rather routine. As Ollie Horning had predicted, Stan Sawell and the 21st Battalion had been among the first over the top. That night, Stan sat down in the unit's new positions to record his experiences:

> Arrived in position at 3AM. Opening of the Battle of Amiens. Jumped off at 4.20AM in a very thick fog. I could not see more than 15 yards. Made several attempts before I found the way. Our objective was Marcelcave nearly 3 miles away. Luckily the fog cleared up somewhat before reaching this place. The Hun fought some in places, but for the most part surrendered easily enough. I did not have a single scrap. Every Hun I saw had his hands so far up in the air they looked as if they were trying to reach the low hanging clouds. I only had 35 rounds for my pistol, so I let them all go back to our rear. With Lt. Hill and about 15 men, I was first to the objective this time and took charge of consolidating. Had a bit of fun firing on retreating enemy who were running about 200 yards away. Our losses were fairly light, but we lost our Col. which was great enough loss in itself. 5th Cdn Bde passed over us about 9AM and continued the attack. 6th Bde passed over us in the afternoon along with tanks and cavalry. Cavalry passed our lines in file at trot for about 3 hours. The battle has been a great success. Tonight we are in open warfare.[38]

Stan Sawell, wearing his Military Cross ribbon. Photographer unknown. (Steven R. Sawell collection)

As a gunner, Ollie Horning had a slightly different experience, as he related in his first letter home to Waterdown after the offensive opened:

France, Sept 6, 1918

Dear Ell,

Just a line to let you know all's well. For the past month have hardly had time to eat, let alone sleep. Have been at war in earnest, chasing Fritz all the time.

I last wrote Dad when down at a town near Amiens, just before the drive started down there. No letters were allowed to go out for some time as they did not want it known where we were. And they certainly put 1 over him this time.

For three nights before the push started we were packing ammunition on horses for 12 miles and dropping it in a wheat field, and put our guns in there the night before the push began.

We were the most forward batteries and all expected us to get cut to pieces as soon as we were seen in the morning. There was a large forest just back of us which was full of tanks, armored cars, cavalry and reserves of artillery and infantry.

The 21st battalion were going over the top just in front of us, and saw Capt. Stan. Sawell the night before it started. Have not heard how he came out.

I was at the guns when it started and have been ever since. At four in the morning of Aug. 8th thousands of guns of all calibers opened fire as one gun. We kept it up until eight, increasing our range as our infantry advanced, by which time we were out of range.

By six o'clock the infantry were through his first line and the tanks and cavalry had him on the run.

It was the grandest sight I ever saw to see the tanks and cavalry sweeping past us, while we were firing, and a steady stream of Fritzies coming back; had them carrying out our wounded and theirs all day.

For three days we had him on the move; sometimes we were supporting Canadian infantry, and other times Imperials (Royal Scots). He made several stubborn stands, in one at a town just in front of Roye; saw over 500 of the Scots killed by his machine gun fire. They rushed up more artillery and took the town with Canadians who worked around the town and only had ten casualties.

We were at it day and night down there for eight days, and the French relieved us.

We were a night and a day marching out over ground captured from the Germans, about 18 miles strewn with dead horses and men, and as the weather was the warmest we have had all summer, the smell was almost unbearable.

Our battery came through rather lucky, with only 15 casualties, but our horses certainly got it; had 40 killed one night. We were told we were going out on rest for a couple of weeks, but instead loaded on the cars that morning at 5 o'clock, and were on our way north again by six o'clock. Arrived at a small station behind the line here at Arras, and marched up ten miles and fired in the barrage here at 5 o'clock the next morning, and again had Fritz on the run, and have been at it ever since.

The fighting has been harder here but we are now on ground which is well behind the Hindenburg line, and have released several villages full of French inhabitants, who have been slaves to the Germans since 1914.

It has been the same program daily for the past two weeks; take up a position close up to the infantry and support them when ever needed until out of range; then move up again, seldom staying a day in one position. And the same program to go through, get the guns into position to fire, clear the dead, generally Germans, out of the nearest dugout, if any; and if the smell is not unbearable getting what sleep you can. Then get something to eat, if the rations have been able to get us, roll up your blankets ready for to move, and wait for orders.

That is what I am doing now, as our Capt., who is in command of the battery, is at present up forward picking out a new position ...

Did you ever send that other suit of underwear. Am at present wearing some I got in a German officers kit; also got a dandy revolver. Nearly all the boys have one hanging on their belt; also field glasses, range finders, periscopes, etc, which are all far superior to our own.

Do not know how much longer we are to be in this offensive, but do not think our infantry can stand it much longer, as most of them have had a great many casualties and are all pretty well tired out. We have not had a straight night's sleep in a month, not one bath or change of clothes, gassed several times, and continually dodging shells. I have had several close calls in the past month; completely buried on one occasion.

Well, Ell, will have to ring off for now, as it is 10:30 and have to have our guns into another position, about a mile forward of here, before day-light, as it is in the full view of Fritz. Good-bye for now and give my best to all.

Sincerely, your Bro,
Ollie[39]

By the time Ollie wrote home, the offensive east of Amiens had been wound down. The gains on the first day alone had been stunning—up to eight miles in the Canadian sector—and by 20 August, the Corps had cleared sixty-seven square miles of French territory and liberated twenty-seven vil-lages. The four divisions had captured over 9,000 prisoners, almost 200 artil-lery pieces, and over a thousand trench mortars and machine guns, at a cost of nearly 12,000 killed, wounded, and missing—roughly a third of them on the first day of the offensive. For what was gained, generals considered the cost to be very modest.

The grieving family of Hart Allen, with whom Richards had shared lem-onade at the Dominion Day sports meeting, was probably less sanguine. He was killed on the first day in front of Beaucourt Wood, which was strongly held by enemy snipers and machine-gun posts.[40] Other local men were luck-ier. "They have got me at last," wrote Sam Cook triumphantly to his mother in Waterdown, "a peach of a Blighty, one shrapnel through the wrist and one near the thigh." His 19th Battalion had been in the first wave of the advance and Sam got as far as the German second line before he was wounded.[41] "It was a grand sight to see the big guns advancing and the cavalry and tanks going into action," he wrote. "In two hours' time after we started I was in the forward dressing station." The next time he wrote, he was at Witley, his wounds healed, well rested after ten days' leave in Scotland, and doing physi-cal drill to get his strength back. He wrote to his mother that he was catching up with Rob Buchan and other old friends from the village—Jim Simmons (whose age and physical condition kept him in England for the entire war), George Taylor (who had just been wounded for a second time), and Earl Ire-land (a conscript who hadn't yet gone to the front) from Vinegar Hill. Walker McGregor, with the Princess Patricias, got a shell fragment in the foot on the first day. Max Buczeg of the 29th Battalion was hit in the back by shrapnel the following day. On the 10th, as the 78th Battalion was fighting for the village of Hallu, near the easternmost end of the Canadian advance, Joe Eager took a gunshot wound to the head. The same day, Edgar Richards was caught by a shrapnel burst near Bouchoir; doctors would remove three chunks of metal from behind his knee. For all of them, the Amiens fight was their last—they were all out of the war.

Stan Sawell was out too, at least for the short term. The 21st Battalion had been relieved on the night of 14–15 August and had moved back to positions at Fouquescourt. It was a hot and muggy day and the men had gone three nights without a proper sleep. As soon as they were given the order, they slumped down in their new positions, most without even bothering to take off their equipment. But within minutes, German gas shells were raining down on them. It was critical that the men be roused so they could put on their gas masks, but many of them seemed dead to the world. Only by taking off his own mask and liberally doling out shouts and shoves could Stan get their attention. But in doing so, he took in a healthy dose of gas himself. Within hours, he was feeling the effects. Wracked by stomach cramps and diarrhoea, he couldn't keep anything down, not even water. Convinced that a few hours of rest would see him right, Stan had no intention of reporting sick but the decision was soon taken out of his hands. Ordered to report to battalion headquarters, he managed to drag himself there but stumbled as he entered the dugout and fell to the floor. His head spinning, he couldn't even muster the energy to get up and just sat there in a heap. With his commanding officer standing over him, he could no longer deny that he was sick. Stretchered to the nearest field ambulance, Stan was crushed: "I felt that my personal efforts had been mostly responsible for the splendid fighting trim that Coy D was in and that they trusted my leadership," he wrote later. "We had only started our advance towards Germany, but we all had the conviction we would not stop until it was all over. I wanted to stay with D Coy until the end."[42]

Looking back, it is tempting to assume that an inexorable sequence of events had been set in motion by the triumph at Amiens, that the Canadian Corps' momentum turned it into an irresistible force whose ultimate triumph was only a matter of time. But to do so is to underestimate the challenges on the path to victory. And unlike the Somme and Passchendaele, where a depressing sameness characterized both the terrain and the operations, ahead of the Corps in August 1918 lay variety—in objectives, in tactics, in ground. As Stan Sawell had written in his diary, they were now in open warfare—and that meant most days brought something different.

Clare Laking was finding that out in spades. He had been at the front since March 1918 and was starting to get used to the experience. The first time an artillery shell landed near him, he thought, "Boy, what have I got myself into?" but before long, it was all in a day's work. It was just as well, because the offensive found him busier than ever. Clare was a signaller with the Canadian Field Artillery and his job was to string the wires that maintained communications between the batteries, their forward spotters, and headquarters. Open warfare meant that the batteries were constantly on the move, which meant that there was always wire to be strung. It wasn't a complicated job, but it made you painfully aware of your own vulnerability. "We had eight signallers and one officer," he later recalled, "and we were trying to get through a low-lying section to a house a half a mile away. The Germans were shelling and the officer said we were to go across two at a time. He pointed at me and said 'You and I will go together.' The officer carried nothing and I had my haversack, telephone and all the wire. The machine-gun bullets would ZZZ, ZZZ, ZZZ all around us. I'd flop to the ground, string out the wire, and run another twenty yards before I'd flop to the ground and string out more wire. Finally we got to the house and a shell came over and hit the house, which was brick. I was leaning against a wall when shrapnel caught me on my steel helmet and put a lump in the helmet the size of a fist."

On 26 August, just six days after the operations east of Amiens ceased, the Canadians were back in action again. The Corps sat astride the main road between Arras and Cambrai, an ancient thoroughfare whose near-perfect straightness betrayed its Roman origins The landscape was cut in one direction by a number of shallow river valleys and in another by a series of German main and connecting trenches (the latter known as switches), each more formidable than the last. The Germans had gone to great trouble with these fortifications because the area held critical significance: it constituted the pivot point on which a withdrawal of their sectors to the north and south would be undertaken. Cracking this tactical nut meant that dozens of enemy divisions in both directions would be vulnerable. This time, though, there could be no surprise; the enemy knew that the Canadians were coming, even if they didn't know exactly when. They came on 26 August, with battalions of the 2nd and 3rd Divisions leaving their trenches at 3 a.m. For the next three days they pushed forward, held up by difficult terrain, heavy rain, and pockets of stiff resistance, until they had covered five miles in places and had captured parts of the Fresnes-Rouvroy Line, the first of the major fortified trenches that stood in their way. The attacking divisions, having taken some 5,800 casualties, were then withdrawn, and the 1st and 4th came up to press on towards the even more formidable Drocourt-Quéant Line. Their attack went ahead on the 2nd of September and two days later the D-Q Line had fallen, at a cost of another 5,600 Canadian casualties. Over the next week, German armies were withdrawing all along the front, giving up almost all the ground they had captured in the spring offensives. As a feat of arms, thought Currie, it was even more important than the Corps' success on the first day of the Amiens attack.

But an even bigger challenge lay ahead: the unfinished Canal du Nord. Construction had begun in 1913 but had been suspended when the war began, leaving the Germans with the makings of an ideal defensive position. Forty yards wide in places and with a fifteen-foot-high bank on the western side, it was surrounded by marshland that had been flooded to render it impassable. Only in the Canadian sector was the land dry enough for operations; only in the Canadian sector could the canal be crossed. It was the kind of operation that, two years before, might have been deemed impossible or, at the very least, led to ruinous casualties. But in the fall of 1918, it was a tactical problem whose dangers could be mitigated by careful planning and preparation by Currie and his staff. The first stage of the operation, the crossing of the canal to establish bridgeheads on the eastern bank, went ahead at dawn on the 27th of September and achieved its objectives all along the front with surprising ease. The second phase, the push towards Cambrai, was tougher, in part because battalions were starting to run short of men. Austin Tudor had his first taste of battle on the 27th, as the runner for his platoon officer, and soon found himself with greater responsibilities: "as luck would have it, he got wounded and I didn't and then we stayed in supports for three or four days and I was made section commander, and believe me, I didn't like the job of leading my section over the top on the 1st of October, as there were some boys in the section who had been in France for two years, and they know more about it than I did, but an order has got to be carried out, so I obeyed, and now I am the only one out of the section that isn't wounded or killed."[43] Small pockets of resistance held up the advance, forcing the staff to rethink plans, and ultimately the Canadian Corps had to settle for smaller gains than it was used to achieving. When the attacking divisions were stood down on the afternoon of 1 October, exhausted and now under-strength, they had advanced just a mile beyond the Canal du Nord, and the city of Cambrai remained in German hands.

But not for long. On 8 October, the Corps began the push through the northern suburbs and the next day, two mounted rifles battalions crossed the Canal de l'Escaut and entered the city. Resistance was sporadic, but the Canadian Mounted Rifles and the engineers who followed them found that parts of the city had been prepared for demolition by the retreating Germans. On the 11th, once the dangers had been cleared, the Corps was relieved, having liberated fifty-four towns and villages and 116 square miles of France. Ollie Horning took advantage of the lull to bring his family up to date on what he had been doing:

France 13-10-18

Dear Dad,

Just a line to let you know all is well, and we are still going strong. Have been steadily advancing ever since we started the Cambrai drive. Are at present about seven miles past Cambrai, and have had a couple of days' rest, and may be here for two or three more. Hope it's a week, as we certainly need the rest. Our guns are still in action. This digging a fresh hole to sleep in every night is rather tiresome, especially when you don't get a chance to sleep in it after you have it dug.

We are at present in a small town living in furnished houses; am sleeping in a real feather bed; have a piano in the parlor; in fact, the house is better furnished than the best city houses in Canada. The civilians have had to get out and leave everything behind.

We have been living on the fat of the land so far as vegetables go, every garden was filled with all kinds of them. I picked three strawberries in a garden yesterday, and was gathering English walnuts to-day. There is no fruit of any kind left behind. No orchards in these parts, just a few trees in each garden.

Well, Dad, the Cambrai drive has been the toughest the Canadians have run up against, as no doubt you already know by the casualty list. Our battery has been fairly lucky—lost 3 officers and 20 men, but only 4 killed; but our horses did not fare so well—lost 80 in two days at Bourlon Wood. Had to borrow some from the other batteries to carry on with. Had to leave two of our G.S. wagons behind, with all extras. But it is easy to pick up anything you want as you go along.

I saw Roy Willis about two weeks ago at Bourlon, and the Battalion which Stan Sawell was in is in this town. Stan returned to them after being gassed down south. Was with them about 6 hours, when he went down the line again with a piece of shrapnel in the arm.

Our leave is open now, have about 20 away, and some going and coming back every day. I am about 60 on the list now. At the present rate of going will get mine somewhere near Christmas. Guess I will go up to Scotland again.

Well, Dad, by the time this reaches you the work will be done for another year. One can hardly realize the summer has gone. But in the morning here now the ground is covered with white frost.

·Will have to ring off for to-night. Give my best wishes to all.

As ever,
Ollie[44]

When next he wrote home, Ollie was on the outskirts of Valenciennes, the next city to be liberated by the Canadian Corps.

France 23-10-18

Dear Dad,

Just a line to let you know all's well, and that we are still going strong, although held up here for a few days, as our friend Fritz has dammed up the canal and blown up the locks, and forming quite a lake between him and us at present. Some houses have just the roofs above water. We are at present in the suburbs of Valenciennes.

Well, the going has been rather strenuous for the past week, as it has been raining and the Germans have done all they can to spoil the roads, mining every cross-road, blowing up all bridges, etc. But this has been more than repaid by the French which have been left behind in the towns. They hardly know what to do with themselves after being, as it were, slaves to the Germans for so long.

Nothing is too good for us, put us in their best beds for the night and gave us coffee a dozen times per day. While passing through Denain shook hands with at least a thousand and every time the battery would stop for a minute out they would come with coffee. It is surprising the amount of flags they have kept stowed away all this time, the streets were lined with them.

It was the first time a good many of them had ever seen the kilts.

The Germans took everything from these people before retreating, not a living thing left behind, not even a chicken, took or damaged all the machinery in the factories and coal mines, as this is a coal district, even took their best farm implements.

The town we are in at present has no inhabitants, as he has taken them all with him, but the houses are all in good condition, all we have to do is light the fire and we are right at home.

Tell Jess or Will to drop a line and let me know what's going on around the old home now that the work must be nearly done for another season.

> Give my best to all,
> Ollie[45]

After all but walking into Cambrai, Valenciennes looked like a tougher test. But with superb coordination, pinpoint timing, and a smothering artillery barrage, a bitter street fight was avoided. A few miles ahead of them lay the Belgian border. Behind them lay thirty miles of battlefield over which they had advanced, the remains of thirty German divisions they had defeated, and nearly 30,000 casualties. For most people, the First World War was defined by trench warfare, in a muddy, alien landscape that swallowed men, field guns, and horses. But it was far more dangerous advancing across the open fields northeast of Amiens than it was fighting from shell hole to shell hole on the Somme or in front of Passchendaele. The open warfare of 1918 was a more dangerous game, with much higher casualty counts. A century later, we can see that cold reality in the statistics. In 1918, Canadians saw it in their newspapers. The *Waterdown Review* continued to print soldiers' letters, but through the summer and fall it was also printing their obituaries, sometimes two or three at once.

Stan Sawell got his wish and returned to the 21st Battalion, expecting to see things through to the end with his men, but it was not to be. The morning of his return, a handful of enemy shells fell on battalion headquarters, killing seven horses and shredding the tent in which Stan was sitting. A piece of shrapnel caught him in the arm and, less than a day after he had returned, Stan found himself out of the fight again—this time for good.[46] Maurice Scott had his foot fractured by a piece of shrapnel.[47] Austin Hearns and Fred James, both of whom had lost their brothers at Vimy, were gassed, and so was George Arnold—twice.[48] One can only assume that he had been scared straight by his brush with military law, for he acquitted himself well through those last few weeks in action. Clare Laking was another soldier whose war came to an end then. He and a pal were carrying a third signaller to hospital when a shell burst knocked the trio flat. Scrambling up, Clare turned to his pal. "Is there a hole in my tunic?" he asked.

A quick look. "The whole back of your tunic is in shreds!" came the reply.

"But is there a hole in my shoulder?" Clare asked. There was. It was just a flesh wound, but it was enough to get Clare sent to hospital. He never returned to the front lines.

George Taylor, the last of the six pals from Aldershot who enlisted together in 1915, was out of the fight too. He described the circumstances in a letter home, saying that the Germans "sniped me right through the right chest and out my back. I was hit on Sept 27th and have been in bed ever since ... The specialist says my chest has switched around the right and I have to stay in bed till it comes back again. Some joke, what do you say? I asked him how long it would be before I was fit again and he said months, so after I get out of bed I may have a chance to make Canada. I wonder what it would be like to be back in old Waterdown again with all my friends."[49]

But others would never make it home to the township. John Springer was killed on 2 September in the 102nd Battalion's attack northwest of Marquion, near the Canal du Nord.[50] So often, tragedy piled on tragedy. John's younger brother, age fifteen, had died of pneumonia in November 1914, and in July 1918 his father succumbed to injuries sustained in a car accident months earlier. Harry Green was killed in a quiet period. The operation against the D-Q Line had finished and the 29th Battalion had moved into trenches at Sains-les-Marquion, near the Canal du Nord. But having fought with the battalion through Passchendaele and in the Battle of Amiens, he was killed by a shell fragment on 6 September, an otherwise quiet day.[51] Harry had married Winifred Mitchel in Carlisle in May 1916, not long before he left the township for the last time. George Fretwell's machine-gun battery was laying down a barrage near Vis-en-Artois in the push towards Cambrai on 27 September. George was bringing up ammunition to one of the gun positions when a shell exploded a few feet away from him, killing him instantly.[52] He had been with the unit just three weeks. Twice his mother had refused to give him permission to enlist earlier in the war, but she couldn't stand in the way when he was conscripted. Years after the war, Margaret Fretwell would write that she still felt "in a measure responsible for his loss."[53] The same day, Ben Rayner was hit by machine-gun fire shortly after the 7th Battalion reached its objective in the attack on Bourlon Wood. He was given first aid and evacuated to a casualty clearing station, but died of his wounds six days later.[54] On the 30th of September, Eddie Crane died when the 54th Battalion was called to attack west of Sancourt.[55] A couple of weeks before, his brother James, a Wentworth County roads worker, noticed an insect bite on his face and casually scratched it; within days, it had become badly infected and on the 18th, James died of blood poisoning. James Robertson simply disappeared. On the 1st of October, fellow soldiers of the 1st Battalion spotted him crossing a railway embankment during an attack west of Blécourt, but no trace of him was ever found after that.[56] The same day, Carlisle-born Ken Hunter of the 102nd Battalion was hit in the head by a shell fragment and killed in an attack southeast of Blécourt.[57] Three Hunter brothers had enlisted; all three were now dead.

One other battlefield death from 1918 generated a family mystery. In October, the *Spectator* carried a short obituary relating to one of Mountsberg's founding families:

> Mr. and Mrs. Berryman [actually Benjamin] Maddaugh, of Freelton, have received the sad news that their son, Pte. Percival A. Maddaugh was killed in action. Pte. Maddaugh was in his 24th year. He tried to enlist early in the war but was rejected. Later he applied and was accepted in the 249th battalion, determined that physical inabilities should not prevent him from serving his country. He was transferred to the 28th battalion, with which unit he was serving when killed. He is survived by his mother and father, one sister, Miss Pearl, of Hamilton, and one brother, Cecil, at home. Previous to enlisting he was a farmer in Binbrook.[58]

But eighty years later, a descendant's enquiry to the National Archives in Ottawa yielded a puzzling response: "Mr. Maddaugh did not die while serving in the Canadian Expeditionary Force and there is nothing in his file to indicate that he is deceased."[59] Nothing—except the *Spectator* article and the fact that Percy's name appears on the local war memorial, although it wouldn't be the first time that a war memorial was wrong. Further research revealed that there was a John Maddaugh on the official casualty rolls, but the family had no record of an ancestor by that name—even though, like Percy, he was living in Oxbow, Saskatchewan, when he enlisted in the 249th Battalion at Estevan, Saskatchewan, and he put Benjamin and Jemima Maddaugh of Freelton as his next of kin. But surely John must be an imposter. He was obviously killed in battle, but who was he? A friend of Percy's from Oxbow who, for some unknown reason, didn't want to enlist under his own name and instead enlisted as Percy's brother? And what happened to Percy if he wasn't killed in France in October 1918? The waters were further muddied by Percy's military record, which indicated that he had enlisted in the 152nd Battalion in Estevan, Saskatchewan, in August 1916, but had subsequently disappeared from Camp Hughes in Manitoba. The army had no record of him after 22 September 1916, when a court of enquiry declared him a deserter and struck him from the unit's nominal roll.[60]

Often, such mysteries are impenetrable, the passage of time erasing all clues that might have led to an answer. In this case, however, a theory presented itself when I started looking closely at the service records. The first clue was that Percy and John had suspiciously similar handwriting. Then, I noticed that their physical descriptions were virtually identical, except for a slight difference in height. With that, I assumed that the scenario must have gone something like this. Percy enlisted in the 152nd Battalion in May 1916 but, for whatever reason, soon decided that it wasn't to his liking and deserted. Then, he had a change of heart. Perhaps news of the armistice for deserters never reached Oxbow and he envisioned spending his life on the run from military authorities. So he decided to re-enlist. Everyone in Oxbow surely knew him as Percy, but for the army he adopted the most common Christian name he could think of, John, and enlisted as his own non-existent brother. He informed his family of the situation, spinning the story that the *Spectator* eventually picked up—that he had been rejected for physical reasons when he first tried to enlist, but had persevered and gotten himself into uniform. To the Maddaughs in Freelton, their son Percy was now in the army, to be killed near Sancourt when his machine-gun section was hit by a shell burst. To the army, however, Percy had disappeared in the summer of 1916 and it was a different person, John Maddaugh, who died that day at Sancourt.

———◆———

THE FOURTH ANNIVERSARY OF THE WAR CAME, with most congregations holding special services. At Waterdown Methodist Church, the Reverend H. B. Storey gave a sermon on the occasion. "After rehearsing the causes of the war," reported the *Spectator*, "and recounting glorious battles of Vimy Ridge, Ypres, etc., in which the Canadians distinguished themselves, the speaker referred to the need for learning the lessons which the conflict teaches: (1) We should be more concerned about crowning a cause than of winning a spectacular fight; (2) don't forget the principles for which the soldiers are fighting, ie. freedom, justice, truth and righteousness, in the midst of our activities; (3) keep the home fires of faith in God burning brightly while the boys struggle and die 'over there'; (4) when the nation gets down upon its knees in prayer, we may count the days to the end of the war. Our cause is right; the God of Righteousness is with us."[61]

But it wasn't really the time to dwell on such weighty issues; it was the start of fair season, the time for prize-winning chickens, massive eggplants, lemon ices, and silly games. At least it was supposed to be. To read the accounts of the 1918 fairs is to be transported back to a world that was trying so hard to be normal, and yet couldn't escape the dark shadow of war. Yes, there were the horse races (in Freelton, a green trot and a free-for-all, whatever they might have been), the pantomimes, the fish ponds and the hot dog stands, the pennants, and a hat for the oldest man at the fair. I'm tickled to see that my grandmother, by then nine years old, took first prize for five Yellow Leviathan mangels in the Wentworth County school fair—she never struck me as the mangel type.[62] And there was always baseball—village teams, company teams, out-of-towners, and, at Carlisle's fair, what I can only imagine was the diamond's equivalent of the Harlem Globetrotters: the Colored Chicken Catchers of Hamilton, under their captain Sir Nell Black Minorca Bantam.[63]

But at every turn was the war. In the person of Colonel James Edgar Davey, a Hamilton doctor who enlisted in February 1915 and gave a short talk at Millgrove's annual garden party on his three years' service in France.[64] In the little tots of the Freelton Sunday School, whose patriotic flag drill "evoked enthusiastic applause."[65] In the exhibition of war bread at the Waterdown Fair, which was judged a signal success: "The directions of the Canada food board had been followed implicitly in the making of the bread, cornmeal, whole

The south end of Waterdown's fairgrounds, showing the James house at the left. Photographer unknown.
(Author's collection)

wheat flour and other substitutes were used and seemed to improve rather than take from the quality."[66] The war was always there—even on fair day, when the rural world revelled in itself, the war was always there. More for some than for others.

———◆———

THE BANG JOLTED SARAH JAMES AWAKE. The family's house was on the southern edge of the Waterdown Fairgrounds, so they were used to hearing strange sounds at odd times—even at 4:30 a.m. It could have been a window slamming shut or a car's backfire—Sarah couldn't be sure, so she called out to the far bedroom, which her daughter Gustie shared with her husband John Miller. She had bid them goodnight a few hours earlier and had left them talking, apparently quite normally, John in bed and Gustie lying beside him, still clothed, on top of the quilt. For a long time, Sarah heard nothing—then a chilling response.

"John has shot himself."

Sarah and Gus James were in the room in an instant. It was a gruesome sight. John Miller lay in bed, blood flowing from a ghastly wound in his head and oozing from his mouth and nose. A deep red stain was spreading across the bedclothes. Remarkably, he was fully conscious.

"I'm going to fetch Dr. Hopper," Gustie announced, and before anyone could speak she was out the back door and into the churchyard. She picked her way between the headstones and then walked south on Mill Street. She was approaching the Presbyterian Church when she heard footsteps behind her. It was her eighteen-year-old brother Storman.

"Gustie, where are you going?" he asked. "Doc Hopper's house is the other way. I'll go with you." But they had gone only a few steps when Gustie stopped.

"I'm not right, brother. I'm feeling so faint," she stammered. Her breathing was quick and shallow and even in the darkness, Storman could see that all the colour had drained from her face.

"You go back home, Gustie," he said. "I'll get the doctor. You go home—we'll be there soon." He turned and ran along Church Street, towards the Hopper house. It was only a few blocks, and it was no more than fifteen minutes before Dr. Hopper was in the James house, standing beside John Miller.

It took him just a moment to see that John's condition was beyond his abilities. The bullet had entered near the temple and come out of his eye socket, close to the bridge of his nose. Storman was despatched to the nearest telephone, in the Anglican church rectory, to call for an ambulance from Hamilton. Incredibly, John remained conscious and lucid. Hopper's first question was obvious.

"Who shot you, John?"

"I don't have any idea. I was asleep and got woke up by a real bad stinging in the side of my head. I put my hand up and there was blood all over it. I looked for Gustie but I couldn't see anything—still can't."

Hopper was troubled. Sarah James had relayed Gustie's first words to her—"John has shot himself"—but Miller's version of events was totally different. By that time the village constable, George Potts, had reached the house, so he and Hopper made a quick search of the room. What they found did nothing to ease the doctor's concerns.

At the bottom of the bed was a spent cartridge, almost certainly from the round that hit Miller. The bullet itself couldn't be found. In the folds of the quilt, Potts found three more cartridges, unused. And then, under Gustie's pillow, Hopper found a gun. Miller thought it was probably the same gun they had borrowed from a friend to go shooting a few days earlier. They had kept it because they planned to go again in a day or two. Hopper looked more closely at it. What he discovered stunned him. The gun had been reloaded with a new cartridge and had been cocked, ready to fire again.

Hopper was no detective, but he knew that Miller, blinded and bleeding freely from a gunshot wound to the head, would not have been able to eject the spent cartridge, locate a new one in the folds of the quilt, load and cock the gun, and place it under Gustie's pillow. It simply wasn't possible. The doctor turned to ask Gustie for an explanation. She wasn't there. In the confusion, no one had noticed her absence and Storman, sent right back out to call for an ambulance, had forgotten to say that he had met up with Gustie near the Presbyterian Church and had told her to go home. Obviously she had gone somewhere else. But where?

Once again, Storman was sent out, this time with Constable Potts, to make a search. They began in front of the Presbyterian Church, the last place she had been seen, and worked their way in all directions from there. Back up Mill Street to the 4th Concession road, east to the mills at the foot of Victoria Street, along John Street to the west. By now, it was dawn and there were a few people around to take up the search, poking around in their gardens and sheds. Storman and Potts continued south on Mill Street, crossed Dundas, and followed Waterdown Road down towards the creek. Just beyond the railway bridge, they came to the Palmer property beside the Great Falls. It was a beautiful August morning, warm and calm, and the sun sparkled on the water as it plunged over the lip of the falls to the pool below. There, doubled over in ten feet of water, was the body of Gustie Miller.

No one will ever know Gustie's agonies, both before and after the shooting, but over the next twenty-four hours, details emerged to suggest why she might have attempted to kill her husband, and then succeeded in killing herself. They seemed to be, as the *Spectator* said, a most affectionate young couple, but the war years had been tough on them. They had only three months together after their marriage in March 1915; John had gone overseas in June to be posted to the staff at Shorncliffe, where he became

Facing page: The Great Falls in Waterdown, where Gustie Miller's life ended. Photo by Will Reid. (Author's collection)

the sergeant in charge of the stables and grooms. In the spring of 1916, he came down with severe bronchitis and tonsillitis and had to be confined to Westcliffe Canadian Eye and Ear Hospital, where his tonsils were removed. The surgery seemed to affect John more deeply and he had a nervous collapse while convalescing. The army decided to send him for a month's furlough in Canada; it was later extended by another month and when he returned to England in September, he was posted to the Canadian hospital at Taplow. Another month in hospital in January 1917, and in June he was back in hospital with appendicitis. In December, John was before a medical board. He complained of a steady dull pain in his right hip that under strain became sharp and disabled him for a few minutes; the doctors put this down to a fall from a horse in June 1916 which caused bursitis and partial loss of function in the hip joint. The board also determined that he was of a "nervous temperament" and recommended that he be returned to Canada as category B3. He sailed home on the *Olympic* in February 1918 and went before another medical board at Ravina Barracks in Toronto in March. That board judged John to be category E, unfit for service. He was officially discharged on 14 March 1918.[67] Curiously, upon his return, the *Spectator* reported that he had been with the field artillery in the First Contingent and had been wounded at Sanctuary Wood, none of which was true. He got a job with Hamilton Bridge Works and he and Gustie moved into a house at 90 Birch Avenue in Hamilton, but in August 1918 they moved back to Waterdown, to live in the James house.

Gustie Miller had been pregnant when John went overseas, but miscarried at six months. The loss of the child seems to have started a downward spiral in her health, both physical and mental. She was in and out of hospital and doctors' offices and had two operations, neither of which improved her condition. The couple had moved back to Waterdown largely because Gustie's health had worsened, but a return to familiar surroundings didn't seem to help. "The past week," reported the *Spectator*, "she had been in exceptionally poor health." She had already attempted suicide once and the family came to the conclusion that Gustie, tortured by seemingly endless health problems and convinced that John too was suffering, decided to end both of their lives. She shot him in the head and reloaded the gun to shoot herself, but was prevented from carrying it out by the alarm raised in the house. Leaving the house, she probably never intended to go to Dr. Hopper's house but instead headed in a different direction—when Storman met her at the Presbyterian

Church, it was only a minor hitch in her plan—and threw herself over the falls in her despair.[68]

Two days later, villagers gathered at the James home for Gustie's funeral. Out front, John Vance's ornate horse-drawn hearse was waiting to take her on her final journey. Leaving the house, it turned down John Street and then south on Mill, the same way that Gustie had gone in the hours after the shooting. East on Dundas Street, the hearse clopped across the bridge over Grindstone Creek and climbed up Vinegar Hill. It turned down George Street and pulled into the Union Cemetery, where six pallbearers tenderly carried her coffin to the grave. As the minister read the rites of committal, Gustie Miller was lowered to a rest that she seems not to have enjoyed in life. No headstone marks the place.

Was Gustie a casualty of the war? Would she and John have had a long and happy life together if they had lived in a peaceful world, or would some other tragedy have befallen them? On 17 October, a young farm labourer named Leonard Gravelle jumped from the back of a moving automobile on Highway 6 to catch a rabbit. But as his brother watched from his buggy behind, Leonard struck his head and fractured his skull. Within hours he was dead.[69] Ironically, Leonard had been conscripted in May but was almost immediately discharged as "Erroneously Ordered to Report" because he was too poor a physical specimen to be of use to Canada's army—so far, at least.[70] If he had gone into uniform, would he have lived to inherit the family farm and grow old with the land? Or would he have fallen victim to something else?

Like Charlie Carson. Charlie, too, was a conscript, called up in June 1918. By August he had reached England and was posted to the 8th Reserve Battalion at Witley. On his first leave, he decided to visit Ireland, from where his family emigrated to Waterdown, but by the time he got back to camp he was feeling poorly—chills, fever, headache, general fatigue, loss of appetite. He'd never been sick much before and was strong and well developed, a typical farmer of nineteen years, but after four days of trying to ignore the symptoms, he decided to see the medical officer. Within a day of being admitted to the military hospital at Bramshott, his condition had deteriorated. His lips were dry, his face flushed, and his tongue coated, he had developed a dry cough that settled in his lungs and gave him only a restless sleep. The doctor reported that Charlie's spirits remained bright, but as he struggled to take in enough oxygen, his face began to take on a bluish-purple tinge. His breathing became even more laboured as his lungs filled with fluid, and his pulse became quicker and weaker. Day after day, his doctor made the same entry on his medical case sheet: "No improvement." On the 25th of October at 5:05 a.m., Charlie died.[71]

The disease that killed him was the Spanish flu, which, despite its name, had emerged from Asia to be brought to North America and Europe by Chinese labourers recruited to work for the Entente armies on the Western Front. Carried by the mass movement of troops and their concentration in vast, often overcrowded encampments, it would eventually kill more people than the war, including more than 50,000 in Canada. Already it had a grip on East Flamborough. It had killed Ashton Johnson, a discharged soldier in Aldershot, and Gladstone Hilborn of Freelton, who succumbed in Halifax, where he had been admitted to hospital on his way overseas with the Canadian Field Artillery.[72] And it drove the township to take the same precautions that were taken everywhere else to quell the spread of the disease. Church services were cancelled and all schools were closed from the middle of October. Dr. Hopper advised parents to keep their children off the streets at all times, because the young were at greatest risk. In East Flamborough, the majority of the dead were under the age of thirty; a third of them were under ten years old. Still, there was always a local poet to make light of a deadly situation:

> When your head is blazing and burning,
> And your brain within is turning
> Into buttermilk from churning,
>   It's the "Flu."
> When your bones are creaking and cracking,
> As if all the fiends were racking
> And all the devils were attacking—
>   It's the "Flu."
>
> It's the Flu, Flu, Flu,
> Which has You, You, You.
> It's caught you, it's got you,
>   And it sticks like glue.
> It's the latest thing in fashion,
> It's the Doctor's pet and passion.
>   So sneeze a bit, wheeze a bit,
>   Ka Chew, Chew, Chew.[73]

With schools and churches shuttered, the concession roads and streets deserted save for a few brave souls, some of them wearing masks, who walked quickly to get their errands done and return home, the township took on the air of a place under siege. But even so, with no end in sight to the war, the next Victory Loan campaign had to go ahead as planned. Most of East Flamborough's campaign committee members had children in uniform—Emory, Horne, Attridge, Horning, Filman—and the township had set its sights high, with a goal of $250,000 in sales. To give some context to such an abstraction, the *Review* told readers what one $50 Victory Bond would buy: 1,000 rifle cartridges, 104 hand grenades, ten gas masks, fifty pairs of soldiers' socks, ten pairs of soldiers' boots, knives, forks and spoons for an infantry company, or 1,000 yards of adhesive medical tape. It would pay Canada's war bill for 4.5 seconds, feed 100 soldiers for one day, or pay one soldier for forty days.[74] More than one reader probably wondered how much longer Canada would have to feed and pay its soldiers.

And then, deliverance. "As we go to press," reported the *Review* breathlessly on the 7th of November, "Waterdown is celebrating the news of Peace with all her might. With bells ringing, whistles blowing, flags flying and school children parading the streets the old town has gone wild with joy."[75] But joy was snatched away as quickly as it had come. It was just a rumour, a false armistice emanating from a mistake by an American press agency that spread around the world before it could be contradicted. The whistles and flags went away again. The agony would continue.

A little before 11 a.m. on the morning of 10 November, Waterdown-born Willie Garvin of the 3rd Canadian Machine Gun Company was riding as brakeman on an ammunition limber in the little Belgian village of Ghlin, west of Mons. Willie was a conscript who had been in France just over a month; this was the first heavy artillery barrage he had faced. Shells burst in front of him, then behind, showering his crew with lumps of earth and brick. And then, a blast right beside him. Willie's right leg was sliced off by a big chunk of shrapnel while another piece cut into his abdomen. Artillery and machine-gun fire was only getting heavier, so there was no way to evacuate Willie, or even bring up a stretcher-bearer to treat his wounds. His pals did what they could with field dressings but Willie probably never had a chance. He remained fully conscious almost until he died.[76] Twenty-four hours later, the guns fell silent.

7

AFTER

———◆———

As the sounds of violence petered out along the Western Front, the din was
building in Waterdown. Factory whistles were tooting ceaselessly and everyone who owned a car (which, in East Flamborough in 1918, meant about a
dozen people) was tooting the horn. Jim Simmons being still in England with
the Army Service Corps, his replacement as bell-ringer was hauling away at
the rope with an energy that few people thought he possessed. The sound of
church bells, each with a different tone, rolled through the early November
air. Ada Flintoft heard the distinctive sound of the bell she had donated to
Grace Church in memory of her son Tom, and smiled. Waterdown's brass
band had never sounded worse, playing with great enthusiasm but little art-
istry, and pots and buckets that had been brought out for the false Armistice the week before were brought out again. Elsewhere in the township, the
hamlets did their best to match Waterdown for noise, but it was difficult to
muster a commotion without factory whistles, car horns, or brass bands. The
emotions, however, were just as intense. "The Great War is over," trumpeted
the *Waterdown Review* a few days later. "Canadians will now kill the fatted
calf and the Yankees shoot the bull."[1]

The war might have ended, but the struggles would continue—to get
home and find a way back to peacetime civilian society, to rebuild lives and

relationships, to shake off the clouds of a war that had already blotted out so much. There was lots of talk about getting back to normal, but what exactly did "normal" mean? The way things had been in July 1914? The way they would have been if the war had never happened? Many people had forgotten what normal felt like, let alone how to achieve it. The weight of the war might have been lifted but it was still a disorienting, bewildering time.

Among the soldiers in the battle zones, the strongest emotion was either joy or relief—or both. Whatever the feeling, it was manifest in a realization that their lives were now much less dangerous than they had been a few days earlier. "It certainly is fine to be able to live like human beings once more," wrote one fellow to his aunt in Waterdown. Their duties didn't end, and no one expected that they would be on the way home immediately—the volunteers had, after all, signed up for the duration of the war plus six months. But the feeling of security was a new experience. "It sure is a great relief to know that we can walk around and not have someone taking a shot at us or shells bursting around us," Lorne Mount told his father. "It sure puts new life in a man."[2]

Judging from their letters home, the soldiers were most profoundly affected by the Belgian and French civilians, whose gratitude towards their liberators was almost boundless: "The Belgian people sure are using us fine," wrote Mount. "They cannot do enough for us. Of course, this part of the county was under German rule for over four years, up till last Monday, so I expect they were glad to be rid of them. It is the happiest day of their lives when the Allied armies march into the towns that the Germans have been holding for so long."[3] At times, their expressions of gratitude were humbling, even embarrassing: "Towards the last the civilians did not have time to get out, so there you would find them huddled up in cellars, and at the sight of a khaki-clad soldier they realized that their term of being prisoners was over and relief from the Bosche is something for which they were very thankful, and showed it in no uncertain manner," one local wrote. "I will never forget one old man, who came out and started shoving two pieces of black bread in my pocket."[4]

The determination of the civilians to restart their lives was also evident. "Mons is a very pretty place, and is now rapidly assuming a businesslike air," as Clifford Shireman of Winnipeg wrote to his family back in Waterdown. "The stores are getting in their stocks and soon it will be itself again." But it was also clear that, because of the destruction wrought by the war, many civilians had nothing to go back to. It wasn't a case of farmers, artisans, and merchants picking up where they had left off, because everything connected to their old lives had been obliterated. "They are also wending their way back to their homes or what was their home in many cases. A good many will find their homes blown to powder when they get there," wrote Shireman.[5] "I feel sorry for the refugees we see pouring back every day; many of whom will find nothing but a shapeless pile of brick and stone, where their homes once stood, and as far as their eyes can see there will be nothing to look at but skeletons of trees, ruined villages and the earth itself with huge shell holes lip to lip for miles," as another local soldier described it. "I don't think I would have the heart to go back to some villages I know, to build a home. It would seem a hopeless task, but still I suppose the most of them will rise again from their ashes. In future years though, tourists will still be able to see some of the devastation of war. Old Mont St. Eloi still stands, a relic of the Hunnish hordes of 1870 and again under fire in this war. It looks down on Vimy Ridge and many a day I have looked up to it and wondered if I would live to see it the next day. In Arras, too, the once beautiful town hall and the great cathedral are being preserved as they are, so that the world may see the work of German kultur. Both are mere piles of rubbish now."[6]

For the conquering army of the Hundred Days, the reward for winning the war was to march farther away from home. Two divisions (the 3rd and 4th) would remain in Belgium and two (the 1st and 2nd) would go into Germany, not as liberators but as conquerors. Their arrival was triumphal, and indeed it had a whiff of the ancient world about it. There was a ceremonial parade across the Rhine, one unit at a time and with each unit falling under the gaze of the official photographer, and then the artillerymen set up their guns on the banks of the river—the victors doing their own Watch on the Rhine, more for symbolic purposes than practical. For the men, it was a chance to see German civilians up close and to tell their families of their appraisal: "The German people I have met don't seem to care as long as they are well fed, well amused, and making money, whether they are free; the French and British want to be free first of all, free anyhow, free even when they might be better off materially under benevolent autocracy. We want to have a voice in the Government, they are willing to be governed by professionals, as long as they make him comfortable."[7]

But no one wanted the Canadian Corps to linger on the continent. Without an external enemy, discipline was almost certain to slip. Everyone, from the ranks to the staffs, knew they were in a holding pattern and the shop-worn maxim, fight the Huns instead of each other, no longer held meaning. Minor slights that might have been shrugged off a few months ago now caused deep offence. Tempers were quick and feathers easily ruffled.

On the 29th of November, the 58th Battalion was putting in time with parades, fatigues, sports, outings—all the things that armies do to keep the men busy and out of trouble. But they weren't working very well anymore. After parade, two privates were having a conversation about the war and what it had cost. When it started to get heated, their corporal told them off, but a couple of minutes later they were back at it. The louder of the two, a Detroiter who had volunteered in 1917, said that when they all got back home, the late arrivals should stay in uniform to make up Canada's standing army. "You're a quitter, you bastard," he said to the other man, Ebon Church of Flamboro Centre.

"And you're a poor whore," replied Church quietly.

"You had better keep a guarded tongue next time," growled the Detroiter, pushing against Church, who swung his rifle around to ward off the fellow. Their two weapons crashed together—with the American's thumb, now just an ugly mess of torn flesh and broken bone, between them. A sergeant was quickly on the scene, and Ebon Church was put on charge.

At his court martial, he didn't deny his actions but claimed that he had been provoked by the American, who had baited him as a conscript.[8] Church had indeed been conscripted but only because, after volunteering for the 205th Battalion in Hamilton in 1916 he had been discharged through ill health. Church also admitted that he wasn't in the best of moods for, just three or four days earlier, he had received news that his mother had succumbed to influenza in Flamboro Centre. The court martial was unmoved: Church was convicted of unlawfully wounding a fellow soldier and sentenced to two years in confinement.

It was just a tussle, not even a ripple in the great struggle, but it was indicative of the problem of keeping large numbers of soldiers out of trouble when their officers had nothing meaningful for them to do. So as soon as possible, the exodus began. Canadian units remained in Germany over Christmas 1918, but in the New Year they started returning to Belgium. For administrative and other reasons, the 3rd Division was the first to cross back to Britain; it was followed by the other divisions, with the last units crossing in mid-April. The men were destined for demobilization camps at Bramshott and Witley, while troops already in England went to camps at Seaford, a coastal resort town not far from Folkestone, and Ripon, a cathedral city in central Yorkshire. Kinmel

Park, an estate on the north coast of Wales, became the final staging point for drafts sailing from Liverpool.

Between 11 November 1918 and 2 April 1919, over 110,000 men returned to Canada, an impressive number to be sure, but not nearly enough for the men who were waiting to go home. No one could have predicted the delays that would plague the process. There was a heavy demand on shipping space, and the government in Washington wielded enormous pressure to ensure that the doughboys got home early. Then there were the endless forms to be completed. The Canadian government had decided that most of the discharge paperwork would be done in Britain, so that once the soldiers reached home, they could be released with few formalities. This was wise in principle, but in practice it meant that Canadians cooled their heels as dozens of separate forms, dealing with everything from their teeth to the state of their kit, were completed and filed for each of them.

All the while they waited, if not patiently then with a degree of resignation. But it was an atmosphere in which the malcontent could quickly become the troublemaker. It started with small-scale disturbances—a half-hearted riot, petty arson, standoffs with local constables—but at Kinmel Park in March 1919, thousands of soldiers, tired of delays, bad food, no pay, and ineffectual officers, went on a rampage, burning buildings and looting canteens. Stan Sawell was in a part of the camp that hadn't yet been attacked. He and his fellow officers were awaiting dinner when their colonel decided that, under the circumstances, it wasn't a good idea to sound the usual bugle call for dinner. Stan was sent out to get to the bugler before he started playing, but as he sprinted across the compound, a well-thrown rock caught him on the back of the head and knocked him to the ground. He needed stitches to close the gash, but never got the third wound stripe that he felt he deserved.[9] Other soldiers were less fortunate than Stan. When the camp calmed down, five soldiers were dead—five men who had just wanted to go home. At Epsom in June, another black eye for Canada. After the police arrested two Canadian soldiers in a street brawl with local men, hundreds of their comrades descended on the police station and demanded their release. When they were refused, they attacked, pelting the building with bricks, rocks, chunks of wood, and pieces of iron railing. The Canadians left with their two liberated pals, but they left behind every constable wounded and one, himself a veteran, dying of a blow to the head.

The riots jolted military authorities. The movement of men was accelerated as much as possible, and by the late summer of 1919 almost all of the CEF was home. Canadian Corps commander Arthur Currie had argued that the men of the Corps should return in their units, and be welcomed by their home communities as units. Such celebrations would provide a fitting ending to a great national experience, and would give civilians a chance to celebrate their soldiers in a very public way. "The men would arrive in Canada happier and feel more contented and with discipline better maintained," military authorities believed, "if the Unit organization were adhered to until the last possible moment." It was a fine sentiment, but it didn't necessarily reflect the reality. Most of the battalions that had left Canada—including, from Wentworth County, all but the 19th Battalion—had been disbanded in Britain, so most communities no longer had a unit to welcome. Other units had changed dramatically, for the simple reason that Canada's largest province had provided the greatest number of reinforcements in the last year of the war. The 54th had gone overseas as the Kootenay Battalion, but came back as the 54th (Central Ontario) Battalion. The 102nd went into battle as the North British Columbians, but came out as the 102nd (Central Ontario) Battalion. And one has to wonder if rural Canadians would rather be welcomed by urban folk at big-city armouries, or by their own kith and kin closer to home.

Sailing lists regularly appeared in Canadian newspapers, and starting in early 1919, almost every issue of the *Review* listed the names of local soldiers who were on their way home. One of the last to get back was Wilf Langford, for reasons that he explained in a letter from Siberia:

> We we are all ready to return to our country as we feel we do not want to make the army our home, and it is a task of many impatient, or patient, years out here I will say.
>
> There are about 20,000 Allied soldiers in this country now. I understand the ones which came last, the Infantry, will go first, leaving us last as we were first here, and are the unit which has carried on the work according to the war plans. The boys get sick, shot, hurt and frozen, and we have to carry on no matter what comes or goes. I have been working in the Hospital wards all winter, but thinking I might need some outside life I am now on the Ambulance section, driving and repairing, and I sure see the country for miles around. It is the most natural and artificial fortified harbor in the world. Hills and valleys to no end, and roads like trails in the West, all

rough but good hard bottoms. Sometimes we find a nice smooth road which the Germans prisoners have built and are still doing so. They are quite contented since the Canadian and Americans have taken charge of them, and that peace is near at hand in their own country. I am pleased to know you are all having a good time, so many dances and parties I am sure it will be a treat after such along siege of confinement due to the flu. We will have it much easier when the Infantry go home. I don't know that I have much more I can say as news is scarce. I hope the contagious diseases let us down light, and that we may spend our summer months in dear old Canada.[10]

It would be May 1919 before Wilf Langford got back to Waterdown, and by then most of the other soldiers from Britain were on their way home to warm welcomes from family and public welcomes from the community, often at the roller rink. But once the banquets and galas were finished, East Flamborough's new veterans faced the challenge of what the government called re-establishment: becoming a civilian again. Some of them had been in uniform for over five years, with the army telling them what to do and when to do it, and providing their room and board into the bargain. Demobilization meant freedom, but it also meant having to find and keep a job. For years, labourers had been in short supply but by 1919 willing workers were thick on the ground, just as the economy was starting to slow down. And employers were happier to keep on the payroll the men who had worked for them throughout the war, rather than retrain ex-soldiers out of gratitude and patriotic duty. Coming back to a family farm or business usually meant a seamless transition, but recent immigrants, who could almost name their price in the pre-1914 labour shortage, often found that they weren't needed. A classified advertisement that appeared in the *Review* in 1922 was all too common: "Two returned men will do any kind of work by the hour or day. Apply to Harry Clark."[11]

The typical ex-soldier also had to get used to living a quieter life. War is hell, but it does offer excitement, travel, the belief that one was engaged in great events, and the comradeship whose bonds were forged in the harshest conditions. After such extremes, an eight-hour day spent sorting cheques in a bank might have seemed punishingly dull. We might assume that young men wanted nothing more than to get back to home and hearth, but the reality was more complicated and many veterans wrestled with emotions that were conflicting and apparently contradictory. Even before the war ended, one local soldier wrote to Will Reid a letter full of confusion and uncertainty: "I'm afraid this life has made a great change to me, being away two years last April, and goodness only knows for how much longer. I sometimes think I have nothing left now. I hear very rarely from home, and the boys never write me, except Gerald, he writes occasionally. I sometimes think I am a widower, and shall have to look after another wife to look after me in my old days ... I really don't know what I shall do after my discharge. I seem very unsettled these days. Am sorry to know so many poor boys have lost their lives in this war. Such is the price for such dirty work ... I put in some good times over here, Will. I am in no hurry to return home yet, things are too good over here, I can tell you."[12]

There was only so much that their families and friends could do to ease the transition. Homecoming parties were appreciated and council struck a Repatriation Committee "to look after the interests of returned soldiers," but nothing in the surviving village or township records suggests that it did very much. New veterans also came to rely on each other, for only another ex-soldier could really appreciate what they had been through, and were going through. A Waterdown and district branch of the Great War Veterans' Association, the country's biggest ex-soldier group, was established in February 1922, with Stan Sawell as the president.[13] For the first few years, it met in the drill shed—an appropriate setting given that the 129th had trained there in 1916.

But only a small proportion of local veterans opted to join a veterans' organization; most had nothing further to do with things military. Their lives would be punctuated not by inspections and battles, but by the things that young men's lives are supposed to be punctuated by—weddings, births, travels, employment. Reading the *Review* in those early postwar years, one sees life going on. Many of them apparently stepped back into their lives with barely a hiccup. They married locally, settled in and around East Flamborough, sent their children and grandchildren to school there, and died there—almost as if, having seen what they saw overseas, their attachment to the township was affirmed. So they remained fixtures in the community. When I was growing up in Waterdown, Wilf Langford filled my prescriptions and I used to read Stan Buchan's hydro meter. I went to school with Careys, Doughertys, Aldersons, Hornings, Cummings, and Binkleys, all with older relatives who had gone into uniform half a century before.

Evelyn Galloway and Edgar Richards married, after meeting overseas while she was a nurse and he a machine gunner. They were born just a few miles apart, but had to travel 3,700 miles to meet. Joe Eager returned to his wife Louise, with whom he had spent just a few weeks after he was commissioned into the CAMC, but their life together would be short. In 1923, Louise and her baby both died in childbirth. Grief-stricken, Joe changed the focus of his practice and became one of the area's most beloved and respected obstetricians. Stan Sawell met and married Elizabeth, the oldest of the Fleming girls from Valley Farm in Aldershot. A few years later, their youngest daughter, Isabell, married Harold Vance. Born in 1903, Harold had watched his older friends go off to war but had been too young to go himself.

The Mason brothers, Frank (the oldest) and Bert (younger by three years) came to Canada before the war with one of the British charitable organizations that brought in orphaned and destitute boys to give them a better life. Some of them got it, but not the Masons. Bert was bounced from farm to farm while Frank ended up with a family near Millgrove that treated him worse than an indentured servant. Not permitted to enter the house, he slept and ate his meals in the chicken coop; the rest of the time, he was kept at work in the fields. But Roland Cummins, on the farm across the road, had a soft spot for the slender boy with the beautiful singing voice. He could always use extra help, so he hired Frank away, moved him into a proper bedroom in their farmhouse, and made him a member of the large and loving Cummins family.

Home Children in Canada had a very high enlistment rate—were they thankful to the country that took them in, or desperate to escape a life of drudgery?—and the Mason boys joined the rush. Both enlisted in 1915; Bert eventually ended up with the 49th Battalion and Frank with the 19th. Frank spent a year at the front, the end of his war coming in November 1917 at Passchendaele, with a chunk of shrapnel in his right knee. It was the beginning of a medical nightmare that is detailed in the 276 pages of his personnel file. The wound got badly infected, and within a month the lower part of Frank's leg had to be amputated. There followed a dozen separate surgeries as doctors chased gangrene up his leg, each time cutting off bits of rotted flesh and bone in an effort to save at least part of the limb. But it was the combination of influenza, double pneumonia, and pleurisy that almost did Frank in. His life was saved only by a nurse at Toronto's Sunnybrook Hospital who set up a cot in the corner of his room so she could care for him constantly. Finally, he rallied and was well enough to go home to Millgrove. Doctors said he would be lucky to survive for five years.

Bert's war was a little less dramatic. He spent two years at the front, during which time he was treated for an infected hand and trench fever; his war ended when he was gassed in September 1918. While in England, Bert met and married a local girl; they had a daughter and after the war set out for Canada to start a new life together.

But the fortunes of the two brothers weren't quite what one might expect. Frank confounded the doctors and went back to farming. He later married a Cummins and, with a small inheritance, bought the very farm on which he had been so badly treated as a boy. The couple had three daughters, whom Frank adored, and he was a favourite in the Millgrove community. As he stood atop a ladder pruning his fruit trees, he would sing vaudeville favourites and army songs (Frank had loved the discipline and comradeship of army life). Neighbours swore they could hear his voice a concession away. He lived a long and happy life, his missing leg almost the only evidence of how much the war had taken from him. The only other hint came during rainstorms at night, which always got Frank out of bed. He would sit out on the veranda until the storm passed—he always said that the thunder reminded him so much of the guns that he couldn't sleep.

Bert came back with no obvious scars but the war's end brought him no peace. He drifted from farm to farm, turning to alcohol to soothe his restlessness. Frank used his inheritance to buy a farm; Bert drank his away. His war bride hated Canada and soon took their daughter back to England—as far as the family knows, he had no further contact with them. Bert came to rely on his brother for all sorts of things—even help applying for his military pension. Shortly after Frank died in 1977, Bert took a taxi from Millgrove to a funeral home in Waterdown, where he paid for a coffin and burial. Not long after, he was dead. The brothers are buried together in Millgrove cemetery. Years earlier, Frank had bought a plot close to his own for Bert. He wanted to know that, whenever he died, his brother would be buried with family.

It's easy to find out what the survivors did, but impossible to say what the dead might have done. Nevertheless, the township did its best to honour them. The armistice was just a month old when the *Review* announced that a Soldiers' Memorial Fund would be opened to "place in Waterdown something which will be a lasting memory to the Waterdown boys who fought in the great war of liberty."[14] By January, a men's committee of the Soldiers' Memorial had been struck to work with the ladies of the Patriotic League and in February a large group of ratepayers went to Township Council looking for support for the construction of a memorial hall as the township's commemorative centrepiece. East Flamborough and Waterdown councils both struck committees to work out the project's details.[15]

Everyone seemed to agree on the importance of a memorial, but opinion was divided on the form it should take. Opposition to the memorial hall idea crystallized around the deplorable state of the high school. The constraints of the war years had only hastened its slide into decrepitude and the first time it was inspected by the Ministry of Education after the war, the inspector was blunt: "[the high school] is situated on the upper floor of the Public School, and is reached by means of a stairway which is a veritable fire-trap ... The class room assigned to Form I is at the far end of the building, and can be reached only by passing through one of the other class rooms. The floors of Forms I and II are worn to a wretched condition. There is no private room for the use of the teachers. The class rooms ... are heated by wood stoves, one of which emits volumes of smoke into the room, and as there is no provision for ventilation except by means of the windows, the pupils are obliged to sit in this smoke-charged atmosphere all day long."[16] The verdict: the local school board would receive no further provincial grants until the problems were corrected. Elementary students could continue to use the lower floor until their new school (then under construction) was completed, but the upper floor would be closed and the high school students would have to receive their instruction elsewhere. For many locals, the idea of older students shuttling between various rented spaces in the village was intolerable. At a meeting in the roller rink, one critic observed that "everywhere they are putting up Memorial Halls" but what Waterdown really needed was a school. Not for the first time, he claimed to speak for the dead: "If those men could speak I feel satisfied they would tell us they would rather have their names perpetuated in a school where the children spend six hours a day five days a week learning the lessons needed to fit them for the years to come, than in a Hall to be used occasionally for recreation or amusement."[17] Local groups continued to support the idea, and continued to raise funds, but opponents got their chance when the village announced plans to issue $20,000 worth of debentures to pay for the hall—and, according to municipal law, all projected debenture issues had to go to a vote.

Nothing survives to tell us about the campaign that was waged, save a single editorial that appeared in the *Review* just before the vote. It is detailed enough, however, to tell us what issues were most concerning. First, on the question of ownership, it confirmed that ownership of the hall would rest in public hands. The Community League had bought the site on Dundas Street (the decrepit Bell House was soon to be torn down, before it fell on someone), but would deed it to the village as soon as the hall was built; council would operate the facility, so there was no chance of it becoming a private clubhouse for one group.[18] Second, there would be little, if any, long-term impact on the mill rate—in any rural community, a phrase that struck terror in the heart of any municipal politician. Because it would house the post office and one or two stores (as well as the council chambers, a public hall, and storage for Waterdown's fire equipment), the Memorial Hall would all but pay for itself. Finally, it was a matter of looking to the future. Short-sightedness had killed the combination public school and high school, and readers were urged not to let history repeat itself. The village needed a town hall because the current building "would be a disgrace to even a back woods, cross roads settlement ... Waterdown will probably never have a better or more economical opportunity of building a public hall than the present one."[19]

It is a curious editorial, less for what it says than what it doesn't say. There is hardly a mention of the war, or commemoration, or our honoured dead. There is nothing about memory, or of enshrining the valour of the fallen for future generations. It is all about practical matters—the hard-headed pragmatism of the rural mind. It would seem to confirm what opponents of utilitarian memorials like halls feared most: that they were shameless attempts to capitalize on public grief to erect something that people might otherwise decline to pay for. If that was the case, it worked—but only just. The by-law authorizing the debenture issue was carried by ninety-eight votes to sixty-seven. The strength of the opposition can be guessed by the *Review*'s comment that the victory was a "surprise to even a number of those who voted for it."[20]

Perhaps because of that opposition, the project languished and other communities in East Flamborough decided to erect their own memorials. Aldershot announced that it would build its own $15,000 memorial hall near Wabasso Park, complete with a gymnasium, recreation and reading rooms, and a hall for concerts and other entertainments. "Great enthusiasm prevails at the present time," observed the *Review*, "over the prospect of having some place where residents of that thickly settled farming section may meet for educational and social purposes, as well as for entertainment."[21] Millgrove unveiled its war memorial in October 1920, and Carlisle Methodist Church dedicated its war memorial gates in September 1921. And still the project for Waterdown's hall languished.

Finally, Reeve Smith announced that "the hall seems to be a dead letter at present."²² This left him with a problem. Shortly after the war, he had applied to the federal government for a war trophy, a captured weapon that could be put on display as a symbol of the victory. The government had announced that it would be bringing back to Canada hundreds of captured artillery pieces, to be given to communities to display as an affirmation of the defeat of the Hun—"tangible demonstrations of a great victory," as it was put. Smith's intention was to place it in front of the Memorial Hall, but in August 1920 he received word that the gun was on its way to Waterdown—now he had to find somewhere to put it. The village adopted the practice of many communities and had it hauled to the school, so that it could serve as a daily object lesson to students. Two primary students even wrote about the gun for the school essay contest:

> I was found in a very large iron mine. I was taken away to a smelting works. When I got there I was tumbled in a large pot. Then I was cooled off and found I was made into a cannon. I was sent out in the trenches and tried to fight as hard as I could for the Germans, but at last I was captured and sent over to France. Then I had to fight for the Canadians, which I did not like very much. When the war was over I was sent over to a little village called Waterdown, and there I was drawn down to the school yard behind a truck. They left me by a flag-pole. On Halloween I was moved down to the front of the school and there I told this story to the boys.

> One day some birds were resting on the cannon. It was telling of its adventures and I heard what it said. "One day I heard someone digging all around under me. I wondered what it was. Alas, I found what it was. They were digging me out of my home in the ground. Then they took me to a factory in Germany and they put me in a hot fire and melted me and made me into a cannon. War was on between Germany and Britain and they took me up to the front lines. I tried to do my duty for my country, and I saw many sad sights. I saw dead horses and men and guns blown to pieces. I surely was frightened when I was first taken up to the lines. I was not there long before

the war was over. One day they sent me to a little village called Waterdown, and placed me by the flag-pole in the school yard. The children pass me on their way to school. The women and men come to see me. And they think of the brave deeds that have been done. I have one friend and that is the flag-pole."[23]

The absence of any strident nationalism in the essays suggests that the children may not yet have taken the appropriate moral lessons from the gun, but it certainly became a popular climber for generations of children. I've seen only one image of the gun from that time—a small, fuzzy snapshot of a well-dressed older man standing beside it. Nearly a century later, the gun is still there, although it has lost its wheels, axle, blast shield, trailing arms—everything, in fact, except the barrel, which sits on a cement plinth behind the old school. Most people in the village have no idea what it is, or why it was put there with such fanfare in 1920. It hardly looks now like a tangible demonstration of anything—except perhaps neglect.

The gun was only one of the many newcomers to the township by 1920—speed-limit signs and a car dealership; a new high school at the west end of the village; a new elementary school, named for Mary Hopkins, one of the district's first teachers, on Waterdown's fairgrounds; churches had new

ministers to replace the ones who had gone to war and never returned. The Toronto-Hamilton Highway, opened in 1917 and cutting right through Aldershot, was starting to see more traffic. The 1921 census would show that the township's population hadn't grown by much since 1911, but there seemed to be more of everything—more trains, more trucks, more businesses, more building. As the restraints of the war years were relaxed, having more was itself a novelty.

But one thing was all too familiar to the township: fire. In March 1917, two businesses on Main Street had been destroyed in a midnight fire; the post office and a grocery store were also aflame at one point, but the firemen battled to save them—and won. In September 1918, another fire struck the heart of Waterdown. Just as in 1915, this one started in the back of a drug store on the south side of Dundas Street. The cause was never discovered but a combination of volatile pharmaceuticals and dodgy wiring probably had something to do with it. Having lost the library, the post office, and a general store two years earlier, the locals weren't about to stand idly by. As the volunteer firemen worked at the back of the store, a small army of men and women were carefully carrying the stock out the front and depositing it in nearby buildings. And when the house next door looked like it too might be in danger, they emptied it of everything portable too—so eager were friends and neighbours to help that they started to get in the way of the firefighting operation. But that wasn't the real lesson as far as the *Review* was concerned. It used the situation as the opportunity to call on council to buy more pumpers and chemical engines, and to hope that "the days of the frame fire traps are numbered."[24]

They weren't. In 1922, in the early afternoon of a warm May day, a worker was tending the boiler at Davies' heading mill. All around him were piles of fine, excelsior-type sawdust thrown off by the shingle saw that cut the headings. The piles stretched almost to the roller rink on the next lot, and every once in a while the spring breeze picked up a few wispy shavings and sent them into the air. The next gust came just as the worker was opening the furnace to tend the fire, and the errant wind puffed a cluster of embers out onto the piles of sawdust. Two nearby workers immediately grabbed a couple

Facing page: Waterdown's war trophy, after it had been installed on the school grounds. Photographer unknown. (Author's collection)

of boards and tried to beat out the smoldering shavings, as they had done so often in the past, but in minutes the fire had got ahead of them. One of the workers dashed off to alert the volunteer fire department, returning with an armful of pails to bring water from the creek that ran through the end of the property. He was followed by the chemical pumper that council had bought after the 1915 fire, and by the venerable old hand pumper, which had been around as long as anyone could remember. This would be its last day. The firemen wheeled it into the creek, dropped the intake hose into the water, and began pumping but before they could generate much of a stream, the fire had jumped to nearby piles of lumber and stacks of barrels. The volunteers beat a hasty retreat and the hand pumper was left to burn in the creek.

By now, the roller rink was fully engulfed and the flames were ready to jump to nearby buildings. Hampered by a lack of water, the locals realized that the fire was already beyond their resources and put in a call to Hamilton. Until the professionals arrived, the villagers could only resort to emptying buildings that seemed to be at risk. But even that was an imperfect science. One family moved their furnishings and possessions three times before they got them out of range of the fire. Dad Alton emptied his billiard parlour, barbershop, and garage but didn't move it far enough and everything burned. When the Bell Telephone building was threatened, strong arms removed the switchboard; it was saved as the building was consumed, but Waterdown was now cut off from the outside world. On the fire's western fringes, flames leapt across Main Street South to destroy a general store; only the Hamilton fire-fighters, reinforced by pumpers from half a dozen local industries, kept it from jumping Dundas Street and razing the Kirk Hotel. Further south, it jumped a sixty-eight-foot gap and latched onto the Springer house; within a few minutes, it too was a mass of flames.

The flames moved inexorably outwards, consuming building after building and relentlessly pushing back the ring of villagers who had already spent hours trying to move furniture and stock to safety. But by this time, the fire-fighters had punched a hole in the small dam on McGregor's property and let the water flow into a pond behind the Kirk Hotel. Now with a good supply of water, they caught another break when the wind direction changed, blowing the fire back on itself. By dinner time they finally had the upper hand. An hour later, there were just a few smoldering hot spots left.

Late that afternoon, an unknown photographer climbed to the roof of the Kirk and captured the devastation. The scene looked disturbingly like the ruined villages that the men of the Canadian Corps had encountered during the Hundred Days—a haze of smoke clinging to the ground, jagged stands of brick wall leaning uncertainly against piles of rubble, people walking around, perhaps dazed by the destruction of what they knew so well. An entire block had been razed, over a dozen homes and businesses. Two of the village's general stores were gone, along with a butcher shop, a grocery, and Dad Alton's premises. McGregor's Hall was burned out, and the roller rink had been reduced to a pile of smoking timbers. On so many occasions during the war, the village had come together in one of those buildings—to raise money, to recruit volunteers, to bid the soldiers farewell or to welcome them home. And now they were gone.

In the background of one of the photos taken from the Kirk that day, it is just possible to make out the foundations of a new building: the Memorial Hall. Since Reeve Smith had declared the hall a "dead letter" two years earlier, work had gone ahead, culminating in the last fundraiser In January 1923, a gala ceremony was held to dedicate the new hall and unveil the large bronze plaque that accompanied it.[25] It is a curious artifact, like so many local memorial plaques, full of errors and mysteries. Elmer Baker is listed twice, once under his real name and once as Roy Burnett, the name under which he enlisted. Tom Flintoft's name is spelled incorrectly, and Achilles Hearn's name is almost unrecognizably rendered as Achilis Herron. Lots of names are missing and a handful can't be identified. It is typically classless (no ranks are given, nor is there any distinction between officer and ranker), although the women are listed separately from the men—at the end.

Mountsberg has its own memorial, as do Carlisle, Millgrove, and Freelton. Most of the township's churches have memorials of some sort, from plaques to gates. But those memorials, either individually or taken together, can't really convey the impact of the war on a rural township like East Flamborough. The statistics say that about 8 per cent of its population served in uniform and about 1 per cent died—or, if you prefer raw numbers, 210 out of 2,400 served and 28 died. But how much do those numbers actually reveal? The scholarly world has come up with an indicator called the impact factor to determine how influential any given piece of research might be. But is there an algorithm that can convey the emotional impact of East Flamborough's enlistments and deaths? Surely not, and the very idea seems repugnant. If losing your husband is worth twenty points, how about losing your son or your father? Is an older brother worth the same as a younger brother? Is a brother-in-law worth anything at all? Perhaps separation from your family for four years counts as six points—does being away for two years count as three points? After the war, Sam Hughes argued that every community in Canada should be given the same war memorial, although in different sizes—the more people you lost, the bigger your cenotaph. And, presumably, the bigger your cenotaph, the more you had suffered. No one listened to Sam's attempt to create a hierarchy of grief in 1919, and trying to quantify the psychological impact of loss makes no more sense today.

I was still flailing away at this when I came across a brief newspaper article in the *Review* about the 1920 funeral of William McMonies, my great-great-uncle.[26] It reported that the pallbearers were six of his nephews: Thomas Allen, William G. Horning, Ollie Horning, W. A. Ryckman, Watson Hamilton, and Blake Binkley. A quick count revealed seventeen men and women with those surnames on East Flamborough's service roll. A little more hunting, and the list of locals who were related to William McMonies grew, and continued to grow. In the end, I determined that about two-thirds of East Flamborough's soldiers were related somehow, by blood or by marriage, to William McMonies, and therefore to each other.

That was a revelation to me, but it wouldn't have been to the people of East Flamborough a century ago. Kinship networks were important to them, and they regularly expressed them in weddings, anniversary parties, funerals, and church picnics. With that, the impact of the First World War on rural Canada finally hits home. It wasn't just the township that went to war in 1914, but a few large extended families. The situation was fundamentally different in Canadian cities. Every city started out as a village settled by people who might be tied together by blood, marriage, or birthplace but growth and urbanization brought anonymity. As cities drew people from across the county and around the world, the interconnectedness of the original village was replaced by alienation. Not that a city dweller was bereft of friends and relatives, but most of the people to be encountered on a daily basis were strangers.

For better or for worse, strangers were rare in a rural community, even one as close to a big city as Waterdown. Rural society was close-knit, with a combination of large families and a tendency to marry locally creating a high degree of interconnectedness, so that any loss rippled through a dozen households or more. I have no way to prove it but I would guess that when Roy Mount was killed in action in May 1917, his death reverberated more strongly in East Flamborough, where he had been born and raised and where his family still lived, than in Hamilton, where he had only recently moved to join the army of wage labourers crowding the city's boarding houses. Only with this realization do I appreciate that the war cut deeply into rural Canada, more deeply even than the raw numbers would suggest. Its memory, grey and opaque like a rain cloud, would hang over that generation, those streets, those homes, those schools, those churches, obscuring what came before—lives that had been cut short, places that once rang with laughter, futures that would never be.

Envoi – Clare

CLARE LAKING PAUSES after another funny story and wheezes as he catches his breath. His pauses have become longer, his stories not quite so animated. I assume he must be getting tired after nearly two hours of reminiscing, but then I see him steal a glance at his watch. It's getting close to dinner time and, like most people his age, Clare Laking values routine. He's far too polite to say anything, but it's time for me to leave. I start to gather up the papers he is loaning me, and ask him if he's been back to his old stomping grounds lately. He pauses before answering, still studying me with his sharp eyes.[1]

"No," he shakes his head, one of the few times that a hint of sadness shadowed his face. "It's not the same place anymore." He tells me that the Laking farm is long gone, the fields from which he plucked rocks now part of the Mountsberg Conservation Area. School Section #2, where he and his pals caught mice to frighten the girls, is now a private home. The train that he took from his farm through East Flamborough to Hamilton stopped running decades ago, and the stations disappeared one by one. Most were torn down after sitting empty for years. The Vance house, or Waterdown South station, fell to an arsonist in the 1960s. Only one of the township's railway stations still stands, now used as the office of a quarrying operation.

Will Reid took no more photographs after the First World War, although he lived another thirty-five years. Perhaps there were practical reasons for giving up his hobby, but I think the real reason was emotional. Will was deeply in love with the old world of horse-drawn buggies, dirt roads, clapboard houses, and gentle breezes on the millpond; he wasn't interested in automobiles, electricity, radio, or progress. I suspect he believed that his world, the world he had photographed so sensitively and with such empathy, had passed. He was not a modern man; the new age ushered in by the war had no charm for him. So away went his camera and photographic plates.

Even the township of East Flamborough itself no longer exists. In successive reorganizations of the area's municipal government it has been many things—the Regional Municipality of Hamilton-Wentworth, the Town of Flamborough, and now the City of Hamilton. Waterdown is now a small downtown amidst ever-expanding suburban sprawl. A few of the old buildings are recognizable. The Kirk Hotel and the American Hotel are still serving the hungry and the thirsty, albeit under different names, and the Memorial Hall remains on Dundas Street, although the symmetry of the original design has been ruined by the addition of a glass-and-steel elevator lobby. The old drill shed was taken down in 1928—a local builder paid the Department of Militia and Defence $100 for the right to cart away whatever good lumber he could scavenge from it.[2] Clunes still stands, but the property has been redeveloped into townhouses; elsewhere in the village, pre-1914 houses share streetscapes with modern split-levels. Aldershot, long ago hived off to become part of the City of Burlington, is even more transformed, the traces of the Generation of 1914 even more difficult to find. Only in the villages on the periphery—Freelton, Millgrove, Mountsberg—can one easily imagine what life was like a century ago. Mountsberg had greeted the twentieth century full of optimism, a tiny hamlet that was bullish about a bigger and better future. But the war had knocked the wind out of the village. Its schoolteacher and its clergyman went away in uniform, never to return. The sons of its founding families dead and disabled, it had no more will to dream big dreams. Mountsberg is now a mere shadow of what it once hoped to be.

And now, Clare Laking too is gone. He died in 2005, one of the very last of the more than 600,000 Canadians who served in the military during the First World War. After years of thinking about the profound changes that the Great War brought to Canada, and to the Generation of 1914, I was glad that I hadn't passed up the opportunity to ask Clare how the war had changed him. This time, he had answered quickly.

"I've lived with that war for most of my life. How did it change me? I know what I am now, but what was I before the war? I'm not sure I can say. All I know is, that war is part of me."

As it was for Clare, so it is for the old East Flamborough, and for Canada. The Great War is part of what we are, even if we can't say precisely how.

NOTES

ABBREVIATIONS USED:

CPC Colin Pomfret Collection, Millgrove, ON
FAHS Flamborough Archives and Heritage Society
JFVC Jonathan F. Vance Collection, London, ON
LAC Library and Archives Canada
LLSC Ley and Lois Smith War, Memory and Popular Culture Research Collection,
University of Western Ontario

INTRODUCTION

1 Interview with Clarence Laking, Downsview, Ontario, 17 July 2001.

2 Arthur Marwick, *The Deluge: British Society and the First World War* (London: The Bodley Head, 1965).

3 Gillian Tindall, *The Fields Beneath: The History of One London Village* (London: Temple Smith, 1977), 18.

CHAPTER 1

1 LAC: RG46 CII-1, vol. 1650, f. 24806, Hugh Drummond, reeve of East Flamborough, to Board of Railway Commissioners, 20 November 1924.

2 Quoted in *Waterdown and East Flamborough, 1867–1967* (Waterdown East Flamborough Centennial Committee, 1967), 33.

3 Quoted in Patricia and Maurice Green, Sylvia and Robert Wray, ... *and they came to East Flamborough: A Celebration of East Flamborough Township's pre-Confederation Heritage* (Waterdown-East Flamborough Heritage Society, 1997), 8.

4 J. H. C. Dempsey, "The Cultivation of our Native Orchids," *Ottawa Naturalist*, March 1906, 228.

5 Kirwan Martin, "The Neutral Nation," *Papers and Records of the Wentworth Historical Society*, vol. 6 (Hamilton: Griffin & Richmond Co., 1915), 25–8; *Pen and Pencil Sketches of Wentworth Landmarks: A Series of Articles Descriptive of Quaint Places and Interesting Localities in the Surrounding County* (Hamilton: Spectator Printing Co., 1897), esp. 74–91.

6 "Exploration of the Great Lakes, 1669–1670 by Dollier de Casson and de Bréhant de Galinée," *Ontario Historical Society Papers and Records*, vol. 4 (1903), 41.

7 T. Roy Woodhouse, "La Salle's Arrival In Burlington Bay in 1669," *Wentworth Bygones, from the Papers and Records of the Head-of-the-Lake Historical Society*, vol. 8 (1969): 2–5.

8 William J. Eccles, "René-Robert Cavelier de La Salle," *Canadian Encyclopedia*.

9 Mabel Burkholder and T. Roy Woodhouse, "Crown Patentees of East Flamborough Township," *Wentworth Bygones: Head-of-the-Lake Historical Society*, vol. 9 (1971), 67–70.

10 *Illustrated Historical Atlas of the County of Wentworth, Ont.* (Toronto: Page & Smith, 1875), 23.

11 George Douglas Griffin, "Historical Recollections of Waterdown, 1806 to 1860," *Transactions of the Wentworth Historical Society*, vol. 2 (1899), 55–61; Justus A Griffin, "Waterdown and Some of Its Early Settlers," F. L. Davis, ed., *Souvenir Book and Programme for Military Encampment Given by the Ladies' Committee of the Wentworth Historical Society, November, 1885* (Hamilton, 1895), 21–8.

12 Lieutenant-Colonel E. A. Cruickshank, *The Origin and Official History of the Thirteenth Battalion of Infantry, and a Description of the Work of the Early Militia of the Niagara Peninsula in the War of 1812 and the Rebellion of 1837* (Hamilton: E. L. Ruddy, 1899); LAC: MG13 WO13, VOL. 3716-B-3194, Muster Roll of Waterdown Guard, 17 December 1837, under command of Lieutenant Henry Young.

13 *Waterdown Review*, 20 June 1918, 3.

14 LAC: RG24 CIA, vol. 6242, f. AHQ-14-315-1, indenture for land to build drill shed, 28 August 1867; JFVC: "Waterdown, written by Agnes Louisa [McMonies] Middleton some few years before she died in 1966."

15 *Evening Times* (Hamilton), 23 November 1867, 3.

16 *Evening Times* (Hamilton), 26 February 1863, 3.

17 FAHS: Minutes, Waterdown Village Council, 8 September 1913.

18 *Globe* (Toronto), 8 January 1914, 2.

19 FAHS: Minutes, Waterdown Village Council, 13 October 1913.

20 *Bulletin* (Edmonton), 28 February 1910, 6.

21 Quoted in Brandon Mendonca, "Agnes Macphail and the Politics of Social Feminism, 1921–1939" (MA cognate paper, University of Western Ontario, 2015), 26.

22 *St. Louis Post-Despatch*, 5 May 1906, 6.

23 *Toronto Daily Star*, 4 October 1909, 6.

24 *Globe* (Toronto), 4 February 1885, 2.

25 Charles A. Millar, "Methods and Manufacture of Sewer Pipe in Canada," *Journal of the American Ceramic Society* 8/7 (July 1925): 452–6.

26 LAC: RG76 IA, vol. 412, f. 595173, reel C-10300, F. A. Whitley, Millgrove, to W. D. Scott, Immigration Branch, Ottawa, 4 February 1908.

27 LAC: RG76 IA, vol. 412, f. 595173, reel C-10300, W. D. Scott to George F. Griffin, Millgrove, n.d.

28 LAC: RG76 IA, vol. 412, f. 595173, reel C-10300, form from George Alderson, Carlisle, 9 March 1908.

29 LAC: RG76 IA, vol. 412, f. 595173, reel C-10300, Walter T. Evans, Hamilton, to L. M. Fortier, Immigration Branch, 10 July 1911; reply, 13 July 1911.

30 Canada, Dominion Bureau of Statistics, *Census of Canada, 1911* (Ottawa: King's Printer, 1911), table 1, no. 135 Wentworth, 94.

31 *Daily Colonist* (Victoria), 16 March 1895, 1.

32 FAHS: Minutes, Waterdown Village Council, 10 November 1913.

33 *Hamilton Spectator*, 28 March 1914.

34 Ontario, Department of Education, *Report of the Department of Education*, 1914, 722–3; "Waterdown Mechanics' Institute," *Papers and Records of the Wentworth Historical Society*, vol. 10 (Hamilton: Griffin & Richmond Co., 1922), 141–6.

35 Burlington Public Library: *Aldershot Tweedsmuir History* (Aldershot: Women's Institute, n.d.), vol. 2, 61; "Come Up to Waterdown and be Happy" (advertising handbill), n.d.

CHAPTER 2

1 LAC: RG24 CIA, vol. 6242, f. AHQ-14-315-1, G. C. Wilson, MP, to Sir Sam Hughes, 11 June 1914; GOC 2nd Division to Militia Council, 15 July 1914.

2 Steven E. Sawell, ed., *Into the Cauldron: Experiences of a CEF Infantry Officer During the Great War* (2009), 2.

3 *Hamilton Spectator*, 31 July 1914, 12.

4 *Hamilton Spectator*, 22 August 1914, 17.

5 *Hamilton Spectator*, 1 August 1914, 1.

6 *Hamilton Spectator*, 3 August 1914, 1, 7.

7 *Hamilton Spectator*, 4 August 1914, 1.

8 T. Melville Bailey, *Hamilton: Chronicle of a City* (Windsor: Windsor Publications, 1983), 87.

9 PC 2067, 6 August 1914, in A. F. Duguid, *Official History of the Canadian Forces in the Great War, 1914–1919*, vol. I, pt. 2 (Ottawa: King's Printer, 1938), 37.

10 Night telegram, 6 August 1914, in Duguid, *Official History of the Canadian Forces in the Great War*, vol. I, pt. 2, 37.

11 *Hamilton Spectator*, 7 August 1914, 14.

12 *Hamilton Spectator*, 22 August 1914, 1.

13 G. M. Pirie to the editor, *Dundas Star*, 30 August 1914.

14 LLSC: Ross Medland, 3rd Battalion, to Mrs John Crake, Toronto, 18 September 1914.

15 G. M. Pirie to the editor, *Dundas Star*, 14 September 1914.

16 LLSC, L.P. Spence, 15th Battalion, to A.E. Spence, Preston, 9 September 1914.

17 G. M. Pirie to the editor, *Dundas Star*, 14 September 1914.

18 *Hamilton Spectator*, 16 October 1914, 15.

19 *Hamilton Spectator*, 11 November 1914, 9.

20 LLSC: George Cargill, 3rd Battalion, to Frank, 3 November 1914.

21 *Hamilton Spectator*, 14 November 1914, 14.

22 *Hamilton Spectator*, 16 November 1914, 11; 18 November 1914, 8; 15 December 1914, 13.

23 Mary F. Gaudet, ed., *From a Stretcher Handle: The World War I Journal and Poems of Pte. Frank Walker* (Charlottetown: Institute of Island Studies, University of Prince Edward Island, 2000), 4 December 1914, 43.

24 *Hamilton Spectator*, 7 October 1914, 14; 8 October 1914, 10.

25 *Hamilton Spectator*, 6 October 1914, 12.

26 *Hamilton Spectator*, 11 November 1914, 9.

27 *Hamilton Spectator*, 31 October 1914, 7.

28 *Hamilton Spectator*, 26 September 1914, 14.

29 *Hamilton Spectator*, 17 October 1914, 9.

30 *Waterdown Review*, 27 February 1919, 2.

31 Minutes of Puslinch Township Council meeting, 21 September 1914, http://www.clarksoftomfad.ca/PuslinchTownshipCouncilMinutes1913to1919.htm.

32 June R. Andrews, *Nassagaweya: A History of Campbellville and Surrounding Area, Its Land and People* (Campbellville Historical Society, 1982), 291.

33 *Hamilton Spectator*, 13 October 1914, 6.

34 FAHS: Minutes of the Waterdown Women's Institute meeting, 2 September 1914; 7 October 1914.

35 FAHS: Minutes of the Waterdown Women's Institute meeting, 4 November 1914.

36 LAC: RG24 C1a, vol. 6242, f. AHQ-14-315-1, memo, 22 August 1914.

37 *Hamilton Spectator*, 20 October 1914, 7; 23 October 1914, 13.

38 *Hamilton Spectator*, 24 September 1914, 9.

39 *Hamilton Spectator*, 6 November 1914, 1.

40 *Hamilton Spectator*, 18 November 1914, 8.

41 Grace Church, Waterdown: Minutes of Anglican Young People's Association meetings, 3 December and 17 December 1914.

42 *Hamilton Spectator*, 12 December 1914, 17.

43 LAC: Militia and Defence Records, RG9 III-D-3, vol. 4911, f. 346, reel T-10703, War Diary, Princess Patricia's Canadian Light Infantry, 24 December 1914.

CHAPTER 3

1 *Hamilton Spectator*, 25 January 1915, 1.

2 Mary F. Gaudet, ed., *From a Stretcher Handle: The World War I Journal and Poems of Pte. Frank Walker* (Charlottetown: Institute of Island Studies, University of Prince Edward Island, 2000), 1 January 1915, 49.

3 Tom Alger to mother, 10 March 1915, http://www.lornesmuseum.ca/page10/page13/page13.html.

4 LAC: Militia and Defence Records, RG9 III-D-3, vol. 4915, f. 59, reel T-10707, War Diary, 4th Battalion, 22 February 1915.

5 LAC: Militia and Defence Records, RG9 III-D-3, vol. 4915, f. 59, reel T-10707, War Diary, 4th Battalion, 1 April 1915.

6 LAC: RG150, accession 1992-93/166, box 3154A, f. 51, service record of #645 T. Flintoft.

7 William Boyd, *With a Field Ambulance at Ypres, Being Letters Written March 7 – August 15, 1915* (Toronto: Musson, 1916), 49–50.

8 A. F. Duguid, *Official History of the Canadian Forces in the Great War, 1914–1919*, vol. I, pt. 2 (Ottawa: King's Printer, 1938), 238.

9 LAC: RG150, accession 1992-93/166, box 6934, f. 314, service record of #29474 M. MacKay.

10 LAC: RG150, accession 1992-93/166, box 3551, f. 342, service record of #11073 W. Gillies.

11 LAC: RG150, accession 1992-93/166, box 4614, f. 11, service record of #10914 W. Humphreys.

12 Richard Hunt to mother, 1 May 1915, *Hamilton Times*, 25 May 1915.

13 Gaudet, *From a Stretcher Handle*, 67.

14 LAC: Militia and Defence Records, RG9 III-D-3, vol. 5027, f. 824, reel T-10914, Lieut.-Col. W. L. Watt, "Field Ambulance Impressions" appended to War Diary, 3rd Field Ambulance, April 1915.

15 LLSC: *Life for Ever and Ever, Sermon by the Lord Bishop of London at the Canadian Memorial Service, St Paul's Cathedral, May 10th, 1915*.

16 JFVC: program, Waterdown Choral Society Grand Patriotic Concert, Wednesday, April 28th, 1915 at 8.15.

17 *Globe*, 1 January 1915, 8; FAHS: Minutes of Waterdown Village Council meeting, 11 October 1915.

18 *Hamilton Spectator*, 23 January 1915, 16.

19 FAHS: Minutes of Waterdown Women's Institute meeting, 7 April 1915.

20 FAHS: Minutes of Anglican Young People's Association meeting, 7 January 1915.

21 *Hamilton Spectator*, 5 January 1915, 4.

22 *Hamilton Spectator*, 14 January 1915, 5.

23 *Canadian Champion*, 27 May 1915, 3.

24 FAHS: Minutes of Waterdown Village Council meetings, 14 June 1915; 12 July 1915.

25 *Canadian Champion*, 15 July 1915, 3; *Hamilton Spectator*, 14 July 1915, 16.

26 LAC: RG150, accession 1992-93/166, box 397, f. 1, service record of J. Ballantine.

27 All of the John Filman correspondence is held in the Joseph Brant Museum, Burlington, Ontario.

28 Filman is referring to the British-issue Lee-Enfield rifle.

29 LAC: RG24 vol. 1385, f. HQ 593-6-1-129, Militia Council to OC, 2nd Division, 12 November 1915.

30 LAC: RG24 vol. 4381, f. 34-7-99, Knowles to AAG, 2nd Division, 6 December 1915; reply, 9 December 1915.

31 LAC: RG24 vol. 4381, f. 34-7-99, Knowles to ADS&T, 2nd Division, 29 November 1915; reply, 9 December 1915.

32 LAC: RG24 vol. 4381, f. 34-7-99, Knowles to AAG, 2nd Division, 10 December 1915; reply, 11 December 1915.

33 *Hamilton Spectator*, 18 December 1915, 47.

34 *Hamilton Spectator*, 18 December 1915, 37; 17 January 1916, 13.

35 *Hamilton Spectator*, 18 December 1915, 1, 47; 21 December 1915, 1.

36 *Hamilton Spectator*, 20 December 1915, 11.

37 *Hamilton Spectator*, 21 December 1915, 14.

38 *Hamilton Spectator*, 24 December 1915, 8; 24 December 1915, 15.

CHAPTER 4

1 Steven E. Sawell, ed., *Into the Cauldron: Experiences of a CEF Infantry Officer During the Great War* (2009), 4.

2 *Hamilton Spectator,* 5 February 1916, 16; 2 February 1916, 15.

3 *Dundas Star,* 15 June 1916.

4 *Hamilton Spectator,* 18 January 1916, 15.

5 *Hamilton Spectator,* 31 January 1916, 12.

6 *Hamilton Spectator,* 7 February 1916, 12.

7 *Hamilton Spectator,* 7 February 1916, 12.

8 *Hamilton Spectator,* 8 January 1916, 5.

9 *Hamilton Spectator,* 7 February 1916, 7.

10 *Globe* (Toronto), 19 August 1916, 15.

11 LAC: RG24 vol. 4381, f34-7-99, Knowles to AAG, 2nd Division, 10 January 1916; reply 13 January 1916.

12 LAC: RG24 vol. 4381, f. 34-7-99, "Appeal from J. J. Grafton to the Citizens of Wentworth," n.d.

13 *Hamilton Spectator,* 1 February 1916.

14 LAC: RG24 vol. 4381, f. 34-7-99, AAG to Grafton, 4 April 1916.

15 LAC: R. L. Borden Papers, MG26H vol. 29, reel C4213, pp16007–16009, George Church to Borden, 11 February 1916.

16 *Globe,* 17 August 1916, 2.

17 *London Free Press,* 9 June 1916.

18 Grace Church, Waterdown: Minutes of the Grace Church Vestry meeting, 25 April 1916.

19 *Hamilton Spectator,* 7 February 1916, 14.

20 JFVC: Testimonial to Maurice Scott, Flamboro Centre, 27 April 1916.

21 Canadian Letters and Images Project: Earl Johns to Mrs Henry Johns, Elimville, ON, 11 July 1916.

22 Canadian Letters and Images Project: Earl Johns to Mrs Henry Johns, Elimville, ON, 13 July 1916.

23 William E. Chajkowsky, *The History of Camp Borden, 1916–1918: Land of Sand, Sin and Sorrow* (Station Press, 1983).

24 Canadian Letters and Images Project: Leslie Scherer to Cath, August 1916.

25 *Globe*, 8 January 1917, 9.

26 LAC: RG150, accession 1992-93/166, box 1709, f. 3, service record of #240388 E. L. Church.

27 LAC: RG150, accession 1992-93/166, box 2194, f. 12, service record of #757510 T. L. Crysler.

28 LAC: RG150, accession 1992-93/166, box 4632, f. 32, service record of #240115 J. Hunter.

29 LAC: RG150, accession 1992-93/166, box 2900, f. 25, service record of #784299 W. Embleton.

30 LAC: RG150, accession 1992-93/166, box 2252, f. 24, service record of #784519 T. A. Cutts.

31 LAC: RG150, accession 1992-93/166, box 865, f. 2, service record of #784575 C. Bomford.

32 LAC: RG150, accession 1992-93/166, box 1769, f. 16, service record of #784178 W. G. Clark.

33 LAC: RG150, accession 1992-93/166, box 2904, f. 55, service record of #784381 J. Emery.

34 LAC: RG9 IIBII, vol. 6, f. 129th Bn After Orders, list of soldiers SOS as deserters.

35 LAC: RG150, accession 1992-93/166, box 962, f. 43, service record of #784572 P. H. Bowman.

36 *Globe*, 28 November 1916, 1.

37 *Globe*, 10 August 1916, 5.

38 LAC: RG9 IIB5, vol. 6, f. 120th-129th Bns CEF, Report of the Annual Inspection, 1916, of the 129th Overseas Battalion, C.E.F., 25 July 1916.

39 *Dundas Star*, 11 August 1916.

40 *Globe*, 19 August 1916, 4.

41 Steven E. Sawell, ed., *Into the Cauldron: Experiences of a CEF Infantry Officer During the Great War* (2009), 10.

42 Cyril Falls, "Byng, Julian Hedworth George, Viscount Byng of Vimy (1862–1935)," *Dictionary of National Biography*.

43 Quoted in Ralph Hodder-Williams, *Princess Patricia's Canadian Light Infantry, 1914–1919* (Toronto: Hodder & Stoughton, 1923), vol. 1, 112.

44 Quoted in Stephen K. Newman, *With the Patricia's in Flanders, 1914–1918* (Saanichton: Bellewaerde House Publishing, 2000), 90.

45 LAC: Militia and Defence Records, MG9 III-D-3, vol. 4914, f. 356, reel T-10706, War Diary, 3rd Battalion, 12 June 1916.

46 Sir James E. Edmonds, *History of the Great War Based on Official Documents: Military Operations, France and Belgium, 1916*, vol. 1 (London: Macmillan and Co., 1932), 241

47 LAC: Militia and Defence Records, MG9 III-D-3, vol. 4930, f. 410, reel T-10731, War Diary, 21st Battalion, 15 September 1916.

48 LAC: Militia and Defence Records, MG9 III-D-3, vol. 4942, f. 445, reel T-10748, War Diary, 54th Battalion, 18 November 1916.

49 LAC: RG150, accession 1992-93/166, box 4360, f. 39, service record of #443595 H. W. Hunter.

50 Cyril Falls, *History of the Great War Based on Official Documents: Military Operations, France and Belgium, 1917*, vol. 1 (London: Macmillan and Co., 1940), 65.

51 LAC: RG150, accession 1992-93/166, box 4493, f. 39, service record of #406729 M. M. Hopkinson.

52 LAC: RG150, accession 1992-93/166, box 64, f. 10, service record of #141367 J. Akam.

53 LAC: RG150, accession 1992-93/166, box 4698, f. 35, service record of G. A. Inksetter.

54 LAC: RG150, accession 1992-93/166, box 4264, f. 20, service record of #142227 C. Hendry.

55 Joseph Brant Museum: J. Filman, A Surgical Ward, No 4 General Hospital, 28 September 1916.

56 Joseph Brant Museum: J. Filman, A Surgical Ward, No 4 General Hospital, n.d.

57 LAC: RG150, accession 1992-93/166, box 3081, f. 20, service record of #406713 J. W. Filman.

58 Sawell, *Into the Cauldron*, 18.

59 Sawell to Velma Sawell, 28 September 1916, in Sawell, *Into the Cauldron*, 19.

60   Sawell, *Into the Cauldron*, 23.

61   LAC: RG150, accession 1992-93/166, box 8738, f. 18, service record of #174673 W. Scott.

62   LAC: RG 150 ser. 8, f. 649-S-14387, court martial of #174673 W. Scott, 28 August 1916.

63   *Dundas Star*, 28 September 1916, 1.

64   *Dundas Star*, 28 September 1916, 1.

65   *Dundas Star*, 19 October 1916, 1.

66   *Dundas Star*, 30 November 1916, 1.

67   For the transactions, see LAC: RG9 IIIA1 ser. 8, vol. 49, f. 8-5-117; and RG 24, vol. 1545, f. HQ683-199-6, Report on 129th Battalion, 7 August 1920.

68   LAC: RG150, vol. 98, f. 129th Canadian Bn, Daily Orders. Part II.

69   LAC: RG24, vol. 1575, f. HQ683-199-2, GOC Military District #2 to Militia Council, 16 February 1917.

70   LAC: RG24 vol. 4381, f. 34-7-99, A. A. Smith to Knowles, 23 August 1916.

71   LAC: RG24, vol. 1575, f. HQ683-199-2, Knowles to Paymaster, Military District #2, 28 November 1916; Knowles to Department of Militia and Defence, 29 May 1917.

72   LAC: RG150, accession 1992-93/166, box 947, f. 30, service record of #784294 W. H. A. Bowden.

73   LAC: RG150, accession 1992-93/166, box 4614, f. 1, service record of #406732 T. Humphreys.

74   LAC: RG150, accession 1992-93/166, box 3141, f. 16, service record of #1102 W. Fleming.

75   JFVC: William Fleming papers.

76   LAC: Militia and Defence Records, RG9 III-D-3, vol. 4918, f. 396, reel T-10710, War Diary, 8th Battalion, 25 May 1915.

CHAPTER 5

1   Burlington Public Library: *Aldershot Tweedsmuir History* (Aldershot: Women's Institute, n.d.), vol. 2, 55.

2   FAHS: Minutes of Anglican Young People's Association meeting, 20 July 1916.

3   LAC: RG150, accession 1992-93/166, box 3386, f. 30, service record of E. G. Galloway; box 3387, f. 24, service record of R. L. Galloway.

4   LAC: RG150, F. 649-G-1923, reel T-8662, court martial of #83788 A. W. Galloway, 20 November 1916.

5   *Canadian Champion*, 5 July 1917, 4.

6   Steven E. Sawell, ed., *Into the Cauldron: Experiences of a CEF Infantry Officer During the Great War* (2009), 55.

7   Diary entry, 8 April 1917, in Sawell, *Into the Cauldron*, 58.

8   Quoted in G. W. L. Nicholson, *Canadian Expeditionary Force, 1914–1919: Official History of the Canadian Army in the First World War* (Ottawa: Queen's Printer, 1962), 244.

9   Sawell, 1934 memoir, in Sawell, *Into the Cauldron*, 58.

10 Sawell, 1934 memoir, in Sawell, *Into the Cauldron*, 59.

11 Sawell, letter to E. T. Sawell, 1917, in Sawell, *Into the Cauldron*, 62.

12 Sawell, letter to E. T. Sawell, 1917, in Sawell, *Into the Cauldron*, 63.

13 Sawell, 1934 memoir, in Sawell, *Into the Cauldron*, 59, 65.

14 LAC: RG150, accession 1992-93/166, box 2798, f. 16, service record of J. C. Eager.

15 University of Toronto Archives: A73-0026/091 (66), Joseph Culloden Eager file, Eager to G. Oswald Smith, 30 March 1920.

16 CPC: Eager to Agnes Eager, 4 August 1916.

17 CPC: Eager to J. E. Eager, 26 November 1916.

18 LAC: Militia and Defence Records, RG9 III-D-3, vol. 5034, f. 851, reel T-10924, War Diary, No. 1 Canadian General Hospital, 5 April 1917.

19 CPC: Eager to Agnes Eager, 10 April 1917. Garth Tassie of Waterdown, a cousin of the Eagers, had joined the 129th Battalion in April 1916, and later transferred to the Royal Flying Corps.

20 LAC: Militia and Defence Records, RG9 III-D-3, vol. 5034, f. 851, reel T-10924, War Diary, No. 1 Canadian General Hospital, 11 April 1917.

21 JFVC: Eager to J. E. Eager, 18 April 1917. Calgary lawyer Daniel Gordon Campbell was killed in action at Vimy on 9 April while serving with the 16th Battalion.

22 National Archives of Australia: Service record of #2407 R. W. Cutter, 47th Battalion AIF.

23 JFVC: Eager to J. E. Eager, 13 May 1917.

24 F. H. Hitchins Collection, University of Western Ontario: card file, Colin St George Campbell; A. H. Young, *The War Book of Upper Canada College, Toronto* (Toronto: Printers Guild, 1923), 13.

25 CPC: Campbell to Agnes Eager, 19 January 1917.

26 The National Archives, Kew: WO 339/65189, RAF Officers' Service Records, 2/Lieutenant Colin St George Campbell.

27 LAC: RG150, accession 1992-93/166, box 6447, f. 25, service record of #784190 R. W. Mount.

28 LAC: RG150, 1992-93/314, Circumstances of Death Registers, vol. 183, #11073 Sgt William Gillies.

29 LAC: RG150, accession 1992-93/166, box 8901, f. 21, service record of #163689 J. Sills.

30 *Daily Colonist* (Victoria), 31 January 1917, 11.

31 LAC: Militia and Defence Records, RG9 III-D-3, vol. 5034, f. 851, reel T-10924, War Diary, No. 1 Canadian General Hospital, 10 March 1917.

32 For the newest account, see Patrice Dutil and David MacKenzie, *Embattled Nation: Canada's Wartime Election of 1917* (Toronto: Dundurn Press, 2017).

33 *Hamilton Spectator*, 15 December 1917, 29.

34 *Hamilton Spectator*, 6 December 1917, 20.

35 Thirteenth General Election, results for Wentworth electoral district, https://lop.parl.ca/About/Parliament/FederalRidingsHistory/hfer.asp?Language=E&Search=Det&rid=802&Include=.

36 LAC: RG150, accession 1992-93/166, box 3750, f. 52, service record of #800166 C. R. Gray.

37 LAC: RG 150 ser. 8, f. 649-G5848, reel T-8662, court martial of #757739 C. J. Greenlee, 5 March 1917.

38 LAC: RG150, accession 1992-93/166, box 3794, f. 53, service record of #757739 C. J. Greenlee.

39 *Waterdown Review*, 12 December 1918, 1.

40 LAC: RG150, accession 1992-93/166, box 1033, f. 27, service record of #467046 R. E. Breckon.

41 LAC: RG150, accession 1992-93/166, box 1033, f. 30, service record of #514124 W. D. Breckon.

42 LAC: RG150, accession 1992-93/166, box 6859, f. 33, service record of #663531 C. W. McGregor.

43 LAC: RG150, accession 1992-93/166, box 1033, f. 31, service record of #931330 W. J. Breckon.

44 Stan Sawell, 1934 memoir, in Sawell, *Into the Cauldron*, 108–9.

45 LAC: RG150, accession 1992-93/166, box 2567, f. 14, service record of #690791 L. H. Dougherty.

46 LAC: RG150, accession 1992-93/166, box 5831, f. 45, service record of #688055 C. H. U. Maddaugh.

47 LAC: RG150, accession 1992-93/166, box 2908, f. 7, service record of #784576 W. H. Emmons.

48 Joseph and Elmer Bishop had both gone west from Algonquin, Ontario, before the war. They both enlisted in 1915 and died three months apart in 1917.

49 Reginald H. Roy, ed., *The Journal of Private Fraser* (CEF Books, 1998); LAC: RG150, accession 1992-93/166, box 2824, f. 58, service record of #240701 A. W. Edge.

50 LAC: RG150, accession 1992-93/166, box 3034, f. 15, service record of #784325 R. Fenning; box 2695, f. 35, service record of #784602 S. Duckhouse.

51 *Hamilton Spectator*, 8 December 1917, 20.

52 *Hamilton Spectator*, 30 December 1917, 1.

53 Sawell, 1934 memoir; diary entry, 25 December 1917, in Sawell, *Into the Cauldron*, 117.

54 CPC: Eager to J. E. Eager, n.d. [Dec 1917].

CHAPTER 6

1   *Hamilton Spectator*, 29 December 1917, 1; 9 January 1918, 12.

2   *Canadian Champion*, 31 January 1918, 4.

3   *Hamilton Spectator*, 17 January 1918, 10.

4   *Waterdown Review*, 16 May 1918, 1.

5   *Waterdown Review*, 16 May 1918, 1.

6   *Waterdown Review*, 23 May 1918, 1.

7   For the only substantial study of conscripts, see Patrick M. Dennis, *Reluctant Warriors: Canadian Conscripts and the Great War* (Vancouver: UBC Press, 2017).

8   *Waterdown Review*, 20 June 1918, 1.

9   *Hamilton Spectator*, 3 January 1918, 4.

10 *Hamilton Spectator*, 18 December 1917, 15; 30 December 1917, 13.

11 *Waterdown Review*, 6 June 1918, 4; 13 June 1918, 4.

12 *Waterdown Review*, 28 November 1918, 1.

13 LAC: RG150, accession 1992-93/166, box 1227, f. 22, service record of #406684 R. O. Buchan.

14 The older brother of Percy Bowman, who had deserted from the 129th Battalion in 1916.

15 *Waterdown Review*, 11 July 1918, 1.

16 *Waterdown Review*, 25 July 1918, 1.

17 Fred had been called up at the same time as Austin Tudor. He served with the 54th Battalion until he took a bullet in the shoulder near Cambrai in September 1918.

18 *Waterdown Review*, 30 May 1918, 1.

19 Waterdown native Lloyd Attridge was just seventeen when he joined the Royal Flying Corps in November 1917. He survived the war and became a dentist.

20 Vern Willis and Roy Wilkinson had originally enlisted with the 129th Battalion; both were eventually transferred to the 123rd Battalion, with which they served at the front. Both survived the war.

21 *Waterdown Review*, 29 August 1918, 1.

22 *Waterdown Review*, 15 August 1918, 1.

23 LAC: RG150, accession 1992-93/166, box 2567, f. 35, service record of #784570 N. A. Dougherty.

24 LAC: RG150 ser. 8, f. 649-A-8920, reel T-8651, court martial of #784551 G. W. Arnold, 28 May 1918.

25 LAC: RG150 ser. 8, f. 649-C-23856, reel T-8659, court martial of #226403 A. A. Clark, 28 May 1918.

26 *Waterdown Review*, 8 August 1918, 1.

27 *Waterdown Review*, 8 August 1918, 1.

28 LAC: RG150, accession 1992-93/166, box 4506, f. 15, service record of #324922 O. M. Horning.

29 *Waterdown Review*, 30 May 1918, 1.

30 *Waterdown Review*, 23 May 1918, 1.

31 Cecil Cummings of Millgrove had enlisted in the 129th, and eventually served with the Canadian Engineers in France.

32 Harold, Edgar Richards' younger brother, was another 129th volunteer. He served in France with the Canadian Machine Gun Corps.

33 *Waterdown Review*, 27 June 1918, 1.

34 *Waterdown Review*, 27 June 1918, 1.

35 The Breckenridge family had lived in Aldershot. Their son Wilder, a pilot with the Royal Flying Corps, was shot down and captured in June 1918. The news of Evelyn Breckenridge's death, however, was greatly exaggerated; she died in 1925.

36 *Waterdown Review*, 26 September 1918, 1.

37 *Waterdown Review*, 26 September 1918, 1.

38 Diary entry, 8 August 1918, in Steven E. Sawell, ed., *Into the Cauldron: Experiences of a CEF Infantry Officer During the Great War* (2009), 146.

39 *Waterdown Review*, 10 October 1918, 1.

40 LAC: RG150, accession 1992-93/166, box 90, f. 48, service record of #663004 C. H. Allen.

41 *Waterdown Review*, 5 September 1918, 1; LAC: RG150, accession 1992-93/166, box 1954, f. 24, service record of #757289 S. E. Cook.

42 Sawell, 1934 memoir, in Sawell, *Into the Cauldron*, 151–2.

43 *Waterdown Review*, 19 December 1918, 1.

44 *Waterdown Review*, 14 November 1918, 1.

45 *Waterdown Review*, 21 November 1918, 1.

46 Sawell, diary entry, 3 October 1918, in Sawell, *Into the Cauldron*, 158.

47 LAC: RG150, accession 1992-93/166, box 8719, f. 38, service record of #784555 G. M. Scott.

48 LAC: RG150, accession 1992-93/166, box 1227, f. 22, service record of #690786 A. B. Hearns; box 4772, f. 35, service record of #784573 F. J. James; box 243, f. 22, service record of #784551 G. W. Arnold.

49 *Waterdown Review*, 7 November 1918, 1.

50 LAC: RG150, accession 1992-93/166, box 9206, f. 53, service record of #2527393 J. A. Springer.

51 LAC: RG150, accession 1992-93/166, box 3776, f. 40, service record of #784569 H. S. Green.

52 LAC: RG150, accession 1992-93/166, box 3312, f. 4, service record of #3310085 G. M. Fretwell.

53 University of Toronto Archives: Department of Graduate Records, f. A73-0026/10 (03) G. M. Fretwell, Mrs William Fretwell to G. Oswald Smith, 18 November 1920.

54 LAC: RG150, accession 1992-93/166, box 8120, f. 2, service record of #784268 B. J. Rayner.

55 LAC: RG150, accession 1992-93/166, box 2112, f. 8, service record of #3314282 E. J. Crane.

56 LAC: RG150, accession 1992-93/166, box 8359, f. 55, service record of #657286 J. H. Robertson.

57 LAC: RG150, accession 1992-93/166, box 4633, f. 38, service record of #687566 K. L. Hunter.

58 *Hamilton Spectator*, 22 October 1918, 11.

59 JFVC: email from Ken Willis, Perth, ON, 1 November 1999.

60 LAC: RG150, accession 1992-93/166, box 5831, f. 48, service record of #925792 P. Maddaugh.

61 *Hamilton Spectator*, 7 August 1918, 10.

62 *Hamilton Spectator*, 8 October 1918, 13.

63 *Waterdown Review*, 12 September 1918, 1.

64 *Hamilton Spectator*, 16 August 1918, 5.

65 *Hamilton Spectator*, 22 August 1918, 4.

66 *Hamilton Spectator*, 2 October 1918, 19.

67 LAC: RG150, accession 1992-93/166, box 6188, f. 3, service record of #51 J. Miller.

68 This account has been pieced together from two newspaper reports (*Hamilton Spectator*, 26 August 1918, 1; *Waterdown Review*, 29 August 1918, 1) and discussions with descendants of the James family. I could find no trace of a coroner's inquest into the event.

69 *Hamilton Spectator*, 22 October 1918, 10; Archives of Ontario: MS 935, Registration of Deaths, County of Wentworth, Division of West Flamboro, Leonard Gravelle, 17 October 1918.

70 LAC: RG150, accession 1992-93/166, box 3744, f. 30, service record of #3234936 L. Gravelle.

71 LAC: RG150, accession 1992-93/166, box 1532A, f. 42 service record of #3235612 C. J. Carson.

72 LAC: RG150, accession 1992-93/166, box 4339, f. 24, service record of #335444 W. G. Hilborn.

73 *Waterdown Review*, 24 October 1918, 2.

74 *Waterdown Review*, 17 October 1918, 5.

75 *Waterdown Review*, 7 November 1918, 2.

76 LAC: RG150, accession 1992-93/166, box 3433, f. 38, service record of #3310498 W. F. Garvin.

CHAPTER 7

1 *Waterdown Review*, 14 November 1918, 2.

2 Lorne Mount to father, 17 November 1918, *Waterdown Review*, 26 December 1918, 1.

3 Lorne Mount to father, 17 November 1918, *Waterdown Review*, 26 December 1918, 1.

4 Clifford Shireman to Uncle and Aunt, 28 November 1918, *Waterdown Review*, 2 January 1919, 1.

5 Clifford Shireman to Uncle and Aunt, 28 November 1918, *Waterdown Review*, 2 January 1919, 1.

6 Russell to Aunt Clara, 29 November 1918, *Waterdown Review*, 26 December 1918, 1.

7 Dick to friends, 16 December 1918, *Waterdown Review*, 30 January 1919, 1.

8 LAC: RG 150 ser. 8, f. 649-C-2810, reel T-8653, court martial of #240388 E. L. Church, 7 December 1918.

9 Sawell, 1934 memoir, in Steven E. Sawell, ed., *Into the Cauldron: Experiences of a CEF Infantry Officer During the Great War* (2009), 172–3.

10 Wilf Langford to friend, 13 March 1919, *Waterdown Review*, 1 May 1919, 1.

11 *Waterdown Review*, 16 March 1922, 2.

12 Edwin Roberts to Will Reid, *Waterdown Review*, 18 July 1918, 2.

13 *Waterdown Review*, 9 February 1922, 1.

14 *Waterdown Review*, 5 December 1918, 1.

15 *Waterdown Review*, 13 February 1919, 3.

16 *Waterdown Review*, 14 August 1919, 1.

17 *Waterdown Review*, 6 March 1919, 2.

18 "The Memorial Hall: An Architectural and Historical Report" (Local Architectural Conservation Advisory Committee, Flamborough Township, 1982).

19 *Waterdown Review*, 1 January 1920, 1.

20 *Waterdown Review*, 8 January 1920, 1.

21 *Waterdown Review*, 12 June 1919, 1; 29 January 1920, 1.

22 *Waterdown Review*, 10 September 1920, 3.

23 *Waterdown Review*, 3 December 1920, 1.

24 *Waterdown Review*, 3 October 1918, 1.

25 JFVC: *Dedication of the Memorial Hall and the Unveiling of the Tablet in Honor of Our Brave Soldiers, Waterdown, Sunday, January 14th, 1923.*

26 *Waterdown Review*, 5 August 1920, 1.

ENVOI

1 Interview with Clarence Laking, Downsview, Ontario, 17 July 2001.

2 LAC: Department of National Defence Records, RG24 C1A, vol. 6242, f. AHQ-14-315-1, Frank Slater to Militia and Defence, 15 March 1928.

A NOTE ON PRIMARY SOURCES

LOCAL HISTORY AND RURAL HISTORY have not been popular topics of late, and local rural history is therefore doubly damned. This is despite the fact that local archival collections tend to be very rich, and there are even greater treasures to be found if one can insinuate oneself into the local community. When I took up this research, it was with the knowledge that part of the battle was already won, in that I was born insinuated into the local community.

The Flamborough Archives and Heritage Society collection, located in the Waterdown branch of the Hamilton Public Library, contains much that is essential to the historian who wishes to understand the tenor of life a century ago. It holds, for example, the minute books of Waterdown Village Council and East Flamborough Township Council, the Waterdown Board of Health, and the Waterdown Women's Institute, township electoral rolls and telephone directories, land titles abstract books, the files of the Local Architectural Conservation Advisory Committee, and the journal of Waterdown business owner Philip Metzger, as well as many cemetery registers from the township and a wide range of family histories. It also holds some church records, though most remain in the churches themselves. Particularly useful were the records of Grace Anglican Church (especially the minute books of the Anglican Young People's Association), Knox Presbyterian Church, and Carlisle and Mountsberg Methodist churches. The society's newsletter, *Heritage Happenings*, frequently prints obscure tidbits from the collection that relate to the township's experience during the First World War.

I have made full use of archival materials that have come down through my family—most directly, the papers of the Fleming, McMonies, and Vance families. My cousin Steven Sawell holds the journals and letters of his grandfather, E.S. Sawell—these he published in part as *Into the Cauldron: Experiences of a CEF Infantry Officer During the Great War* (2009). I was also able to use Stan Sawell's unpublished memoir of his childhood in Waterdown before the war. As the village lawyer (like his father before him), my father came into possession of a wide variety of documents from families in East Flamborough, as well as printed material and photographs; I have found much information of value in these materials. Years ago, he acquired a large collection of papers related to the McGregor family that have been very useful (there is also a small collection of McGregor material at the William Ready Division of Archives and Research Collections at McMaster University). Also many years ago, my mother had the foresight to buy at auction everything she could that came from Will Reid's family—not only his own photographic equipment and glass-plate negatives, but diaries, letters, ledgers, business accounts, and ephemera of all kinds, from get-well cards to the family Bible. Included in this collection was wartime correspondence between Peter Mitchell and his wife Sarah (née Reid). On eBay, I was able to acquire letters written by East Flamborough soldiers Joe Eager, Percy Thomas, and Ernest Todd.

Other local collections also proved to be immensely useful. The Joseph Brant Museum in Burlington holds the Filman family correspondence, and the Burlington Public Library holds the two-volume Tweedsmuir History of Aldershot. Dr. Raymond Cummings, formerly of the University of Toronto, has assembled a mass of material relating to various lines of the Cummings (also Cummins) families in the Flamboroughs. The late Colin Pomfret of Millgrove shared with me his collection of local military correspondence, a collection that, sadly, was auctioned off piecemeal after Colin's death. Smaller troves of documents are held by the descendants of Ingle Bousfield, Russell Carey, the Galloway sisters, Oliver and Henry Horning, George Inksetter, the Mason brothers, Maurice Scott, Joel Stonefish, and Vern Willis.

Although East Flamborough didn't have its own newspaper until May 1918, other local papers proved to be fruitful sources of news from the township. The most useful were the *Hamilton Spectator*, the *Dundas Star*, and the *Canadian Champion* (Milton). Occasionally, the area made it into the national newspapers and, once in a while, American dailies.

The CEF personnel files and unit War Diaries held at Library and Archives Canada are the basic elements for reconstructing the soldier's experience during the First World War. I have also used, from the Department of Militia and Defence, records of courts martial (for George Arnold, Archie Galloway, and Bill Scott), unit inspection reports for Wentworth's infantry battalions, the records of Military District No. 2 (Toronto), and files covering the history of Waterdown's drill shed. Various other record groups at LAC were mined: the Canadian Transport Commission (for reports of railway accidents and railway stations in the township); the Post Office Department (for mail services in the Flamboroughs); the Sir Robert Borden Papers (for correspondence with respect to machine-gun fundraising in Waterdown); and the Grand

Trunk Railway Company and Canadian Northern Ontario Railway Company (for proposed rail lines through the township).

The Archives of Ontario holds a number of useful records: Waterdown village and East Flamborough township financial returns; the papers of Dr. William Philp, one of Waterdown's doctors in the late nineteenth century; baptismal records of Knox Presbyterian Church; an inventory of the Tweedsmuir Histories; and applications for graduation diplomas. Other government records, indispensable to any historian of this period, are the manuscript census records, the annual reports of the various government departments (particularly Education, Labour, and Roads and Highways), and birth, marriage, and death records available through genealogical websites.

Anyone who has used local history publications knows that they straddle the line between primary and secondary sources; they vary greatly in quality, but are nothing if not earnest. Among the volumes (mostly privately published) that I found particularly useful are:

Ariel M. Dyer, *The Laird of Woodhill* (1983)

Gary Evans, *The Prints of Aldershot: A Photographic View of Another Era* (Burlington: North Shore Publishing, 2000)

Patricia and Maurice Green, Sylvia and Robert Wray, … *and they came to East Flamborough: A Celebration of East Flamborough Township's pre-Confederation Heritage* (Waterdown–East Flamborough Heritage Society, 1997)

Patricia and Maurice Green, Sylvia and Robert Wray, *From West Flamborough's Storied Past: A Celebration of West Flamborough Township's Heritage* (Waterdown–East Flamborough Heritage Society, 2003)

Stanley Mills, *Lake Medad and Waterdown* (1937)

The Mountsberg Heritage (Mountsberg Historical Society, n.d.)

Alan Parker and Diane E. Woods, *Exploring the Past: Waterdown* (1984)

Dorothy Turcotte, *Carlisle Beginnings* (Carlisle Book Committee, 1994)

Waterdown and East Flamborough, 1867–1967 (Waterdown–East Flamborough Centennial Committee, 1967)

Donald R. Woods and Diane E. Woods, *The Mills of Waterdown: The Growth of an Ontario Village, 1790 to 1915* (Waterdown–East Flamborough Heritage Society, 2010)

Sylvia A. Wray and Maurice H. Green, *Dundas Street, Waterdown, 1793–1993* (Waterdown–East Flamborough Heritage Society, 1994)

INDEX

Thomas, Percy, 134–35
Titanic, RMS, 118, 132
Toronto, 16, 17, 52, 54, 56, 62, 66–67, 99,
    110, 116, 118, 135, 150, 162, 169, 182,
    236, 249
Townsend, Thomas, 165
Tudor, Austin, 195–99, 224, 279n17

Union Cemetery, 11, 26, 33, 37, 237
Unionists, 166–69, 181, 187
universities, 121; McGill, 122, 162;
    Michigan, 40; Toronto, 16, 67, 101,
    207; Western, 118
Upper Canada College, 162

Valcartier, 49–53, 61, 65, 69, 90, 144
Valenciennes, 226–27
Vance family, 32–34, 82, 85–86, 98, 237,
    249, 261
venereal disease, 57
Verdun, 125, 129, 154
veterans, 246–48
Victoria Cross, 5, 146
Victory Loans, 175, 181, 239
Vimy Ridge, Battle of, 91, 109, 154–55,
    163–64, 173, 191, 209–10, 228, 231,
    243, 277n21
Vlamertinghe, 74, 81

Wabasso Park, 41, 86, 150, 186, 252
Ward, Frank, 183–86, 188

Waterdown Choral Society, 82, 183
Welland Canal, 64–65
Wentworth County, 9, 16, 32, 46, 51, 55,
    86, 98–99, 104, 139, 166, 179, 229,
    231, 246
West Flamborough, 12, 14, 97–98, 109,
    116, 175
West Sandling, 94–95
Whalley, F.W., 20, 87
Wilde, John, 109
Wilkinson, Roy, 197, 279n20
Willis, Vern, 107–8, 197, 226, 279n20
Wilson, Gordon, 140, 167–69
Winnipeg, 5, 54, 143, 242
Witley, 133, 137–39, 191, 194–95, 198, 221,
    237, 244
women's organizations, Daughters
    of the King, 88; Imperial Order
    Daughters of the Empire, 61;
    Knotty Knitters' Klub, 150;
    Women's Institute, 41, 46, 62, 83,
    112; Women's Patriotic League,
    61–62, 83, 112, 149–50, 250;
    Women's Patriotic Society, 61

YMCA, 133, 148, 180, 210
Ypres, 73, 83, 90, 119, 141, 144–46, 172
Ypres, Battle of, 111, 163, 171, 231
Yser Canal, 75, 78

zeppelins, 94, 106